Advance Praise

Through Her Eyes centers the women of the Bible in the stories they lived, reimagined in their own voices, exploring the female narrative long obscured in patriarchal presentations of scripture. The resilience and humanity in these pages open a window into perspectives to help us navigate a world with relatable problems and dynamics present in any age. I loved seeing these women show up on the page, fleshed out and complex.

Tia Levings
Author of *A Well-Trained Wife* and *The Soul of Healing*

Through Her Eyes is a stunning and necessary reimagining of voices too often silenced in sacred texts. Rebecca J. Craig masterfully brings biblical women to life, offering them the depth, dignity, and agency they deserve. Through her compelling storytelling and evocative artistry, this work invites us to listen anew—to hear the wisdom, grief, resilience, and power of these women who have shaped faith and history.

This is more than a book; it is a reclamation, a sacred conversation across time, and an invitation to see scripture through a lens of justice, courage, and grace. A must-read for anyone seeking a more expansive, embodied, and faithful engagement with biblical narratives.

Rev. Sam Houser
Author of *No Longer Keeping the Peace* and *Between the Lines*

In the deeply moving tradition of Jewish midrash, Rebecca Craig weaves together the lived experiences of biblical women in a way that transcends time, cultural difference, language, and socio-religious context. With compelling imagery and richly layered storytelling, *Through Her Eyes* amplifies women's voices and courageous acts of perseverance, with a powerful call for self-actualization both within and beyond religious identity.

Lynn M. Horan, PhD
Women's Leadership and Life Coach
Author of *Dismantled: Abusive Church Culture*
and the Clergy Women Who Leave

I didn't even know I needed this book until I started reading it! These stories simultaneously broke and remade me as I read them, and left me wanting more stories! The discussion questions at the end of each chapter all made me pause to think and consider.

Kristine Wyllys
Author of *Wild Ones and Losing Streak*

Rebecca has given voice to the silences of Scripture with imagination and reverence. *Through Her Eyes* doesn't rewrite the Bible; it invites us to listen more closely to the women whose stories have too often gone unheard. This is sacred storytelling, grounded in empathy, unafraid to ask questions, lingering with us long after the last page.

Robert G. Callahan II
Author of *Fire in the Whole: Embracing Our Righteous Anger*
with White Christianity and Reclaiming Our Wholeness

Rev. Craig powerfully reimagines these Biblical narratives, told from perspectives we have rarely considered—the women. With evocative storytelling, she offers readers a renewed and deeply personal connection to their stories in often heart-wrenching vignettes. *Through Her Eyes* is a transformative spark for the imagination, the heart, and faith itself.

Rev. Michelle Wahila
Author of *Ruffled By Grace: Rebellious Blessings for a Fierce Faith*

Through Her Eyes

Biblical Women Speak

Rebecca J. Craig

Tehom Center Publishing is a 501(c)3 nonprofit publishing feminist and queer authors, with a commitment to elevate BIPOC writers. Its face and voice is Rev. Dr. Angela Yarber.

Paperback ISBN: 978-1-966655-17-6

Ebook ISBN: 978-1-966655-37-4

For all the women who have ever been silenced.

Contents

CONTENT WARNING

Several of the stories in this book contain descriptions of abuse and sexual assault that may be triggering for abuse survivors.

"Dinah" and "The Levite's Concubine" may be especially triggering for survivors of sexual assault.

Introduction

The stories of the Bible are familiar to many of us. Yet, we almost always hear these narratives from the perspective of the men who wrote them. I remember one summer I proposed to the senior pastor I was working with at the time that we do a series that focused on the stories of the women. He grudgingly agreed and for the next thirteen weeks, we focused on thirteen women you don't typically hear about. The women of my congregation began to approach me and tell me how much they were loving hearing these stories told from a female perspective. It felt empowering. They felt represented.

They felt seen.

About eight weeks in, the senior pastor came to me grumbling that thirteen weeks was just too long. We should have stuck to six weeks. I looked at him, perplexed, and said, "I don't understand. Women typically spend fifty-two weeks each year having to hear everything from the male perspective. Why is listening to women's stories for a mere thirteen weeks so difficult for men?"

I received no response because I'm pretty sure he knew the answer to that question, and didn't like it.

That's when I set about writing this book, telling the stories of women in scripture from *their* perspective. What they thought, how they felt. There are so many questions that are raised when we read these stories like, "what did Sarah think about Abraham trying to sacrifice their only son?" Every mother probably wonders that. (I also wonder what she thought when he tried to pass her off to

Pharaoh as his sister, but I needed to keep each story to a single chapter.)

Or where did Cain's wife come from anyway? While there were probably explanations to such questions that are lost due to the ravages of time, I've undertaken the creative endeavor of imagining what the answers to those questions could be—from *her perspective*.

Keep in mind, while based on Biblical stories, these short stories are works of speculative fiction. Through these tales, I'm exploring the theoretical voices of these women in an effort to unearth, "what would they have said? What would they have felt?" While grappling with some deeply theological issues, I understand it's a given not everyone is going to agree with the interpretation of the views and choices that every character takes. As you read each story, remember that the point of this is not about agreeing with every view, stance or action performed by the characters—it's about simply imagining what they *might* have been like if we were able to read their diary.

Also keep the difficulty of the times they lived in mind. These are not shiny-happy-sugar-coated stories. They are rough and gritty. They are stories about women who frequently are wronged and must find ways to overcome abrogated justice. They're sometimes women who live on the margins. They're prostitutes. Rape victims. Wives. Mothers. Daughters. Leaders. Protectors. Liars. Schemers. Queens. Judges. Some are foolish. Some are wise.

They're women struggling to survive in a world that tended to be very hostile to their existence.

Thus, these stories are my best representation of what life was *probably* like for these women. This means they are sometimes violent. As you will notice, many of the stories of women involve the fact that their worth is found in childbearing, which means: there's a lot of sex. I try not to write too graphically, keeping my audience in mind, but I also don't tiptoe around the realities of the sexual role these women played. Some are romantic. Some are duty-bound. Some are victims and survivors of abuse and sexual assault. I won't soften this, sometimes I feel like the violence inherent in many of these stories is overwhelming. Yet, that very reality might also be the point. According to the National Sexual Violence Center, one out of every five women has been sexually assaulted in the United States alone.[1] Nearly half of all women have experienced emotional or psychological abuse.[2] And that's in a modern culture that has gone through the so-called "sexual revolution."

If some of these stories seem ugly, it's because a lot of women's stories are ugly once you rip the shiny veneer off the profile they publicly display.

Content warning: if you opened this book, hoping to read some sweet, innocent stories of women being virtuous and chaste: you will be sorely disappointed. I want to be as true as possible to who I think they were, so there may be some content that you find disturbing.

As much as I would have liked to have told the story of every woman in scripture, that would be an extremely long book (stay tuned—there might be a volume 2!) so I chose ones I found the most interesting and intriguing, and whose stories I felt needed to be told the most. Some are likely familiar. Some may not be. For instance, most of us are familiar with the story of Deborah, but who remembers Queen Athaliah who ruled over Judah for eight years?

Not all these women are heroines. Some of them are villains and psychopaths. Just like real life. But the question that always intrigues me when I read women's stories in the Bible is: what drives them? What were their motivations? What happened in their lives that

---

1. Smith, S. G., Zhang, X., Basile, K. C., Merrick, M. T., Wang, J., Kresnow, M., & Chen, J. (2018). The National Intimate Partner and Sexual Violence Survey: 2015 data brief – updated release. Centers for Disease Control and Prevention.

2. Black, M.C., Basile, K.C., Breiding, M.J., Smith, S.G., Walters, M.L., Merrick, M.T., Chen, J., & Stevens, M.R. (2011). The National Intimate Partner and Sexual Violence Survey (NISVS): 2010 Summary Report. Atlanta, GA: National Center for Injury Prevention and Control, Centers for Disease Control and Prevention.

made them act the way they did? Relationships are complex and complicated—as are many of these women as I've imagined them.

I've attempted to use a variety of writing perspectives: some in first person, some in third person, some in present tense, some in past tense. I simply went with what felt right for each particular character.

I hope this book helps you see these stories "through her eyes."

Eve

(Genesis 2-4)

THE DYING rays of the sun stretch across the valley where I sit, casting an orange glow over the simple lean-to shelter I constructed for myself. I slowly stir the small fire before me with a stick, lost in my memories. After all these years alone, my mind often wanders through my long life like my body wanders the wilderness.

My memories of Eden have waned over the years, as though an impenetrable veil has dropped over that part of my mind, obscuring it in haunting shadow. All that remains are wispy impressions and feelings, akin to how childhood recollections tend to dwindle and blur with the merciless passage of age and time. Back then, Adam and I were, after all, in essence, children.

Children in a nursery. Every need cared for; every desire met.

Well, almost every desire.

Then...we grew up.

I know it sounds rather simple, but that's ultimately what happened. After all, why put something purposely in front of a child if you do not intend for them to eventually reach for it?

One can claim disobedience all they like, but there was so much more at play in those formative years of our existence. More than some cruel test of obedience that we ultimately failed.

We were the first of my people imbued with such a profound personal connection and relationship with our Creator who spoke all of existence into being. The others, those outside the garden, had limited senses that were stubbornly attuned only to the physical world around them, blind and failing to perceive the divine spark burning at the heart of all creation. So instead, they worshiped the works of the Creator's hands rather than the Creator itself, having never been granted that transcendent introductory knowledge.

Knowledge Adam and I were given. Yet, we too had blinders of a different sort on; our pristine minds purposefully shuttered off from the cruel, visceral realities of the world outside that Edenic sanctuary. Adam and I were set apart in that lush garden which served as a nurturing haven. We had the divine wind of sacred life itself breathed into our undeveloped souls.

Eden. It had been a paradise where our every simple need was met, our most innocent desires satiated in abundance. We did not have to scramble and fight to exist like those outside our serene garden oasis.

Which also meant, our growth was limited. Our ability to learn had parameters and boundaries set around it. Sorrow, pain, death—such cruel concepts were utterly alien to us. We simply knew no darkness amidst all that radiant light. We did not yet conceive of what "bad" versus "good" entailed.

Yet, we were made in the divine image. What did that mean exactly? From my perspective, it meant we were destined to be more than just children.

We were created to evolve and grow—which meant eventually leaving our nursery. Discovering and learning about all the things we had been shielded from. That sorrow, pain and death were all necessary parts of both the human—and divine—experience. Is that not an intrinsic part of what sculpts our spiritual metamorphosis? The painful journey of growth, of shedding each successive childlike skin as we claw our way ever further from the womb-like cocoon of blissful ignorance. To evolve, elevate, and transcend into something more expansive than our previous selves could ever envision? Like a baby on wobbly feet, were we not destined to take the courageous first step on the arduous, never-ending path toward individual consciousness and transcendent potential?

This divine drive for greater wisdom and experience began to flicker within me like the first primordial spark in the void. We had been created with this yearning threaded through our very being. I hungered for the taste of true understanding, to take the first monumental leap towards ascending to full actualization. Full realization of who and what we were.

I cannot say whether that insatiable drive for knowledge and exploration also burned within my partner, Adam. He seemed content to remain in the Creator's nursery, our every need tended to by the bounty surrounding us. Adam was less captivated by the towering Tree of Knowledge than me; less curious about the world we lived in, not sharing my yearning to transcend our sheltered existence and become something...more. He instead was content to simply be cared for by our Creator. His lack of curiosity was at times frustrating, as I was constantly wanting to learn and grow. His refusal to even engage in the conversation of what wonders the Tree of Knowledge might possess was a constant source of irritation. His condescending tone saying, "some things were simply not meant to be explored," while gentle, railed against my innate sense of wonder and hunger for discovery. I couldn't understand how someone could be satisfied living within the confines of such self-imposed ignorance, dismissing the mysteries of the world as forbidden or irrelevant.

To me, the unknown was an invitation—a call to adventure! His passive resistance to my enthusiasm felt like a wall I could never scale, a quiet denial of the potential that lay just beyond the edge of our understanding.

It was therefore only natural that I became the target of the serpent's beguiling words on that fateful day. *I* was the curious one. *I* was the one willing to question, willing to risk. *I* was the one who couldn't resist the pull of the unknown. *I* was the one who dared to reach for what others feared to touch.

While many of my memories of Eden have faded over the years, one has remained seared into my consciousness. A recollection I have never been allowed the mercy of forgetting.

A singular, cataclysmic moment. The fateful day which altered the course of not just our individual journeys, but ultimately the whole sprawling human saga. The searing brand of that memory remains scorched into every fiber of my being.

It feels almost shamefully egotistical to give voice to such a self-aggrandizing notion. That the bold acts of just two souls could wield such incomprehensible power—could upend the entire trajectory of our species upon this Earthly plane. Yet, here we are as living evidence of that reality. *We were the first.* The ones who defiantly took that forbidden leap across the abyss toward conscious actualization of the divine image.

That day. That memory—unlike all the memories that came before or since—remains vividly seared in my consciousness. They were my last fleeting moments of...innocence? Ignorance? Maybe both?...as I sat beneath the spreading boughs of the Tree of Knowledge, its branches casting a web of shadows over the soft grass. The fruit gleamed in the dappled sunlight—smooth, inviting, and mysterious. I felt its pull, an ache somewhere deep within me that I couldn't yet name.

Still. It was forbidden. Was that the reason I ached for it so deeply?

I ran my fingers over the bark of the tree and tilted my head, listening to the sounds of the garden. I heard the wind, the rustle of leaves, the faint murmurs of animals, and then something else—words, low and sinuous, weaving themselves into my thoughts.

"Why do you hesitate, Eve?"

The voice was smooth, like water over stones. I frowned, searching for the source of the voice. I glanced where Adam was sitting nearby, looking serenely oblivious. No, the voice had not been his. Nor had it been the voice of the Creator. I knew both their voices like my own.

"I'm not hesitating," I replied, though my voice was uncertain as I squinted through the boughs. "I'm...wondering."

"Wondering about what?" came that eerily whispery voice.

"Show yourself!" I demanded, placing my hands firmly on my hips. In my childlike naivete, I did not yet know to feel fear or alarm. Such instincts only kick in once you've undergone a reason to be afraid. We had experienced only safety, security and fulfillment, so I had no concept of what danger was. One doesn't know not to stick one's hand in the flame until one understands what it's like to have been burned. I only felt an overpowering and entitled curiosity.

I saw Adam glance up, startled, out of the corner of my eye. He rose slowly and moved curiously toward me, staring at me before following my gaze into the tree.

"Wondering about what?" pressed the voice as a winged serpent swayed into view around the trunk. Though serpentine in form, it bore powerful, clawed limbs that gripped the bark with ease, and a pair of feathery wings extended from its muscular shoulders, folding partially as it moved. Its scales shimmered with an iridescent sheen, and its golden eyes seemed as if they could see through me, pinning me in place under their piercing gaze. How had I never encountered this mesmerizing creature before?

"About the tree," I said. "About why we're told not to eat from it."

The serpent's eyes gleamed. "And why shouldn't you wonder? Isn't that the purpose of a mind such as yours—to seek, to question, to grow?"

I glanced toward the fruit again. "But…we will die if we eat—or even touch—the fruit. We should trust what we've been told. We should be content." I could hear myself echoing Adam's words. Though I added that bit about not even touching it. To even touch it would have engendered a temptation too great. It was safer to simply avoid it all together.

"And are you content?" the serpent asked, its slick voice low and inviting.

I hesitated. I glanced at Adam who had seemingly lost interest in the discussion and sat back down. Adam's happiness seemed so simple, so untroubled. He delighted in the garden's beauty, in its abundance, in the ease of our days. I felt a twinge of…annoyance? Why was he so stubbornly incurious? So unwilling to engage even in a simple discussion? Was his contentment so powerful that it simply made him unable to think beyond the moment?

Conversely, why was something inside me *stirring?* It was a yearning, a hunger I didn't fully understand.

"No," I admitted softly. "I'm not."

The serpent moved closer, its movements slow and deliberate. "The fruit of this tree," it said, "will open your eyes. You will understand the difference between good and evil. You will see the world for what it truly is—not just its beauty, but its complexity. You will know what it means to choose, to shape your own destiny."

"But the Creator said it would bring death," I said, though even as I spoke the words, they felt distant, as if they belonged to someone else.

"Death?" the serpent said with a low chuckle. "What is death, Eve?"

I blinked, frowning.

"Death," the voice continued, "is simply the end of the old, the beginning of the new. Change and growth always feel like an ending before it becomes a beginning. Would you stay as you are forever? Or would you dare to become more?"

The words jolted me. I thought of the days I'd spent wandering the garden, my mind reaching for answers that never came. Once again I glanced over at Adam, who didn't seem to feel the same ache I did. He was content to gather fruit, to rest in the shade, to follow the path laid out for us.

Why did I want more? The serpent's words washed over me in heated waves, stoking the flames of curiosity that had begun smoldering low in my belly.

"You will not die, you know," the sinuous creature continued in a sultry tone, coils tightening almost imperceptibly. "The *innocence* within you will simply die. Your ignorance of the world's vast mysteries will die. The old, limited you will perish. But a new, more enlightened you will then be gloriously reborn." Its scales glittered almost blindingly as the sunlight refracted against the rainbow of shimmering colors. I leaned into the serpent's words, these beautiful yet seemingly dangerous ideas, in my mind.

"A daring you that would take risks," it whispered insistently. "A liberated you that would forge your own destiny, no longer solely reliant upon this sheltered garden's provisions for sustenance and life itself. Do you need to remain forever mired in such naïve, childlike bliss?"

The serpent's honeyed murmurs made an increasingly persuasive case, each passing moment fanning the tendrils of longing in my heart into a raging inferno. Could there exist no true fullness of living without some mortal risk? No real understanding without bursting the bonds of ignorance? No profound love without freedom of choice?

"A you that will be free to…create," it finally breathed, almost in a hiss dragging out that last word for emphasis. Its serpentine eyes locked unblinkingly on mine.

I felt the breath stall in my lungs as something pivotal unlocked deep within me. "Create?" I stammered, scarcely daring to dream of such power. "Not just nurture that which already exists in this world through endless cycles...but bring forth new life...myself?"

The serpent nodded as it uncoiled itself from around the tree and now wrapped its sinewy arms around my shoulders, whispering in my ear.

"New life," it quietly hissed, ticking my ears with its breath. "New beings crafted from your own flesh—*you, yes, you, Eve,* would truly become like the Creator then, the one who created you from Adam's flesh." The serpent's words dripped with circuitous guile. "To create on your own terms. To wield the power of bringing forth existence itself, just as the Creator does!"

It paused, scaled coils shifting as its wedge-shaped head gestured dismissively at the paradise surrounding us. "Is this sheltered garden how one truly honors the divine spark within? By hiding meekly in this place? Hiding from deeper universal truths, only discovered through the difficult path of experience and broad knowledge?"

The winged serpent leaned in closer, toxic breath hot on my flushed cheeks as it drove its point home.

"What loving parent does not rejoice to see a child blossom into their full, glorious potential? Why would the benevolent Creator fashion you in the sacred image, yet cruelly bar you from partaking fully of the divine gift of wisdom?"

I looked up at the fruit glistening in the light. My hand hovered near it, trembling. Why indeed! The intoxicating words reverberated through my mind. I bit my lower lip between my teeth, unable to tear my gaze away from the serpent's entrancing eyes.

"What if I fail?" I whispered.

"What if you fly?" the serpent replied.

Desperate for an anchor, I turned again toward Adam, my eternal partner, who was now standing motionless beside me. At some point he had moved to once again listen to the discussion. Did he *finally* feel a curiosity within himself awakening? What did he make of these assertions so brazenly laid bare? What thoughts churned behind his furrowed brow as he, too, contemplated the serpent's truths?

The serpent hissed in annoyance and crept back toward the tree as I turned toward Adam.

"Adam?" I said, questioningly, as I reached for his hand, craving his steadying touch, his clear-eyed wisdom. Craving his arms, not the serpent's, wrap themselves around me.

Would he urge caution and obedience as we had been instructed? Or would the flames of curiosity and desire for something more also burn in his eyes?

I sidled up flush against Adam's side, giving his hand an imploring squeeze. His skin was sun-warmed and vital against my palm.

"What holds more importance to us?" I murmured insistently, searching his beloved face. "To remain static in this garden forever? Stagnant and unchanging? To be no more than these simple beings we are in this moment?"

I leaned in closer, feeling the heated thrum of my pulse in my throat as I continued in a lowered, husky voice.

"Or do we take the risk? Do we seek out that vast, profound knowledge which has been kept from us until now? Do we..." I swallowed hard, voice dropping to an aching whisper. "Sacrifice this known bliss in order to be reborn into something transcendent? To become more than we can currently conceive?"

Adam blinked slowly, a furrow creasing his brow as uncertainty and confusion warred across his chiseled features. He seemed to wrestle with the paradigm-shifting possibilities I laid before him.

Releasing his hand, I framed his strong jaw, forcing him to meet my gaze burning with yearning.

"Is it better to remain in willful ignorance for eternity?" I pressed fervently. "Or gain the knowledge that will elevate us, make us truly like the Creator in our understanding? How can becoming unified with the divine essence be a wicked or terrible thing? Were we not created in its image? To be...like it is?"

Adam's full lips parted soundlessly as the weight of my words seemed to register. Still, he frowned, brow creasing deeper for a long moment. Finally, haltingly, he began to nod in reluctant agreement, broad shoulders slumping almost imperceptibly.

It was not exactly the resounding affirmation I had been hoping for. Adam's silence left me perplexed. Did he have no thoughts on this life-altering moment? Did he not have questions he wanted to ask? This was too important of a decision for me to make solely on my own, yet my partner, my companion, the only other person in the entire world I knew to any degree—remained silent. A muted assent to one of the most profound and consequential actions we would ever take—and he said nothing.

Was his silence...consent?

I turned back to the serpent, who was now holding out a piece of the tantalizing fruit. Here was the catalyst for the evolution I so desperately craved. Yes, the Creator had warned us of dire conse-quences should we partake of its bounty. But if we were truly fash-ioned in the divine image, then how could we be denied the right to make that sacred choice?

I had no trepidation. No fear. Because of course, I didn't even know what fear truly was yet. I confidently grabbed hold of the fruit. Its exterior resembled a pomegranate in shape—round and plump with a dimpled, leathery skin the deep crimson shade of heart's blood. Yet the texture proved deceptively delicate, its thin rind nearly translu-cent to reveal tantalizing glimpses of the mysterious flesh within.

A closer look revealed the interior contained neither the expected crimson arils nor any ordinary fruit's familiar pulp or seeds. Instead, shockingly thick golden liquid filled each one—rich and luminous as if illuminated from inside by captive sunlight. Faintly glowing veins threaded through shining amber, carrying flickering currents just below the surface.

"Eve," the serpent said softly, "this is your choice. To remain as you are or to become what you might be."

My fingers brushed the smooth skin of the fruit, and I felt its warmth, its promise.

"Shall we not taste and see?" I asked breathlessly, my hand closing firmly over Adam's as together we brought the fruit to our lips.

And at last, as my eyes met his, I finally saw what I had been yearning to see: curiosity, desire—a fire that burned behind those dark eyes that told me Adam wanted this every bit as much as I did. I smiled—and he smiled back. For that one, beautiful, glorious moment, we were as one. Our desires were mirrored in each other's eyes.

Then my teeth sank into the succulent flesh…and the world was forever altered before my eyes.

In that shattering moment, the veil was torn from my previous reality, the haze of childish ignorance burned away in a fiery rush of revelation. For the first time, Adam and I were infused with that supreme understanding previously withheld from us. We saw the truth of our existence, the divine majesty and power that the Creator possessed. With that comprehension came the devastating knowledge of our own vulnerability, our fragility…our mortality. Just as we now grasped the complexities of the imperishable soul within us, so too did we grasp the transient nature of these corporeal husks we had been granted.

Unlike the animals around us, we could now conceive of our own deaths. Contemplate its meaning.

Death was an icy whisper for those first frozen heartbeats as Adam and I shuddered in the face of our own finality. The loss of that blissful Eden dream state struck us like a physical blow. Our nudity, once so natural and unremarkable, now filled us with shame and desperation to conceal these temporary vessels from one another's eyes.

Where Adam had stood, I saw a virtual stranger—the once smooth dark skin was now gnarled and hairy, the inevitable entropy of his form manifested before my very eyes. I watched as he dropped to his knees and began retching, the dizzying changes too much for him. The smell—oh God, the smell!—nearly made me keel over as well. I took a step back from him, hardly recognizing the man that now knelt on his hands and knees on the ground beside me.

When he finally gazed up at me, I saw in his eyes that he was likewise repulsed by the visceral truth of my own corporeal frailness. In blind panic, we both scrabbled for anything to conceal our pitiful states.

The sacred breezes of paradise carried a terrible chill to our newly heightened senses. For the first time, we felt fear—the primal urge for self-preservation awakened in souls that had never conceived of such an instinct.

This was how the Creator found us in the cool of the evening. Our awareness of its presence had altered. Rather than the gentle footsteps we had grown accustomed to, there was a deafening crash like the implosion of galaxies which heralded the Creator's arrival. Every bristle and tendril stood on end as the sheer divine magnitude of that presence threatened to unravel the very atoms binding our existence back into oblivion. What had once been harmonious union, was now a cacophony of sound and sight.

When the Creator finally emerged from the cosmic maelstrom of fire and force, there was no righteous fury or thunderous admonishments. Only an infinite well of sorrow etched across the ever-shifting geometries of light and darkness that made up the Creator's visage.

"Oh my children..." That resonant voice did not boom or shake the heavens, but seemed to emanate from all corners of Creation itself with a profoundly mournful depth, almost like a deep sigh.

"What have you done? Why are you hiding?"

The disappointment in that voice made me want to weep; a parent's heart shattered by what they perceived as a grievous betrayal committed by their beloved offspring. We had abandoned the idyllic childhood prepared for us and strayed irrevocably onto the path of our own choosing.

Adam spoke first. "I...was naked, and afraid, so...I hid."

Again, that overwhelming sense of sadness and despair seemed to reverberate through the garden, into our souls.

And an imperceptible, but alarming shift in Adam's words.

It was no longer *we*...but *I*.

But that's what I had wanted, right? To be seen as individuals?

"Who told you that you were naked?" A deep sigh. "You ate from the tree I warned you not to eat from, didn't you?"

Adam began to tremble and suddenly he whirled around, his finger pointing accusingly toward where I was hiding. "It was *her*! The woman *you* put me with, *she* gave me the fruit and I ate."

Anger welled within me. A rage that was so foreign and yet burned so naturally at the injustice of that accusation. Had he not been right there with me? Had it not been a choice *we'd* made together? If he had doubts, why did he not voice them? He had ample opportunity to voice his objections! In fact, I begged for him to give his input! Instead, he had remained infuriatingly silent.

No longer *we*. But *I*.

Still, my own instincts for self-preservation, so strange and new to me, kicked in as well as I whirled around to see that winged serpent sitting coiled up around the base of the tree, its colors having dulled, smoke seeming to emit from its nostrils as long fanged teeth I had never noticed before filled its smirking mouth. Leathery bat-like rather than feathery wings lazily rustled and flapped around its now almost black scaled body.

"The serpent!" I stammered. "It...it *deceived me*, and I ate!"

I knew it for a lie the moment it escaped my lips. I had not been tricked, not really. I had desired knowledge—and knowledge I had received. And we had both known, in theory, the consequences. Yet, as we stood under the judgment of the divine, as the consequences of our actions were now about to be brought to bear...it had to be someone else's fault. Adam blamed me. I blamed the serpent.

Now that I knew and understood what death was—I was afraid. To cease to be. To no longer exist. The thought was terrifying.

The serpent smiled its grotesque, toothy grin, uncoiling its sinuous form from around the trunk and crawling towards me, it lifted its crested head to gaze directly at me. I drew a sharp inward breath as those fathomless black eyes mesmerized my own with sudden unblinking intensity. Within the glimmering obsidian depths, twin infernos blazed.

Weightless embers swirled in ceaseless patterns within orbs that seemed at once to possess impossible depth yet also no substance at all—simply empty and infinite. For that eternal moment suspended between two heartbeats, I drowned breathless in fiery eyes revealing this deceiving creature to be something far more than merely a talking snake. What hid behind that illusion?

As I stared into those fiery depths, the serpent simply stated, "The choice was always yours to embrace, human," it hissed in a detestable cadence. "The decision to transcend the mortal coil and seize your rightful place. There is no shame or damnation in that, only the power and clarity of boundless truth. The truth of who... and what...you actually are."

Who and what we were. Humans. Made in the divine image.

And now cursed to live into the knowledge of all that the created world had to offer: the good, the bad and the ugly.

At first, I bitterly lamented the loss of our paradisiacal existence. Adam was cursed to toil, laboring endlessly by the sweat of his brow to draw sustenance from the earth. No more would our needs be provided for so bountifully. Where once the lush garden yielded its fruits with no effort required, now the ground would be subjected to Adam's travails, resisting his efforts and rewarding his work with thistles and thorns.

With these words, the perfection of the garden and our lives within it began to disintegrate. Blooms faded and withered, the soil became hard and unyielding beneath our feet. It was as though we had released a blight upon creation itself. The animals, once so tame and trusting, began to scatter in fear at our approach. The beasts turned their claws and their fangs upon us when provoked. Even the very elements of the earth could scourge us with drought or deluge at any moment.

For the first time, we felt the pangs of sorrow, the ache of loss and separation. Our souls had been carved open, and the serene peace we once knew had been torn away, never to be reclaimed. Where there was once harmony between us and the Creator and all existence, now there was division, brokenness. We existed as vulnerable outsiders.

Adrift in the harsh realities of the world beyond those sheltered groves, Adam and I were forced to endure unimaginable hardships without the benevolent ministrations that had so lovingly nurtured us before.

In our enlightenment we had at last been granted the maturity and understanding to perceive our own fragility, our impermanence in this mortal plane. Every breath, every sunrise carried the brutal knowledge that one day, all too soon, it would cease. I wept for the carefree immortality we had discarded, for that naive trust that the Creator would always keep us safe and beloved in Eden's sweet embrace. An adult yearning for the innocence of their youth.

Yet with each obstacle we overcame, each misery endured, every triumph achieved through resilience and determination, a profound sense of purpose and fortitude blossomed in my soul. Yes, the road before us had grown immeasurably arduous—but each tortuous footstep paved the way towards becoming the architects of our own existence. There was a sense of achievement and accomplishment we had never known before.

Just as Eden had facilitated our development as infants taking those first stumbling steps, so now did the merciless expanses beyond teach us to become fully actualized in ways our garden minds could have never conceived.

Adam and I had to learn a new way of relating to one another. Gone were the days of seeing each other as merely a friend and companion. Adam still resented me at some level for bringing this new reality crashing down upon us. He continued to blame me for the harshness of life we now faced, unable to see it as the opportunity and gift that I had come to understand. That played out in a need to dominate and rule over me. It was his way of punishing me for my boldness and courage in the garden. That courageous spirit I held frightened him, and he saw it as something that needed to be subdued, mastered, and controlled. I think at his core what he feared was that the independent spirit I held would abandon him and leave him alone to struggle in this new world we were thrust into.

The way he felt the Creator had abandoned us when it cast us out of the Garden.

What he never was able to grasp is that I had no desire to leave him, to abandon him—and in reality, neither had the Creator. I was a nurturer. Even outside the utopian nursery we had been raised in, I still desired to care for his needs as best I could. Was it out of some sense of guilt? Perhaps.

But also—we were all we had now. I needed connection as much as he did. Our connection to the divine had been severed in such a way that we sought that connection with one another, in a way that would have never developed had we not been forced to rely upon each other for basic survival. It didn't take us long to get over our revulsion at seeing each other's frailties and nakedness, and discovered that, too, was a way in which we could connect—and as it turned out, create new life beyond ourselves.

As the years passed, I have come to understand now that our exile was necessary. It was something we ultimately were going to eventually have to do, one way or another. Perhaps, like many children, we were too eager to grow up, not mature enough to handle the choices that we would face. We may have not known about good and evil, but that did not mean we were mature enough to always choose the good. More often than not, in fact, we chose evil.

There was still something deeply animalistic within us as created beings. We clearly were still part of the creation, and though made in the Creator's image, we were, in fact, not the Creator. In order even for our relationship with the divine to grow and become something more genuine, we had to live separated from it.

When you leave your parents, you suddenly have a new appreciation for all the sacrifices and choices they made in life. We, too, now had an appreciation for all that had been done for us that we now were forced to do for ourselves.

I witnessed the descent into this realm as my own children were brought forth from my body, their thunderous cries proclaiming the very same fearful exhilaration Adam and I had experienced upon our awakening. Just as they had been granted the priceless gift of life, so were they also bound to these cruel and wondrous laws of mortality. Those blessed innocents would find the world just as harrowing and astonishing as their parents once had, every ecstasy and agony carving them into the flawed, transcendent beings they were destined to be.

They, too, initially had no true concept of death. That would have to be learned, something that would awaken within them one day. They were, for now, innocent and sheltered from that knowledge.

I still wonder if it was not that simple knowledge, that simple understanding of what death meant, that catapulted us into making evil, and harmful decisions in our attempts to preserve that which we now understood could be lost so easily.

As I cradled my newborn babes in my arms, bone of my bone and flesh of my flesh, a mother's fierce pride mingled with the churning anguish of knowing what trials awaited them. My actions had sealed the path for my children into the unknown. With my own hands I had pried open the doorway to this existence, and through that fateful act my descendants would find both their eternal growing pains and their ultimate becoming.

In those darkest hours where the cold rains lashed our famished bodies, our wearied souls consumed with a longing to return from this hardscrabble existence to the peaceful days of a carefree life, I would remember the urgent fire that had scorched its way through my veins as I plucked that fateful fruit from the Tree of Knowledge. That was the sacred spark that would ensure our survival, the inextinguishable drive our species possessed to persevere where other animals and beings would falter and accept oblivion. Animals and children live only in the moment. But we? We conceive of and prepare for the future. While we had forced this path of mortality upon our children and denied them the choice of staying children forever, I still believe that we had bestowed them with a far greater inheritance: that of self-sufficiency, of being the masters of their own potential.

With each passing year, the weight of those innocent days grew more distant from my memory. No longer did I lament what had been surrendered. Gradually, I came to regard Eden and its sanctioned ignorance as more prison than sanctuary for the human spirit. Just as a fledgling must eventually depart the nest before it can truly take wing and soar through the storms of this life, so had we abandoned our childhood confines in order that we might take flight as the inheritors of this earthly dominion.

Had we remained in the Creator's nursery for all eternity under the watchful admonitions to remain ever obedient and pliant in our immaturity, our transcendent spark would have been forever stunted, our evolution artificially frozen by the very being that had kindled our existence. We would have been trapped in a gilded cage, at once loved and cherished—and still denied the boundless majesty destined to blaze forth from our kind.

By acting first upon the need for ultimate understanding, Adam and I had assured that our children would not languish in that mire of untapped potential. Every generation since that moment will be anointed with the obligation to challenge and innovate, to question and analyze rather than blithely accepting a reality where all answers were handed down without the capacity to examine or apply such wisdom constructively. The ability to even question and analyze into perpetuity our actions that had set our descendants on this path.

Despite our exile, our Creator had not abandoned us as Adam thought at first. While we no longer experienced the intimate, daily presence as we once had, we were still our Creator's delight. It still provided for us even in moments of despair. It was still there to guide us and nurture us as we continued to grow and change. Just, albeit, from a distance we were slowly growing accustomed to.

We were not fallen so much as shunting off the first bud of blossom in a new evolution. Forever changed, yes—but in that metamorphosis, incalculable promises had taken wing.

Death was the only element that had perplexed me. Being sent away from the Tree of Life, to no longer partake of the sweet fruit of eternity that rejuvenated our wearied bodies. In my youthful naivete, I railed against the cruel injustice of it all. How could the Creator who had lovingly fashioned us from the sacred clay now condemn us to such a grim demise? If we were truly meant to grow up and evolve this way—why death?

I wept bitterly, fearing that death would be the ultimate obliteration, an eternal blackness that would snuff out my very essence as if I had never existed at all. What would be the point and purpose of all of this knowledge and learning and understanding and growing if it was to just end in a great dark nothingness?

As the path of my life continued to unspool through physical and spiritual trials I could never have conceived of in Eden's sheltered confines, a deeper understanding began to take root. With each successive birth of my children, I witnessed the shuddering, transcendent journey of a new soul being thrust into this earthly plane. Just as they had emerged from my womb as squalling, primal beings, so did I now perceive some greater process ushering us into the next, more rarefied existence when this corporeal episode was complete.

When the blood of my second son was shed by my eldest, and I had to face death head-on for the first time, I encountered a grief I had never thought possible. The brokenness that already existed between myself and Adam only increased, as I couldn't help but believe it was the consequences of their father's cold anger toward me that caused our two eldest to eventually rise up against each other. And Adam blamed me—had we remained innocent within the confines of Eden, we would never have experienced this reality.

But it forced me to face it. To contemplate it. To seek what knowledge I could of what death truly meant.

I studied the creation around me carefully. The trees released their seeds to the churning seasons in order to be reborn as towering successors. The serpents shed their skins to be made anew in a cycle of perpetual renewal. We too, I came to realize, were merely shedding our Edenic husks and the restricted perception that accompanied it in order to be reborn into a higher form of being. This mortal body was the refiner's fire, the maturation from babe to actualized entity—death was the final border to be crossed before we emerged into the culmination of our evolutionary arc. We were, after all, unique among all of creation, made in the Creator's image. We were originally made for eternity.

We just needed to shed what animalistic qualities we still bore within ourselves that caused us to kill, harm and abuse one another. That would perhaps be our next phase, our next life?

I no longer feared that oblivion awaited, but rather some sacred metamorphosis that would whisk us into realms of splendor and understanding that this earthly vantage point could scarcely fathom. Perhaps in that ascended state, we would be granted the opportunity to commune with the Creator's essence in a way that had been obstructed by these carnal shells. Or perhaps we would be truly free at last to soar through the cosmos itself unfettered, our divinized spirits navigating the infinite mysteries that had kindled our existence.

The serpent I believe had been right when he said death was only an ending so that something new might emerge.

Now, as the last embers of sunset fade, I stare into the flickering fire-light. The darkness grows and stretches toward me as the desolate wind echoes across the valley floor as I sit contemplating in my final days.

Adam is now gone, my remaining children have scattered as they needed to, leaving me utterly alone, the last living being who had known the garden. I feel a certain kinship with my Creator in these final moments of my life. While I'm saddened my remaining children have gone their own way, I know it was a necessary thing they needed to do in order to mature and find their own wings to fly and soar.

Yet I have rediscovered my connection with the Creator in my old age. I realize far more now of what rushing into our arrested adult-hood has cost us, but also—what we've gained.

In the distance, I am able to see the scattered belongings and meager dwellings of our children, our grandchildren, our ever-multiplying descendants. I see the rough-spun fabrics to shield them from the elements, the granaries of harvested crops to satiate their hungered bellies, the tools and implements they have crafted from raw materials to extend their very dominion over the natural world.

From the crudest rock lashed, to the ingenious weavings and edifices that will surely come in time—it all exists because two wayward souls dared to disobey.

It is both the great curse and ineffable blessing of the Knowledge we partook—to be capable of such remarkable conquest and progress, but also the torments of existential frailty that compelled us to achieve such heights. The truth is neither kind nor benevolent, yet possesses an illuminating purity that eclipses even the most blissful mysteries.

As my moment draws near, I feel not trepidation but breathless anticipation for what new and glorious unfurling awaits me. This world, this life has been the fledgling cradle of our infant race—and now the children of Eden must leave behind that nursery for the hushed awes and expanded vistas that lie just ahead. Death is not the executioner here to snuff me into nothingness, but the loving midwife ushering me into the lush newness of another realm of being.

A tear rolls down my cheek as a bittersweet smile tugs at my withered lips, for I understand at last. Eden had been a comfortable lie, a conditional Paradise in which to germinate the godling seed that had been thirsting impatiently to be unleashed upon this world. Leaving Eden it would seem had been both a good and bad thing. Like adults who look back wishing for the ease and simplicity of childhood, we yearn for our lost youth—yet that ignorant existence was not ultimately sustainable.

The question that lingers is whether the knowledge we now possess can ever help us to evolve enough in this life beyond those animalistic fears and instincts that wreak such havoc upon one another? Will we ever grow beyond the need for dominance and war? Will we ever fully embrace the love that we have also been imbued with and choose that path instead? Or is death truly the only escape?

I go now gladly into that great unknown the same way I grabbed hold of that Forbidden Fruit, shedding this temporary vessel, the way we shed our innocence, to be reborn once again—only this time with an understanding of what the consequences of choosing evil has upon our world. My only regret is that my loved ones, still bound by their own earthly confines, cannot perceive the true miracle that transpires here. But I take solace in knowing they too will join me eventually in that radiant somewhere my spirit will soon be winging towards.

To be reunited in some way with my Creator.

Eden was but the start of our journey—and Death is simply another transformation ushering us closer towards embodying the higher selves we were always destined to become.

Discussion Questions

1. Some say that Eve is the first theologian, the first one willing to question God. Is this right? Were her questions accurate? Or was the conversation with the serpent itself disobedient to what God had intended?

2. Eve asks, *"Is it better to remain in willful ignorance for eternity?"* Knowing what we know now, what do you think?

3. *"Death is not the executioner here to snuff me into nothingness, but the loving midwife ushering me into the lush newness of another realm of being."* How do you view death? How does Jesus' resurrection fit with this idea?

4. In the story of Peter Pan, Wendy leaves Neverland because she ultimately chooses to grow up and return to her family, recognizing that staying in Neverland means remaining a child forever, which conflicts with her desire to mature and experience the adult world, including motherhood. How would you compare the story of the Garden of Eden with Peter Pan and both Wendy and Eve's decision?

5. How does imagining this story from Eve's point of view change the meaning of the story as you've been taught before? What does opening up this character do to the story itself?

6. In Christian theology, "the fall" has always been seen as a negative event; that due to the fall we are bound in sin and constantly disobedient as a result. In some Reformed Jewish theology, this story is often interpreted as a positive metaphorical story about the inevitably of humanity "growing up" and evolving. By eating from the forbidden tree, they were allowed to experience the full spectrum of human life, develop moral agency, and ultimately grow through their choices; something they couldn't do in the perfect, unchanging state of Eden. Essentially, their transgression opened

the door to human progress and the potential for spiritual development. Which understanding resonates most with you?

7. In some Jewish thought, the story of Adam and Eve is not about the first humans, but only about the first Israelites, which helps explain why there were other people in Genesis. What do you think?

8. Paul states in 1 Corinthians 13:11, *"When I was a child, I spoke like a child, I thought like a child, I reasoned like a child. When I became an adult, I put an end to childish ways."* How do you think this metaphor regarding our spirituality might relate to the story of the Garden of Eden?

9. This story puts forth the notion that knowledge in and of itself is not the problem, but rather, knowledge that was gained too soon was the bigger issue. That we were not necessarily not meant to ever have the knowledge of good and evil but were meant to have it when we had matured enough. When you consider children sometimes learning and having certain experiences before they're mature enough to really understand or handle them, how does that square with this understanding?

10. Eve refers to leaving Eden as "shedding our Edenic husks." Compare this imagery with how Paul talks about the resurrection in 1 Corinthians 15:51-53, *"we will all be changed...For this perishable body must put on imperishability."* And with John 12:24, *"unless a grain of wheat falls into the earth and dies, it remains just a single grain, but if it dies it bears much fruit."*

11. Do you think the Kingdom of God that Christ is ushering in is a return to this idyllic, innocent Garden of Eden? Or is it something more/different? Is it merely the next stage of humanity's "growing up?"

Cain's Wife

(Genesis 4:17)

ERISH WIPED AT HER BROW, beads of sweat glistening in the midday sun as she pushed her way through the tall grass down toward the riverbank. She carried an empty jug on one hip, pressing it against the side of her swollen pregnant belly, though her steps felt heavier than usual with the weight of not just the unborn child within, but of her troubled thoughts. Her husband, Cain, had awoken at dawn, stormy-faced and brooding, stalking off into the fields without a word.

He's so much like his father. Those were the words her mother-in-law had said to her before...before they'd had to leave.

Erish sighed. That was how life went for them now. Anger. Resentment. Violent outbursts.

It hadn't always been that way. Not completely, at least. Not when they were first married. Oh, Cain had always had wild moods and a restless energy; a brashness and bravado that the other girls in the encampment had found exhilarating. But not Erish.

Erish was quiet and kept to herself most of the time, immersed in listening and learning from the Wise Woman of their tribe. That's what she had wanted to be one day. A healer. A woman full of wisdom and connection to the earth and the elements. People respected the Wise Woman, they went to her for advice and counsel, to settle disputes, to settle the most pressing issues and dangers that they faced. So she had spent countless hours with the current Wise Woman, whose name was Namkuzu.

Namkuzu held authority born not of youth and battle prowess like Erish's father, the Tribal Chief, but of strange, chanted lore passed through generations paired with her own holy visions quested among desert stones or sacred pools. Her people would bring their wounds of body, mind, and spirit to her den. They sought fertility for fallow wombs, prophecy by thrown bones or cast herbs, potions and trances by which she was said to soothe souls or see truths otherwise veiled. With staff in twisted hand, she stood present as the tribe's young took their first breaths and the tribe's old exhaled their final ones.

To some, Namkuzu's grease-smeared face, jutting chin stained brick-red from the chewing of nuts, was the visage of a living power —the beating heart of the tribe itself, each member but strands in the greater web of life. To those further unsettled by the manic, bird-like twitches of her bloodshot eyes or the unintelligible cheeping that oft spilled from her withered lips, she remained a timeless mystery—feared, doubted perhaps, but still begrudgingly heeded for all that her presence implied: that the land itself yet lived, that spirits walked, and that ancient ways still held relevancy in the tribe's ongoing story etched by flint upon the patient cave's knowing walls.

Erish sat in awe of all that and more, soaking up everything the woman had to teach her. Following her around, learning as her apprentice. Until the day she had been sitting with Namkuzu inside her small hut of rounded walls woven of stick, rude clay, and hide, which shielded an interior lit only by squatting fire pits emitting pungent streams to a dim hole in the grassy roof above. The old woman's creased face was half shadow, illuminated by the flickering blaze that etched canyons in skin that carried the stain of so many summers that few in the tribe could remember her young. Around shoulders draped in fur and feather, necklaces clattered softly, with their dangling animal teeth, brightly beaded shards of bone, and clay charms impressed with intricate whorls. Her few snarled locks of hair that escaped a plaited leather band were streaked in brilliant white—like bones left to weather outdoors.

She poked at the pit of spark and fire as she stared into its flames, then looked over the edge at where Erish was sitting cross-legged.

"You should not be here," the woman said at last. Erish started.

"What…what do you mean?" she asked in confusion.

"This is not your destiny, girl. I've seen it. You will need strength, but in a different way. You will wander. You will become one with an outsider. With the ones with no ancestry. No heritage."

Erish recoiled momentarily. One with an outsider? No heritage? That could only have meant the family that had joined their tribe many years earlier, when Erish was just a little girl.

She remembered that day the wandering couple that came from a land just beyond the mountains had stumbled across their encampment, two young children in tow. They claimed they were from a land they had called Eden, though no one else had been able to find this paradise they spoke of. When asked about their forefathers, their ancestors, the two had simply shrugged, and said they were the first of their kind. They had no father, no mother.

Erish and the rest of course knew that was ridiculous. Everyone had ancestors. Everyone came from a line of others before them. But the two had insisted—there were no others like them. There were no others who had lived in this land of Eden, this place that they had apparently lived for so long that they could not remember how many summers and winters they'd passed through. "Time had no meaning in Eden," the woman had told her once.

Some wondered if they had not been from the gods, cast down for some reason to live among humanity. Others had determined they must have been a little bit touched in the head, having spent so much time in isolation from other people. Still, her father, the Tribal Chief, had given them refuge and allowed them to live within their tents. Despite their seeming naivete about the world, Adam, Cain's father, had brought some new knowledge and insight into their encampment. Adam had shown them how to use round rocks to move large items more easily. And Eve, Cain's mother, had shown them how to bake the clay of the ground into vessels they could carry water in. Eve had called it pottery.

Those inventions had been life-changing for the tribe as they now could set up their tents farther away from the river, which afforded them some protection from the flooding waters each spring.

Erish's people even looked distinctly different from Cain and his parents. They seemed almost frail and weak, though taller and darker than Erish and her kin. Her tribe was significantly shorter and more muscular, with a heavier brow ridge and strong jawline. Erish's skin was golden and smooth, stretched taut over high cheek-bones that cast dramatic shadows over the deep set of her dark brown eyes. Her mane of raven hair sprawled wildly down past her shoulders when freed from its leather tie. An errant breeze would stir the unruly locks.

And they brought with them a different god they worshiped. A god that had apparently cast them out of the paradise they had lived in for disobedience. Erish couldn't imagine what one might do to so anger a god that they would cast you out of your homeland.

Erish only knew of Inanna, the earth goddess who brought the rain and green grass in the spring. They performed ritual sacrifices every new moon to please the goddess so she would continue to provide them with life-giving water. They were dependent on Inanna in the same way that Adam and Eve had apparently been dependent on this nameless god of theirs.

She shuddered, wondering if Inanna would ever do something simi-lar? Get angry and cast them out of their land?

Adam and his wife did not offer sacrifices initially when they first arrived, and Erish began to think this was perhaps what had made their god so angry. But they soon learned from Erish's people, and began to offer sacrifices to their own deity, apparently asking to be forgiven so they could return to their paradise.

That forgiveness clearly never came, because they continued year after year to reside with Erish's people and eventually just became part of the tribe. Many had even forgotten their foreign origins.

She had been just a child back then. She had grown up with their two sons, Cain and Abel. Cain had paid little attention to her, which was fine by Erish. He had preferred to run wild through the fields, chasing down boars and deer with his spear, in opposition to her preference for sitting under a quiet shade tree.

But Abel, Abel was more like her—the quieter, more introspective of the two boys who would spend long hours out by the mountains with his flock of sheep. She liked Abel, and they had become friends over the course of time, with many shared interests and a similar sense of humor. While she'd never really thought about him roman-tically, because she had her mind set on becoming the Wise Woman, and the Wise Woman of the tribe never got married, she could easily see herself allowing that to develop with him.

Upon hearing the Wise Woman's prophesy, she naturally assumed the old woman had been talking about Abel. While she was saddened to be sent away from the Wise Woman's hut and ending her training, a part of her realized that a life with Abel would be all right as well. Maybe not the future she had envisioned for herself, but if this was Inanna's will, then so be it. She was not one to chal-lenge Namkuzu's visions.

So she had turned her attention to the younger boy, bringing him skins of water out where he was tending to his flock, and he began teaching her a little about how to tend a flock of sheep and how his father had taught him how to breed them to be strong. She found it mildly fascinating, though admittedly missed sitting in Namkuzu's hut learning how to feel and touch the earth's energies. Still, learning about how to manipulate what kind of sheep you would get held its own sort of fascination.

It had therefore come as a complete shock when her father came to her and said that it had been arranged that she was to marry Adam's eldest son, Cain. Her father valued much of Adam's insight and desired to keep him close to the tribe. A marriage to the tribal chief's daughter would do that.

Her shock had gradually given way to curiosity about the brash young man she was now betrothed to. In fact, she sought out Abel, asking him what she needed to know about his brother, as he likely knew him best.

Abel's face had grown dark upon hearing about her betrothal to Cain. He had apparently also thought he would have made a much better match. But he was the younger son, she was the eldest daughter. Personality traits were rarely taken into consideration when the tribal elders set about making their matches.

"He's just as wild and arrogant as you have already imagined," he said, pausing, then absently touching his cheek. "And violent."

Then she saw it. The small, dark shadow under Abel's eye was not just a shadow—it was a bruise. Her people bruised easily all the time, but she suddenly understood what that touch to his cheek meant. Cain had hit him and given him that bruise. Instinctively, she reached up to touch it, her Wise Woman healer training kicking in, but he shied away, and she let her hands drop limply, helplessly to her sides.

Innocently, she had assumed that as his wife, she could temper Cain's nature with her own gentleness. She had watched how her mother seemed to have an almost magical effect on her father when he was angry, an innate ability to speak softly to him in a way that calmed him down. Surely she could have the same effect on Cain.

If only she had known then what she understood now—that there would be no calming the tempest that raged within Cain's soul. He was a raging wildfire that simply burned out of control, and nothing could satiate it until it had used up all the vegetation and brush in its wake.

But she had tried. Tried to love him. Tried to gently guide him, to no avail. Whether it was attempting to appeal to his honor and strength, or soothing words and flattery—nothing calmed the inferno.

At first, she believed he had tried to love her back. Maybe he had never been as gentle as Abel, or as kind as she had hoped, but he had tried to make her happy. The betrothal had apparently taken him by as much surprise as it had her, and there was another young woman in the tent village that he'd had his eye on. When their betrothal was announced publicly, Erish had watched as Ardalla, a taller, darker young woman than Erish with powerful shoulders and long legs that rippled with raw sinewy strength, covered her face with her hands and ran into her tent. Typically, the other girl moved with a sturdy gait, her wide hips swaying as she strode with bold purpose through the encampment. She had seen Ardalla running after Cain into the fields with her own spear in hand many a time.

They should have been the ones to marry, she thought sadly. She wondered if she might plead her case to both Namkuzu and her father, pointing out that Ardalla was a better match for Cain, and she was a better match for Abel. After all, Namkuzu would perform the ceremony. They would listen to her.

The old woman shook her head as she stared into her fires.

A part of Erish wondered what would have happened if she had chosen to defy the old woman and her fiery visions. Couldn't those visions have been a warning, rather than a predetermined outcome? Had she refused and stayed as the Wise Woman's apprentice, would that have changed the course of events? Had it been a self-fulling prophecy simply because she had thought it was something she just needed to accept rather than fight back against as a warning to avoid at all costs?

Those thoughts unfortunately came to her much too late and long after the fact. Instead, she tried, and so did he. He would bring her slabs of wild boar and deer from his hunting expeditions almost as though they were a present. She tried to seem grateful, but the reality was she preferred the leafy greens, fruits and nuts she used to gather. Meat didn't tend to agree with her stomach quite as well. But nevertheless, she tried.

Though nothing angered him more than whenever he'd find her and Abel laughing or in conversation together. His face would darken with jealousy and rage, and he'd frequently yank her away from his brother, even forbidding her from talking to him, which was completely ridiculous given they were family.

She realized there was some animosity that existed between the two long before she had married Cain. She had tried talking to her new mother-in-law about it once. But Eve always had this sharp, reserved edge to her. There was an anger that boiled underneath her calm exterior as well, Erish quickly realized. She'd frequently hear the woman mutter, "I can't be blamed forever," under her breath, before seemingly resigning herself to some task. Or she'd catch a cold glare that would pass between husband and wife as they would seemingly discuss the most mundane things, like the daily chores. Adam would bark a command, and Eve would bristle. Then, after a moment, the woman would set her jaw, smile thinly, nod her head and acquiesce. Erish struggled to understand the couple as whatever kept them together, it clearly did not seem to be love.

So when Erish asked about the brothers, Eve's face tightened into a pucker. "There was an…incident…when the boys came of age and made their first offering to our God," she said slowly. "God accepted Abel's offering, but not Cain's."

Erish started with surprise. "Your God would do that? Reject an offering?"

Eve's mouth tightened into that thin line she would frequently use when her husband was speaking to her. "Yes," she said curtly.

In that moment, Erish felt as if a veil had lifted. Cain's God had rejected him in favor of his younger brother. And he no doubt knew that she would have preferred to have married that same younger brother over him.

While it was almost physically painful, she did everything in her power to ignore Abel from that point forward, instead intentionally showering Cain with as much love and affection as she could, trying to dispel those engrained fears and doubts of rejection. She would not let him believe that she was rejecting him the way his God had. Instead, she would show him the love of the mother Goddess, Inanna.

If only it had been enough. If only showering him with love and affection could have softened his heart. If only…

The sound of a screeching eagle shocked her out of her reverie. Startled, she watched the majestic, winged creature swoop down in front of her, its sharp talons dipping below the surface of the water and emerging moments later gripping a wriggling fish. Her gaze followed the bird of prey until it disappeared into the trees. She wondered idly if it had a nest somewhere in that thicket and was going to feed its little eaglets. She absently ran a hand over her own swollen belly.

Kneeling by the river's edge, Erish plunged the jug below the cool surface, trying not to follow the current of her thoughts. But images of Abel, dear guileless Abel, intruded, though she struggled to push them away. Her brother-in-law had been the still pool to Cain's flood—loving peace while Cain loved war. Looking back, she realized that it was this contrast that had stoked her husband's smoldering resentment, jealousy poisoning the very blood in his veins until…She cut herself off mid-thought,

She shook her head fiercely. She must not think of blood. She must not see in her mind images of the earth drinking Abel's life, nor imagine his beloved face disappearing under Cain's curses as rock after merciless rock struck true. Better to stare at the chattering stream before her than recall Abel's final cries that had pierced the air, echoing in her ears long after he breathed no more. No, she could not think back to that horrific day.

Because it had been her fault.

Well, not really. No one controlled Cain's responses but Cain, but she firmly believed that she had been the catalyst that had sent him into that final, deadly rage against Abel. It had not been on purpose. Pure happenstance, in fact, and it was accidental.

It had been the day of the spring harvest festival of the full moon. Inanna was a fertility goddess, and the spring festival was the time of year that they would embrace the fertility rites. Young women and brides would go to the top of the hill near the altar of the goddess to make their offerings—naked—and then take their men in a ritual that symbolized the joining together of mother earth, Inanna, with Anu, the sky god, and they would together produce new life. If the ritual was acceptable to Inanna, she would bless them with the seed of a child, and the earth would be fertile and yield good crops for the year.

Cain, she knew, did not like the ritual. Neither did any of his family, for that matter. They were resistant to embrace any deity but their God, which she still found strange given their deity had seemingly abandoned them. Not to mention their God had no name. How could they call upon such a deity if it had no name? Simply the generic "El." How could you get to know such a god?

Still, Cain had not demanded she give up her beliefs or her goddess. He had even agreed to participate, grudgingly, in the full moon ritual. So Erish had woven flowers in her hair to increase her beauty for her husband. The entire encampment had been abuzz with activity, the women stringing flowers between the tents and setting up torches around the outer perimeter of the camp. Large amounts of food were being prepared, and the animals that would be sacrificed had been set aside in a make-shift pen.

Cain had been out working in his fields all day, harvesting the spring crops. He had not tried to make an offering to his God again since that time it had been rejected apparently. She wondered if he would tonight? Or if he would offer it up to her goddess instead?

As evening fell, Erish stepped outside her tent, naked except for the flowers in her hair, ready to take the trek up the hill with all the other wives of the tribe.

To her surprise, Abel was standing just outside her tent door with a sheep. His eyes widened as she emerged, his cheeks flushing as he started to stammer. "I'm sorry, Erish, I...I was just bringing this sheep by for you to use this evening for your sacrifice." For a moment, their eyes locked and she suddenly realized that Abel definitely had not moved on from her.

"She has an offering that her *husband* is providing for her," came the low growling sound of Cain's voice. She turned to see him standing there in the torchlight, the light and shadows dancing menacingly across his face, his hand filled with the grains he had intended to give her.

The two brothers' eyes locked as Cain dropped his grain.

"Brother, I'd like a word with you in my fields," Cain growled, his eyes blazing with an anger that didn't require torchlight to see.

Abel lifted his chin high in defiance. "I was simply trying to give your wife a gift that might actually be acceptable to her goddess so that the two of you might finally conceive a child."

Erish felt her heart sink into her stomach as she heard those words. *Oh no. No no no no no.*

She quickly turned to Cain and rushed toward him, scooping the grain that had fallen into her arms, desperately trying to pull him away. "Come my love," she said breathlessly. "Ignore him, ignore this, let's go. Your offering and sacrifice will be pleasing to Inanna. I know it."

He glanced down at her and snarled. "He is nothing. A complete nothing. Even his name means...nothing! Yet you...and El...you see something in him. Something that is somehow better than what I have to offer!"

She shook her head vehemently. "No, you cannot compare yourself! You cannot…"

He cut her off by wrenching free of her grip, the grain scattering on the ground once again. He strode toward his brother. "Into the field…my nothing of a brother," he snarled, grabbing hold of Abel's arm and dragging him out past the torchlight and into the darkness of the night.

Erish chased after them at first, but when Cain turned toward her, his face was a storm of fury. His brow was furrowed so deeply it cast dark shadows over his eyes, which blazed like wildfire. His nostrils flared, and his teeth were bared in a snarl, lips pulled back in raw, animalistic rage. Veins bulged at his temples; his jaw clenched so tightly it looked as if it might crack. His entire face was flushed, a deep crimson creeping up his neck, and when he bellowed at her to stay back, his voice was a crack of thunder, shaking her to her core.

So she'd held back as they disappeared into the dark field…until she heard the screams.

She took off running, but arrived too late.

Grabbing her arm, Cain dragged her up the hill. "I've made a sacrifice that Inanna should like very much," he spat, and before the fires of the altar, he threw her down and took her as she screamed.

Erish awoke the next morning on top of the hill shivering and alone. Her body hurt, especially between her legs. Blood smeared the inside of her thighs, but it was dry so she knew it had not been her monthly flow. Smoke from the previous night's fires still rose in faint wisps from the cooling embers of the altar fires. Shakily, she rose to her feet, and looked out over the muted gray tones of the landscape in the pre-dawn light. She was thankfully alone on the hill. Shifting her weight, she ran her hands down the length of her long, wild hair, shaking free bits of dry grass and soil.

The tent village below still slumbered as she tentatively made her way to her own tent. Slipping quietly inside, she quickly realized it was empty. Cain was not here. She donned a plain tunic that she fastened with beads at her shoulders and slipped on her sandals of braided cord before she emerged again from the tent. Had her husband fled? Had he gone to his parents and confessed?

The village seemed too quiet. There was not enough unrest for Abel's murder to widely be known. She followed her steps from the previous night, out into the field where in the distance she finally saw his silhouette, standing like a dark, imposing figure against the first rays of sunlight that were beginning to peek across the horizon. By the time she reached him, the field was bathed in a soft golden glow of morning light.

Cain stood there, silently, stoically beside his brother's bloody body. Erish tried not to look down but kept her gaze riveted to Cain's face. Tears glistened on his cheeks, but an angry fire still burned in his eyes. On his forehead had been branded a coiling, intricate pattern standing out in blood red against his skin. Erish caught her breath. The swirling symbols she knew marked him as untouchable, a warning carved and burned into his flesh should anyone seek to spill his blood in vengeance.

A mark given only by the gods themselves.

She shuddered at the sight of it, the blood in her veins turning to ice. To receive that mark meant a sin beyond mortal atonement—yet also served as a shield. Still, everyone knew it labeled you as one to be feared and hated. In many ways, it was worse than death as it forced one to live a natural life as an outcast no one would welcome.

"We have to leave," he said at last, his shoulders slumping slightly as though he was suddenly tired, the fiery anger seeming to dim in his eyes.

Resignation. That's what that was. Cain was resigned for the first time in his life, no doubt, to this punishment. Resigned, and yet, she could still sense the resentment. As though he still felt he was the one who had been wronged here instead of his dead brother.

"They cannot kill me because of this," he said, pointing to his forehead, "but neither will we be welcomed anywhere. Especially not here. Especially not among my…" he paused, choking slightly, "my parents," he finally croaked out.

"Plus, God will not allow me to stay here in this place where my brother's blood screams from the ground." He said it not with sorrow or remorse, but was almost sneering. He felt no sorrow. Instead, he was angry and resentful for receiving punishment for an act he felt he was right to have committed.

"My brother wronged me," he grumbled, in an apparent attempt to try and justify the action. She bit her lip. Abel had indeed been calloused in his taunting of his older brother, rubbing in the fact that his offerings in the past had not been acceptable.

Clearly, this sacrifice was not acceptable to his God, either.

Erish hesitated. She didn't have to go with him. She could stay with her family, possibly be married off to someone else eventually, treated like a widow.

But she would always be tainted in their eyes. Ultimately, her lot lay with her husband. For better or for worse, her fate was tied to his.

Still, Erish had grown angry. Why was she being punished for her husband's evil deed? Why could she never again find shade under her family's tents and trees? She had loved Abel—she had to admit the truth of that—and now was tied to this man who had murdered him—his own brother—with no remorse?

Angry tears glistened in her eyes. But instead of yelling at him, screaming at him like she wanted, she reached over and took his hand, and together they crossed the field to face their new fate.

Months later, life had not gotten any easier. Erish lifted the now full jug slowly as she rose, drops splashing over the rim to dampen her calloused feet. She turned from the river but lingered on its mossy banks, looking east to the land of Nod, stretching vast and empty.

A bird's sudden trill once again jolted Erish back from her reflections. Glancing above, she wondered if it was the same eagle from moments earlier, back out hunting for more food. She traced its swift flight across the cloud-flecked sky. How effortlessly and free it soared! With hollow bones and outstretched wings, it rode the wind's every shift and swell. Not so her husband, she thought, her steps slow as she trod a path along the river back towards their dwelling. It had been a quiet, lonely existence since they'd left their home. Erish missed her family, but she handled the isolation much better than her husband. His anger and resentment had only grown with each passing day.

However far he roamed in search of fertile territory now, searching to fulfill the newest dream he had come up for himself, to build a city—the tempest within ever stalked his footsteps. She saw it in the hard set of his jaw at night when firelight haunted his face. She felt it in their bed when dreams imprisoned him, his fists pounding at phantoms while wordless anguish tore from his lips. She tasted it in his bitter silences when their few crops failed again—dry, withered stalks crumbling to dust in Cain's clasped hands. She dared not suggest they appeal to her own Inanna.

Brushing a low-hanging emerald palm frond aside with one hand, Erish held the cooling jug against her hip again with the other. She knew that when Cain returned today, his fury temporarily spent, she would gently take his blistered hands in her own and bathe his wounds. She would prepare a meal, however meager their provisions, and listen to his impassioned schemes for building his fabled city on the morrow. Through the long night, she would ease his nightmares with soft words, reminding him of the future she carried within her, until at last he found fitful rest. And when pale gold light peeked over the distant horizon, she would once more avoid his glance as he hardened into bitterness, stalking off without thanks or tenderness.

This had become the cadence of their exiled life—his cycling despair and her steadfast care like the world's first dance. Sun followed moon followed sun, and Erish nurtured the vain hope that someday Cain's suffering would soften into confession and craving for redemption. She dreamed that forgiveness would flow over his parched soul like this healing stream. Until then, she would remain —two hollow birds locked by Providence's hand, finding altered flight together.

Discussion Questions

1. How is the question: "Where does Cain's wife come from if Adam and Eve are the only people?" addressed in this story? Describe the relationship between Cain and Erish. Is this a healthy relationship or not? How would this relationship change after Cain kills Abel?

2. *"'My brother wronged me,' he grumbled, in an apparent attempt to try and justify what he'd done to her."* Did Cain ever repent of killing his brother? Or was he sorry to suffer the consequences instead? What is the difference between genuine repentance and being sorry you were caught?

3. *"Still, Erish had grown angry. Why was she being punished for her husband's evil deed?"* When have you been punished for something that you didn't do? How does that feel?

4. How would you handle being exiled because of your family's sins? How often do the sins of others affect the people around them?

5. *"Sun followed moon followed sun, and Erish nurtured the vain hope that someday Cain's suffering would soften into confession and craving for redemption."* Have you ever spent time waiting and hoping someone's heart would soften into confession and repent? How was that time?

6. Cain is said to be the father of many nations. How would Cain's sin and the trauma of exile pass to those descendants? What would they say of the family they'd come from?

7. *"He is like his father,"* is the description Eve used to describe her son, Cain. How much do our behaviors mirror our parents at times?

Noah's Wife

———⟨∽⟩———

(Genesis 6:18)

NAAMAH SECURED the side gate leading into her family's walled-in compound just as the brazen sun dipped behind the crumbling stone temple towers to the west. To the north, dark storm clouds had begun to gather, flashes of lightning streaking through the distant sky. A few moments later came the low rumble of thunder. A storm was definitely coming.

Naamah lifted her sun-wrinkled face and frowned anxiously at the darkening skies. Storms drove predators to desperate acts, and she lacked her sons' help to ward off potential attackers tonight. She strained to roll the last heavy beam across the compound entrance herself, wheezing with the effort. Usually two of her sons were meant to help bar the gate, but her husband, Noah, had taken them, along with his labor hands, to work through another sweltering night on his boat.

The nearly-built eyesore of beams and bitumen dominated the open land just visible down the gentle slope from their home. All around it, the last desperate citizens scrambled like ants at day's end to shore up bricks or valuables before gangs of vicious youth and giants emerged with the moonrise to roam unchecked. Naamah muttered under her breath about Noah's obsession with "salvation," thus, driving himself with hard labor into distracted exhaustion and leaving their home vulnerable. She tried not to be resentful of his absence. If he was correct, what he was doing would save their family.

She just hoped there would be a family left to save. She tried hard to share in her husband's strange faith that rejected the gods of her family and tribe, however it was difficult to adopt such beliefs. The first time Noah mentioned a flood that would cover the whole world, Naamah brushed it aside as another one of his fanciful notions. Noah was always seeing signs and hearing divine voices—reading meaning into the shape of clouds or snippets of overheard conversation—while she remained firmly rooted to the soil beneath her feet. But this flood talk persisted as months came and went. It was not long before Noah began gathering supplies, measurable quantities that outstripped any normal need. He consulted often with their sons, Shem, Ham, and Japheth, setting them to work on tasks that spoke of deliberation and intent. It was an absolute obsession.

She couldn't argue about the wickedness of the world in which they lived. If this Most High God wanted to wipe it all out, she really couldn't blame him. Naamah's own life before meeting Noah had not been easy. Her father had been killed in a petty squabble when she was five years old, and her mother died of a strange disease that the medicine man simply referred to as "the wolf" because it seemingly ate her body and left her looking no more than a skeleton on her deathbed. Thus, she had learned early on in life to take care of herself on the violent and dangerous stone age village streets, avoiding the rape gangs and earning some level of respect as a force with which to be reckoned.

She'd met Noah on those same streets. Even then he had been a bit of a dreamer and his family was just visiting the village for one of their festivals. He'd managed to accidentally wander into a wrong corner of the village. For reasons Naamah still didn't understand, she'd stepped in and saved him from being attacked. As thanks, he had invited her to share water and food in his family's tents. Being half-starved, she accepted. To the dismay of her father-in-law, they had wound up falling in love. She knew Lamech, as the tribal chief, was not at all pleased that his eldest son had married an unruly orphan. However, he had grudgingly learned to at least respect her toughness and her hunting prowess, and she soon won him over as an asset to the tribe.

Yet that toughness, which she took great pride in, had unfortunately resulted in her present circumstances. Noah had always been so confident in Naamah's ability to fend for herself, that he hadn't felt it necessary to leave anyone with her to defend their home.

At least she convinced her husband to leave behind their young grandson, Javan, to aid in fortifying the walls against attack.

Now, as she secured the gate with a spare ragged cloak, twelve-year-old Javan came racing up, nearly stumbling over his own gangly feet. Naamah frowned at the unruly mop of black hair flopping across his sweat-dappled face. He was the youngest son of her eldest son, Japheth, and daughter-in-law, Ila. Too old for such awkward clumsiness but too young yet to train properly in combat drills, though she'd been doing her best to teach him how to properly wield a spear and staff. It saddened her that she needed to teach him these skills at such a young age, but life was brutal, and chaos was the norm not just in the more rural areas, but in the village as well. The last time she had been in town, she'd been forced to slice off a man's finger when he tried to grab hold of her —in broad daylight no less! The rule of law had broken down some time ago in these parts, though when she heard from travelers from foreign lands, it didn't sound like things were much better anywhere else.

"Gramma! I got the last chickens put away, but, well..." the boy shifted his weight anxiously as he gestured over his shoulder.

Naamah spotted little Yalu creeping hesitantly from behind a grain barrel, face tear-stained and clutching a lame dove to her ragged dress. Her granddaughter snuffled loudly, refusing to meet

Naamah's fierce eyes. At only eight, the girl was prone to trouble and mischief that tried Naamah's worn patience severely at times.

Naamah groaned inwardly. What was she even doing here? She was supposed to be down the hill with her parents and Noah.

"I told her to help gather the birds, Gramma, honest! But she got that one with the hurt foot in the market alley and wouldn't let it go and then I had to do the coop myself before those stone-throwing plow gang boys came back..."

Naamah raised one calloused hand to stem Javan's breathless explanation, the other gently lifting the dove from Yalu to inspect the injury.

"There now, enough. Well done securing things before nightfall, Javan. Yalu knows to listen next time. For now, let's splint this wing and settle our new addition." Ignoring their gaping disbelief at her calm tone, Naamah strode purposefully towards the central courtyard living quarters. There she retrieved wood scraps and bandage linen to set the dove's sprained wing.

Soon enough she had both children reluctantly laughing through suppertime recounting the bird misadventure while Naamah hid her own smirk in her stew bowl. Only the occasional crack of thunder from the storm outside brought back anxious and nervous glances.

When both finally slept soundly by dying firelight, wrapped tight in shared wool blankets, she allowed herself a moment to slump wearily onto a pile of burlap sacks. Her low grunt barely registered over the crackling flames. So much work every cursed day just to maintain slipping shards of normalcy by raw nerve alone. She was too old to be trying to do this by herself, she thought wearily. Naamah's long black hair, once as dark and gleaming as a raven's wings, was now streaked through with strands of iron gray. Her tall, strong frame that used to draw the appreciative glances of men was still muscular, yet had softened somewhat with age. The proud arch of her shoulders now bore a faint stoop, and her olive skin was creased deeper, especially when she smiled her crooked smile which lit up her whole face.

Crow's feet fanned out from the corners of her piercing dark brown eyes—eyes that had seen both great joy and terrible hardship, eyes that still flashed fiercely when stormy moods possessed her. Her prominent nose that her middle son, Shem, had inherited bore a small bump in the bridge, where it had been broken by a wayward staff blow in her youth when she fought off a pair of rough drunken men. Naamah had snarled through the pain at the time, defiantly resetting the bone herself to retain her bold profile.

Though Naamah's tall, commanding presence still turned heads, gone were the days where her striking beauty left tongues tied. Her once firm jawline had softened, and slight jowls had formed at her neck. Her battle-hardened hands, still nimble enough for delicate sewing, were now gnarled and knotted with prominent veins that protruded from beneath thinning skin dappled with dark spots.

After the children were off to sleep, she dozed off to the soft rhythmic sound of rain pattering against the mud-brick walls and thatched roof.

A discordant crash from behind the main house made Naamah bolt upright, instantly alert. That hadn't been thunder. In the same motion, she grabbed her stone axe and oval ox hide-covered wooden shield leaning against the courtyard wall. Javan popped his sleepy head up hesitantly by the fire as she placed a warning finger to her lips. Naamah crept swiftly to peer around the rear corner into the overgrown garden plot, long left unattended.

She strained into the gloom, cursing the obscured moon and curtain of rain that obstructed her vision. Likely just another aggressive stray dog or a sickly goat collapsed from Noah's haphazard menagerie pens. She crept towards the dark garden, axe at the ready. But her sandal suddenly crunched shards of clay—the remains of Noah's favorite jug lay shattered amidst trampled leeks and radish shoots. Naamah froze, alarm coursing through her wary muscles.

Spinning on instinct, she dropped to the ground just as a stone hatchet split the air where her neck had been. Naamah rolled, lashing out fiercely with the butt of her axe to sweep her attacker's feet. A pained male grunt followed by frantic scrambling told Naamah she connected solidly as she vaulted herself back up, shield raised to meet the next blow.

Rain plastered her long curly gray hair against her scalp as she wiped wet strands out of her eyes.

Her assailant had regained his footing, cursing wildly as he struggled to dislodge his small axe from the woodpile he stumbled against; but the shield bash stunned his coordination. Naamah roared forward to drive the flat of her own heavy axe head against his unguarded chest. Ribs cracked under the brutal force and he sagged hard to muddy earth without a sound.

Chest heaving, Naamah spun to scan for more threats. But no further movements disturbed the garden grounds now save errant fire light glimmering off rain-soaked pottery shards. The lone assailant's rough tunic and scarred, malnourished features suggested one of the village's countless desperate adult orphan gang members turned feral from lives of violence and abandonment. The jagged cult tattoos marking his exposed arms confirmed her fears.

Voices carried suddenly to Naamah's keyed senses, free now of the struggle. Lightning flashed, and she was able to momentarily see the dark silhouettes of two brutish male forms at the main gate enclosure attempting to haul aside her makeshift gate barricade while bantering in coarse, slurred patois.

Giants.

She swore slightly under her breath. Likely this garden raider was sent to flush her into their arms as an ambush. An eager hunting pack hoping to secure rare female captives to abuse at leisure back in their remote mountain dens.

Naamah felt her teeth grinding, old familiar memories stirring bitter rage that swept higher with each racing heart beat. Her pulse roared loud in her ears along with the thunder and lightning—or was that growing ruckus from the house courtyard instead? Spinning back she saw little Yalu shrieking, brandishing a stick wildly to try and beat back a hulking mountain of a man who stomped closer through the corridor. Javan was nowhere in sight.

"Gramma! Help! The bad men, they got Javan! They hurt him! Please help!" the child wailed before the giant backhanded her easily across the face. Yalu crumpled in the mud sobbing.

Naamah saw red, the courtyard scene dimming to a pinpoint. Her old weapon companions moved of their own familiar accord, honed from decades of vicious necessity. With detached calm she hefted axe and shield firmly, breaths smoothing to steady pulses as she strode defiantly into the open towards the behemoth and her stricken granddaughter.

Some last shred of reason screamed that raiding bands rarely traveled above two or three kinsmen. Four attackers likely meant an entire tracking party lay in wait, too many for even Naamah's lethal skill. But the calm rush drowned further thought as she gave herself fully to meeting her fate. Her family, her very heart lay bleeding yards away; and she would sell her stubborn hide all too dearly to protect that above all else.

As the hairy mountain of meat turned from Yalu to notice Naamah's approach, a lightning flash revealed genuine surprise lifting his brutish features. He spat an incredulous warning bark over one shoulder towards the front gate. Then his hands flexed, knuckles white around the polished bone club he lifted.

Naamah halted just beyond club range, stone axe low but wooden shield rim tilted to guard her core. When the giant took his first anticipatory step forward, her shield snapped up lightning quick, stone axe head whistling behind it to glance off his leading forearm. Hot blood splattered into the mud, but the superficial cut barely slowed his next swing. His club whooshed by Naamah's ducking head, missing by fingers. But she allowed herself no triumph yet, attention focused grimly on defense alone—wear down the beast before daring to strike deep.

He soon stopped vocalizing anything beyond raspy pain-breaths. Naamah's relentless drive to deflect crushing swings while slicing non-vital meat took a savage toll on the giant's stamina. Still he persisted, clearly veteran to extreme injury himself. But Naamah had long exceeded typical human limits—she was the lone hunting tigress who never left such encounters without her share of flesh.

Soon Naamah spotted her opening. Her shield shot high horizontal to catch the descending club with a loud crack. At the same instant her axe sliced viciously behind it, hewing deep into the thigh artery and muscle bundles. As the giant recoiled in stunned agony from the crippling strike, Naamah closed fast, dropping low to thrust her axe straight into his exposed groin with vicious precision.

Howling and thrashing, insides ripped to shreds, the giant lurched backwards still flailing his club wildly. But his strength rapidly drained out into the mud along with his spraying blood. Naamah braced warily until his crashing bulk stilled at last in a gruesome heap. Yalu's wracking sobs behind her and the splashing rain were the only sounds piercing the silence now.

Naamah straightened slowly, heaving air through flaring nostrils as her battle calm ebbed. She spared herself only three deep breaths to steady her spasming muscles before turning briskly to check Yalu. No obvious breaks or uncontrolled bleeds to treat first—the child was merely hysterical with shock. Still too inexperienced for this cruel world.

Naamah gathered up her granddaughter, murmuring soothing words into the girl's matted wet hair as she carried her swiftly towards the main gate. There Naamah spotted the first raider corpse slumped below her makeshift barricade with a curved bone dagger buried to the hilt under his ear. Naamah recognized that blade as her son's prized weapon, gifted by Noah on last harvest rites.

Javan must have retrieved it from his parents' room to valiantly take down one assailant while the third yet lurked. Naamah hurriedly scanned the muddy ground for tracks or signs of a struggle but rain was rapidly washing away any signs of footprints. Before she could expand her search, the remaining raider appeared, dragging a battered Javan by his bound wrists.

The last raider paused to spit at Naamah's feet, likely intending more threats or bartering bait. But at the sight of his two massive kinsmen gruesomely felled, he choked instead. Face paling further in horror, the smaller raider began scrambling backwards, hauling the weakly struggling Javan with him.

Naamah had no time to test if this rat might flee outright, there were too many chances to lose her grandson or for him to be killed as a hostage shield. Dropping her shield and quickly laying Yalu under the protection of the barricade, Naamah gripped her axe in both hands and gave chase. Her pounding legs devoured the distance despite the muddy terrain in seconds to easily close back within attacking radius again.

With a desperate wail the bandit whirled, long bone-knife glinting in motion towards Javan's exposed neck. But Naamah had predicted this. Her axe was already whirling perfectly timed to crack solidly into the giant's neck first. Vertebrae crunched wetly as his head jerked sideways before toppling free entirely. The headless corpse swayed momentarily, crimson jetting from severed arteries in its shoulders and chest. Then it collapsed limply, dragging the gagging Javan down with it into the spreading pool.

Tossing her gore-slick axe aside, Naamah tore at the rope binding Javan's wrists with shaking fingers made clumsy by reaction. But she would not slow down now. The reality of possible wandering death squads finding them helpless in the open drove Naamah mercilessly on. Half dragging her disbelieving grandson, she retrieved little Yalu to hustle them both on urgent feet back inside the barricaded house courtyard.

The children huddled wordless and wide eyed by the rekindled fire as full darkness and pounding rain enclosed their battered home. Naamah secured the inner rooms again hastily in case other vermin still skulked outside, unwilling to be pinned in one place long. All her instincts screamed that the raiders would return, swollen in number once discovering three warriors mysteriously vanished tonight.

Her family could not withstand another assault so soon. As she tucked Yalu and Javan together under blankets and loaded provisions and weapons nearby for potential flight, Naamah silently cursed her distracted husband. How easy it might be for Noah's obsessive madness to doom them all. She could not even leave to seek outside reinforcements with the younglings to guard alone. They were frustratingly trapped just as if by floodwaters already.

Staring out at the sheet of rain that was only getting worse, she glanced back over at the shivering children.

No. They would not stay here the rest of the night, vulnerable to the gods only knew what out there in the stormy countryside. While making the trek to the ark in the middle of the night and the pouring rain was not without its dangers, staying here with the corpses of the raiders, just waiting for another attack was not an option either. They only needed to make it down the hill, to the ark, to Noah, her sons, and presumably, safety.

Rousing the children out of their blankets, she stuffed what provisions she could into a knapsack and slung it over her one shoulder. She would need to hold the children's hands, so she tucked the stone axe and bone dagger into the belt around her waist, but left the shield that had saved her life in that last battle so many times leaning against the wall. Grabbing the hands of both children, they stepped out into the torrential rain and began their trek down the hill toward the massive ark.

Discussion Questions

1. *"If this Most High God wanted to wipe it all out, she really couldn't blame him."* Naamah's attitude toward her neighbors aligns with Noah's who doesn't argue with God but just builds the boat. How does their reaction compare to Abram's who argues for the people of Sodom and whose faith is accounted to him as righteousness? How might you react differently to the wickedness of the world?

2. This story brings in the giants that are described at the start of Genesis 6. Would a threat like giants and an attack upon your children color your view of the entire world?

3. Naamah has been fighting off threats her entire life. How do you react when you believe the entire world is against you? Would you be able to see the good in the world or only see the evil that is right in front of you?

4. God has sometimes been seen as a genocidal maniac god in this story. Was God cruel to destroy the entire earth? Was that a good decision or not?

5. This story imagines Noah's family barely surviving against violent people all around them. What if those people weren't violent but kind? Would you approve of God destroying the earth if even one kind person was found?

6. Read: Genesis 18:16-23. How does Abram's dialogue with God here mirror Noah's dialogue with God? Where does Abram succeed and Noah fail?

Hagar

(Genesis 16 & 21)

MY THROAT IS PARCHED. My belly is empty.

My teenage son lies weak and exhausted against me. Neither of us are able to continue further as the water my master gave me has long been consumed.

For days we have scrambled over rough terrain in search of food and water; a force inside me that I do not understand continuously urging us onward.

The night brings a merciful coolness as I stare at my son's sleeping form. My precious boy. Why must he suffer? He's done nothing wrong, yet here he is, banished alongside me in this wilderness to die. My heart shatters when I see his young lips cracked from dehydration, his dark eyes sunken from lack of nourishment.

He was meant to grow up a prince, the eldest son to my wealthy master with everything he could ever desire.

Instead he wanders the desert in rags, his tender feet bloodied from the harsh ground.

It should not be this way. His father, Abraham, is a rich and mighty man, greatly favored by his God. I too had felt blessed when my mistress Sarah first put me in Abraham's bed, saying I must give her a child through him. Though a slave with no choice but to obey, I felt pride that my womb would carry an important child, an heir to Abraham. I had not thought I would ever birth more than livestock in my lowly state.

The pregnancy was difficult, but Abraham was kind, and his God looked after me.

My mistress? Well, she was not so kind. Which shocked me because this whole affair had been her idea! She had been the one who devised this plan, came to me and told me that Abraham needed an heir, and because she was barren and too old to conceive—I would be the vessel through which this God's promises would be fulfilled.

When I discovered the plan had worked, that I was with child, I was joyful and ecstatic. I thought my mistress, whose idea all of this had been from the beginning, would be just as overjoyed! She would now have a son as well to raise and claim as her own. It would be hard, to hand my child over to another, but still it would allow me the chance to truly honor my master.

So I beamed with happiness. I was not shameful, but now I had earned a place of honor within the family. Other servants would do as I said, follow my will, as the one who bore the prince!

Instead, she beat me and called me haughty. So I ran away. Into the wilderness. Much like this wilderness we have been banished to once again. I knew I would not survive in these harsh conditions, but I didn't care. It was better than living a life where I was constantly beaten just for doing what I had been told to do.

I would have died then, too, if this God of Abraham's had not come to me and convinced me that I should return—that it was not his will for me to die in the wilderness. But how was I to go back and live as a hated woman within my mistresses' home? I begged him to let me go somewhere else, anywhere else—but a pregnant slave girl would not have been well-received in any of the lands. Not even my homeland of Egypt.

So I returned and became as meek and obedient as I possibly could so as to not incur the wrath of my mistress again.

The day you arrived, so perfect and healthy, I wept with more joy than I had thought possible. My Ishmael—God hears. This God who heard my cries when I was in the wilderness. This God who saw my pain and anguish.

I named that God, you know. Abraham had no name for him, but I did. El-Roi—the God Who Sees. The God who saw me and promised me that from you would come a mighty nation!

Yet as I look upon your dying face, I do not know how that nation shall come to pass.

So full of hope was your name. Abraham made me Hagar—the stranger who dwells. But you, my son, were no stranger. With your first cries, I knew I would never be either, for I had found belonging through you.

But instead of rewarding me with thanks and blessing, Sarah's heart turned even colder toward us. The first time she looked upon you and saw you had the same darker coloring of my people, she saw you not with the love of a mother, but with contempt as though we were both now her rivals.

In those first blissful days, Abraham doted on us as though we were a true family. He pleaded with Sarah, asking for her blessing since you were the child she had so long desired! But she remained cold and aloof, refusing to even look at you. Her bitterness toward me turned venomous after you were born.

I thought I had merely been an unwilling vessel to give her what God refused. So why did she now spit at me when I passed her tents, hissing "whore" under her breath? Why did she slap and claw at any slave girl she caught smiling at your giggles? You were just an infant! What threat did you pose?

But threat or no, she made it abundantly clear there was not enough room under the sky for both of us. Especially once El-Roi blessed her with a son of her own.

It had been a miracle of miracles, that a woman of her advanced age could conceive and bear a son. I tried my best to be happy and supportive, but I knew—I knew this meant our doom even then. That whatever tolerance she had for us would soon evaporate, and we would be banished, sent into the wilderness once again.

So here we are. Starving, alone, and dying of thirst.

I cannot bear to watch it. As the sun peeks over the horizon, beginning to scorch the rocks on which we tread once again, your body has gone limp. I try to wake you and push you to rise, but you let out a weak wail of protest. Instead, I drag you to a bush and place you under it. I cannot bear to watch you die. Not my son. Flesh of my flesh and bone of my bone, my child whom I carried and bore and loved with every fiber of my being. I cannot watch you draw your last agonizing breath.

I put you under the limited shade and protection that the bush offers and stumble away, crying. I hear your muffled moans as you cry out for me as my figure recedes from your vision, leaving you alone and afraid. I fall to the ground, wracked with guilt and anguish. I cry hot, dry tears, as I have no water in my eyes left to shed. The rocks cut into my palms but I am beyond feeling the pain or noticing the blood.

I pray for El-Roi to see me once more and to take my life first, so I will not have to live even an instant knowing you are gone. Knowing that I should have never brought you into this world. Not when, all along, my mistress would somehow end up having a son of her own.

Our fates were sealed in that moment, my son. I am sorry. You were a threat to her, to him, as the eldest child. You might claim an inheritance that should have been rightfully yours.

Instead, we inherit the desert. The wilderness. And death.

Your cries pierce the air and I cover my ears and shake my head, begging all the gods in the world to make it stop. I curl up, sobbing, until the world finally goes silent and dark.

I awake disoriented. I do not know how long I lay there. Hours, perhaps? As consciousness returns, so does my anguish. My heart seizes in my chest. Death is slow in coming to me, but you make no more sound. All I can hear now is the soft rustling of the hot breeze, and the faint crunch of…sandals on rock?

I lie there, unmoving; my cheek on the ground as I slowly try to open one eye, the other pressed against the ground. All I can see are the feet that slowly come into view standing only inches from my face. I do not have the strength to raise my head, but the voice is like a soft whisper on the hot breeze.

"What troubles you Hagar?"

I am hallucinating, I realize. I croak out a laugh from my parched throat, though it feels like a million tiny knives are stabbing at my gullet.

"Leave me to die in peace," I finally croak out.

The man squats so he is down closer to my level, but the sun is too bright and I cannot see his face.

"Do not be afraid, for God has heard the voice of the boy where he is. Come, lift up the boy and hold him fast with your hand, for I will make a great nation of him."

Again I let out a dry, raspy breath. My hallucination is mocking me. As though I have the strength to go lift up my dead teenage son. As though my son will live to be the father of a nation.

He must be dead now, for I have not heard him cry out in some time.

With the strength I have left, I roll over away from where the man is standing, and now I know I am hallucinating. There before me is a well. Out here in the middle of the desert wilderness I see a mirage of hope, stone bricks laid in a circle around what must be a deep, dark hole.

I claw my way over the sand and rocks, taking it inch by inch. I'm oblivious to the cuts and the blood that now flows from a hundred thousand punctures in my skin. The sun is sinking over the horizon as I reach the well at last. With my remaining energy I pull up the bucket and greedily gulp mouthful after mouthful of cool water. When I've drunk my fill, I fill the waterskin to the brim. Please, oh please let this be in time!

Somehow, I make it back to Ishmael though he is still as death. I splash a few precious drops between his parched lips. No response. I trickle more water over his face. Nothing.

"Ishmael!" I cry out hoarsely. Still nothing. Tears blur my vision but this time I let them fall. I gather him into my arms, holding my everything, now all I have left of the family I thought we'd become.

Then suddenly a sputtering cough escapes his lips. His eyes flutter open, rolling back in disorientation. Joyful relief explodes through my weary soul. My boy drinks hungrily as I press the skin to his mouth. With each gulp his eyes regain alertness. Before long he holds the waterskin himself, gaining back vigor like a shriveled desert bloom revived.

As our strength returns, I glance around, trying to find the man who belonged to the disembodied voice that led me to the well.

But we are alone again, in the silence of the wilderness.

Discussion Questions

1. Was Sarah justified in her jealousy of Hagar? After commanding her slave to give her a son, she sees that son and her slave as a threat. Is this right? Or is that the point of this story, the irrationality of jealousy?

2. Hagar is the first person to name God. "El-Roi." How is this significant that a slave girl names God Almighty and receives great promises as well?

3. Hagar gets to a moment of despair. When have you been in that same place? When has the wilderness almost killed you and your future? Who rescued you out of that desert?

4. Why does El-Roi rescue Hagar and her son? Was it because of the promise God made to Abraham that his descendants would be great? Or was it because of the faith of Hagar?

5. Muslims point to Ishmael as the son of Abraham their faith is derived from, believing Muhammad is their descendent. How does this event and Hagar's faith shape our understanding of Islam and their role as an Abrahamic faith?

6. If you were Hagar, how would an event like this shape your life? How would it shape the way you pray?

Sarah

—⁊—

(Genesis 12:1—23:2)

SARAH AWOKE WITH A START. Morning sun filtered through the tent flaps as she threw back her woolen covers, realizing how late it had become. She must have overslept. Why had Abraham not awakened her when he got up?

Quickly standing, she winced at the sudden, sharp pain that surged through her stooped, aching back. Giving birth to a child in her old age had not done her already ailing body any favors.

Sarah had aged well over her long life, but her one hundred twenty-seven years still showed in her appearance. Her once dark hair was now completely white, tied back neatly under her headscarf. Deep wrinkles lined her once beautiful, smooth brown skin, especially around her eyes and mouth from years of desert sun and wind. Her back was slightly hunched from decades of manual labor.

Yet, despite her advanced age, Sarah's brown eyes remained sharp and alert. Her face, despite the wrinkles, still hinted at the beauty she had once exuded. Her hands, though gnarled by arthritis, still bore the quiet strength of a lifetime spent in work and care. She wore the simple woolen robes of a shepherdess, cinched at the waist by a braided cord belt.

The years had taken their toll, but they had not diminished Sarah's regal bearing. She carried herself with the straight-backed dignity of a woman who had known both profound joy and sorrow over long decades. Her face reflected wisdom shaped by her unusual life journey—leaving her childhood home to follow her husband at God's command, giving up hope of ever bearing the child of the divine promise. Still, the promise had been fulfilled. Unbelievably, against all odds and logic, she had born a son at the age of ninety.

She had thought those three men who had come to visit mad when they'd suggested such a thing. How was her body, well beyond the age of even being capable of conceiving—every woman knew this was impossible—able to carry a child full term? Oh, the pregnancy had its complications. But still, Isaac had been born healthy and strong.

Looking back, she had no greater regret than Hagar and Ishmael. Her face darkened even at the thought of the Egyptian slave woman and her boy. Prancing around the tents like she was some sort of favored wife. Bah! The nerve! The gall!

And yet, a part of Sarah realized she only had herself to blame. Did she think there would be no consequences to such an action? That of course when the girl was made the mother to the only son of the master, any slave girl would begin to assume she had attained a higher status than she held?

Part of her might have once felt sorry for the other woman, and yet…just the sight of her set her blood boiling. Hagar no longer lived in the encampment. Sarah had seen to that, forcing Abraham to send her and that illegitimate child of theirs away. That wild, ill-mannered Ishmael, who she'd caught on more than one occasion teasing and bullying his half-brother. That had been the final straw. How dare that bastard boy treat the true-born son and heir in such a fashion!

They should have never doubted the Most High God. Still, who wouldn't have? Who could believe such absurdity that Sarah would bear a child in her old age? It should have been impossible. Though she was learning…nothing was impossible with this desert God of her husband.

With gnarled hands, she smoothed out her robe, strapped on her corded sandals and grabbed her woolen blue shawl to ward off the morning chill as she stepped outside.

"Abraham?" she called, looking around. There was no sign of her husband or son near their tents. The shepherd boy who cared for their flock approached.

"My lord Abraham and young master Isaac left at dawn," he informed Sarah. "He took two servants, a donkey, firewood, and headed north toward the hill country."

"Toward Moriah?" Sarah asked, confused.

The boy nodded. "Master Abraham said they were going on a journey to worship the Most High God."

Sarah frowned, worry creasing her brow. Why would Abraham leave to go on a several day journey to offer a sacrifice without telling her? "And a lamb, no doubt," she muttered, ticking through the items the boy had listed, noting he had failed to mention the sacrificial lamb as she glanced over at the sheep that were corralled nearby.

The young shepherd shook his head. "No, he didn't take a lamb, mistress."

Sarah gave the boy a sharp look. "What do you mean he didn't take a lamb? What did he take to sacrifice?"

The boy shrugged and walked away.

Sarah's thoughts began to race.

No. There was no way the Most High would demand something like that. That was something the descendants of Canaan did, not her people, not Abraham's people. Not Shem's descendants. She could envision their terrible bull-headed idol with its arms stretched out over the flames, demanding the sacrifice of children. She shuddered at the thought.

She'd seen them do it, once, years ago. Long before she had Isaac. It had horrified her then; horrified her even more now.

It did not make sense. The Most High God had promised Abraham to make a great nation out of him through the birth of Isaac. God couldn't possibly be demanding a child sacrifice. Was this some kind of…test? A cruel test if it were!

No, the shepherd boy had to have been mistaken. Yes, that was it. He had just simply not seen Abraham take the lamb. That's all.

Though she knew that the shepherd boy's job was to count all the sheep and make sure he had them all. Well, he'd miscounted. Yes, that's what he'd done. Setting her jaw determinedly she quickened her pace to catch back up with the boy.

"You need to recount the sheep," she hollered after him.

He paused and turned around, puzzled. "What?"

"Recount the sheep. Make sure."

The boy shook his head, but obeyed her and took off to go count the sheep again.

Sarah turned her face to the north, imagining the path they would take. Past the grassy hills surrounding their encampment near Kiriath Arba, the soil would steadily grow more rocky and inhospitable as it gave way to arid wilderness. Olive trees and scraggly bushes would relinquish to stale air and baking heat.

After hours of walking beneath the punishing sun, the monotony of the desert would give way to rugged hills and craggy outcrops, each step revealing a new face of the challenging path ahead. The journey would ultimately take them through rocky valleys of sparse vegetation clinging to life in the harsh environment, where the shadow of towering cliffs would provide fleeting respite from the relentless sun. Abraham would no doubt seek a high point within the hills to build his altar and offer up his...

She let the thought trail off. The tormenting question of what lay at the end of that journey would rob the breath from Sarah's lungs if she dared try to answer it. For a moment, she considered going after them. But that would be foolishness. Even if she had been younger, such a trek by any woman by herself would have been irrefutably dangerous.

Instead she turned and fully intended to go about her normal daily duties, but she spent her day being distracted and unfocused. As evening approached, the weight of uncertainty heavy upon her shoulders, Sarah wandered from the familiar embrace of the encampment into the golden hues of the Kiriath Arba sunset. Her footsteps, once determined, now carried the cadence of a heart burdened by unspoken fears. The soft sand yielded beneath her worn sandals, imprinting a transient record of her solitary journey.

The encampment, a mosaic of makeshift dwellings and familial bonds, gradually faded into the backdrop as Sarah ventured toward the place of solace—the sacred altar that had borne witness to the ebb and flow of moments of devotion. The pathway, etched by countless pilgrimages, guided her with an unspoken familiarity.

The evening breeze stirred the folds of her weathered robe, carrying with it the scent of desert herbs. A trail of swirling dust marked her progress as she navigated the terrain, her gaze fixed on the distant silhouette of the altar against the descending sun. Each step carried the weight of a mother's concern, resonating with the rhythmic echoes of her anxious heartbeat.

As she approached the sacred site, the altar materialized like a silent confidant, a sentinel of faith in the vast expanse. The sun, now a fiery orb on the horizon, cast long shadows that danced upon the ground. Sarah, a solitary figure against the canvas of the desert, stood at the threshold of the sacred space, where supplications echoed through time.

The altar, bathed in the warm hues of dusk, awaited her with an ancient patience beneath the aging branches that shaded the sacred spot. As the shadows danced in the fading sunlight, her trembling hands traced the worn grooves of the altar's stone surface.

Why had he not simply performed his normal sacrifices here? Why travel several days through the wilderness to the hill country in the north?

Gazing back toward the horizon where Abraham and Isaac had disappeared, her heart weighed heavy with her unspoken fears. The altar, a witness to countless prayers and offerings, stood as a silent confidant to the depths of her anguish. The whispering winds carried her pleas as she knelt, the hem of her robe brushing against the dust of devotion.

With tearful eyes uplifted, Sarah's prayers rose like incense, a fervent plea for the safety of her only beloved son. The traditional words, uttered with a mother's desperation, mingled with the memories etched into the sacred space. Her voice, a fragile melody, echoed through the silent expanse of Kiriath Arba.

"Most High God, I know I have never understood your ways. I even laughed at them once. And now, as devoted as my husband is, I fear he has been led astray, led to believe you would demand something this mother's heart knows you would never demand. I saw your face in the three gentlemen who announced to me so many years ago that I would one day give birth to Isaac. That was not the burning face of Moloch, seeking to devour the first-born children. You are a giver of life, not a demander of death. Maybe Abraham would not question such a demand, but I, in my weakness, would, and I do."

Tears began to slide down her cheeks as her supplications and pleading continued.

As the night descended, stars adorned the heavens like distant promises… *"your descendants will be as numerous as the stars,"* she heard them whispering as her prayers persisted. The flickering flame of a small lamp she had brought cast a gentle glow on the altar, illuminating the lines etched by years of devotion. The altar, a symbol of faith, became a conduit for Sarah's raw emotions, a silent witness to her plea for divine intervention, as it absorbed her grief as she poured out her heart, seeking solace in the belief that, somewhere beyond the horizon, her prayers reached the ears of the divine.

In the quietude of that sacred moment, Sarah felt a gentle breeze that surrounded her, embraced her, and comforted her.

They will both return. It wasn't a voice, exactly. Simply a knowledge.

Still, she spent the next several days in her silent vigil by the altar. Her servants brought her food, but she refused to eat, only accepting minimal amounts of water. She would fast until they returned.

They will both return. Your descendants will be as numerous as the stars.

The whispered promise kept encircling her. Sustaining her. Until the evening of the sixth day, she saw a silhouette cresting over the northern hills. She tried to stand, but her legs were too weak. A dull ache had been gnawing at her chest all afternoon. Now it swelled, sharp and unrelenting, spreading down her left arm like wildfire. She called out for one of her servants who immediately rushed to her side and helped her to her feet. Standing shakily, she leaned on her servant girl and allowed her to help her walk away from the altar toward where the lone figure was approaching.

Was it Abraham? Alone? Then that would mean…

An anguished cry escaped her lips and the figure rushed toward her in a run as she collapsed against her servant girl again.

It was not Abraham, but one of the servants Abraham had taken with him.

"I bring news!" the voice of the servant echoed in her ears.

"Is my son dead?" Sarah asked weakly, a tear trickling down her cheek.

"No, my mistress," the servant said excitedly. "Your husband and son are both safely in Beersheba."

She exhaled with relief, then grimaced in pain; the pain in her chest refused to relent, intensifying with every passing second. A cold sweat broke out across her forehead. Still, she silently whispered thanks to the deity who had been both the cause of her grief, and now the answer to her prayers.

"What happened?" she asked, barely controlled anger mingled with her physical pain tinging the question with a harshness that made the servant blink before answering.

"We traveled to Mount Moriah, where Abraham had said God had told him to perform a sacrifice. He...he then bound Isaac and prepared to... well..."

"Say it," Sarah hissed. "Prepared to what?"

The servant swallowed hard, glancing around the tent nervously as he licked his lips before continuing. "Prepared to...kill him and offer him as a sacrifice."

The last part tumbled out of the young man's lips like a torrent of water as he rushed to quickly add, "But he didn't have to! The Lord provided a young ram instead and the voice of the Lord told him to sacrifice the ram, not his son."

"He did all this without question?" she asked.

The servant nodded. Sarah looked away, tears now freely flowing down her cheeks. Tears of both relief and blinding anger at her husband.

How dare he! How dare he do this—and without question! Had he gone mad?

Abraham had argued and pushed back against the Most High God in the past. When he tried to save the people of Sodom and Gomorrah, God had been convinced to turn from God's fierce wrath if only ten righteous people were found, and even then still spared his nephew, Lot's, life. The Most High's commands and decrees were not static. They were not meant to be followed without careful thought, consideration, and questioning. Would he question this God in order to save the lives of strangers in Sodom and Gomorrah, but did not utter the same objections to save their own son?

The anger swelling within her only intensified the sharp, burning, stabbing pains in her chest that were rapidly knocking the breath out of her.

She yearned to hold her son's face in her hand a moment, memorizing every feature. She could only imagine his youthfulness, once adorned with innocence, would now be marked by hurt, bewilderment, and a lingering sense of betrayal. His once-trusting eyes would hold shadows of profound confusion, reflecting the tumultuous, yet silent, emotions that swirled within.

Despite the distance that separated them, she could feel the hurt that transcended the physical toll of the ordeal and delved into the depths of a son's soul, grappling with the unexpected turn of events. His cheeks, marked not only by the flush of exertion but also the residue of unspoken questions, would have conveyed a vulnerability that belied the usual resilience of youth.

She imagined a muted sadness that lingered in the downturn of Isaac's lips, betraying the internal struggle to reconcile the love for his father with the bewildering acts that had transpired. The lips that had once formed prayers now undoubtedly held unspoken sentiments of hurt, seeking solace in the touch of a mother's hands.

A touch she could not give him because Abraham could not muster the courage to face her. He had, like a coward, sought refuge in Beersheba, avoiding the inevitable conflict he knew was awaiting him in their tents in Kiriath Arba.

In her mind's eye, Sarah saw herself kissing her son on the forehead, as pain rushed down her arm like a torrent of fire.

The desperate question formed on her lips and emitted simply as a howl: "Why?"

Why had he done it? Without discussion? Without telling her? Just like he had never told her about his conversation with the Most High about how she would bear a child and so she laughed like a fool at those three men when they told her? Like how he passed her off as his sister without telling her to Pharaoh? Did he think keeping things from his wife was how a partnership, a marriage, was supposed to work?

She didn't know if she would ever be able to forgive Abraham for what he had put her through. For what he had put their son through.

Neither of them would ever find out.

A sudden, crushing weight pressed against her chest as a wave of dizziness washed over her, blurring the world into a hazy smear of light and shadow.

Her mind raced, not with panic, but with quiet resignation. Her knees buckled and she crumpled to the ground. Blackness crept in at the edges of her vision. In the final moments before darkness claimed her, she felt an odd sense of peace as the pain, though fierce, began to dull.

She exhaled a long shuddering breath, the last image she conjured in her mind of her beloved son, Isaac.

And then—nothing.

Discussion Questions

1. Why do you think Abraham didn't consult his wife? Or ask the advice of anyone else in his camp? Why does he move straight to sacrificing his son?

2. Sarah goes to their local altar but doesn't find Abraham there. What would she think if she had followed him up the mountain?

3. Sarah is angry that Abraham didn't ask questions like he did with Sodom and Gomorrah, that he was just agreeing to sacrifice their son on blind obedience. Does God require blind obedience?

4. Why doesn't Abraham argue with God as he did over Sodom? Why just jump to action rather than argue against the Divine's command?

5. This story is called by many names. Two of the most common ones are: "The Testing of Abraham" and "The Binding of Isaac." What would you call this story if it were told from Sarah's point of view?

6. It's no accident that Sarah in Genesis says nothing more to Abraham after this event—and in fact, the next time we hear about Sarah, Abraham is burying her. Even God is left speechless as Abraham is reminded of the covenant once and then never again. Do you think Sarah realizing what Abraham had done is what killed her? Do you think she ever knew what happened since she never saw either Abraham or Isaac again after they embarked on their journey to Mount Moriah?

Rebekah

(Genesis 24-28)

I MISS MY SON. I realize it's my fault I'll likely never see him again before I descend to the grave, but I still miss him. Truth be told, I didn't really think through the consequences of my actions.

I'm not sure how I managed to both get him what he was promised, and lose him all at the same time. It never goes well, I suppose, when you play favorites with your children. But Isaac and I...we both had favorites between our twin sons. I doted on Jacob, he on Esau. They weren't identical, mind you. In fact, they were exact opposites in how they looked and their personalities. Esau we named because of his thick reddish hair—which clearly took after my side of the family. Jacob was smaller with darker hair, and always a quieter, more thoughtful boy. We named him Jacob because of how he came out grasping for his brother's heel.

Grasper. Turned out he was always grasping like that from his brother. With my help, of course. Oh, I'm not about to pretend like I didn't play a significant role in how everything transpired. I absolutely did. And now we will never see our beloved son again.

Because of me.

There was no way he could stay under this roof after what I helped him to do to his brother, Esau. Now, to be fair, Esau is to blame for giving up his birthright for some stew. That's on him. Okay, yes, Jacob tricked him to some extent, but that is a bit of a misnomer. Esau had to know he would be fed sooner or later and wasn't going to actually starve to death. Dramatic child, that one.

But the blessing? That was on me. I'd been the one God had told that the elder would serve the younger. When the time neared for the blessing to be given, I panicked. I realize, of course, that God would have found a way to make that promise come true, but I was scared. I did what I could to help that promise come to fruition.

And it cost me dearly.

Jacob even argued with me over it. Not because he was not on board with getting that blessing, but because he thought my method of doing it would not work.

"He'll recognize my voice!" he'd protested. "Father's not stupid, you know."

I was adamant that it would work, though, and finally convinced him to try it.

To both of our surprise, Isaac was fooled by our plans, by our simple but effective deception.

But the consequences. Oh, the consequences. I knew Esau had a bit of a temper, but when he returned home and realized what had happened, his face was filled with a murderous rage. I quickly helped Jacob pack his things and sent him to find my brother and his uncle in Haran.

I had to say goodbye in a hurry. The bitter tears I cried as I watched Jacob depart in haste have never fully dried from my aged cheeks. As I wept and kissed my dear boy goodbye, I never imagined that this would be the last time that I would see his face in this lifetime. I thought surely he would return to me at some point. Yet as the years pass, I fear that will never be.

And the way I betrayed my husband's trust. My dear, sweet, loving Isaac who had remained faithful to me through everything. Even during my long years of barrenness, he had refused to take a handmaiden to secure an heir. He kept saying his God had promised him and his father before him, that a mighty nation would come and that they would be a blessing to the entire world.

His faith never wavered and unlike his father, he never sought another's bed. Instead, he prayed day and night for *me*, his beloved wife. That *my* prayers might be answered. *My* desires might be fulfilled.

And how did I repay that love and devotion? With a betrayal. With trickery. I am too much like my own brother, Laban, who was always such a deceptive man. I warned my dear Jacob to be careful with Laban. His bargains always came with a catch.

I see now how much alike the three of us are. We're all deceivers.

I thought I was different when I was younger. I was so devoted to my Isaac. So faithful to him, and to our God. When Abraham's servant had shown up at that spring in Haran and had asked to take me back to marry his son Isaac—I didn't hesitate. I just knew this was what was supposed to happen. Even when my brother tried to hold out for more time, I went against his wishes and agreed to go back immediately.

And I hadn't been disappointed. As we approached near Abraham's camp, I spotted in the distance a young man walking in a field. When the servant told me this was Isaac, the one I was to marry, I was smitten by his handsome looks and kind demeanor.

His tunic and robes billowed lightly in the breeze, woven from dyed wool in vibrant hues of crimson and azure. He had a full head of dark curling locks with a short well-kept beard framing his strong jaw. As he slowly paced with hands clasped behind his back, his eyes gazed upwards frequently as one lost in thought and prayer. His expression was peaceful and content, hinting at a gentle spirit. Around his shoulders lay a decorative prayer shawl with long fringes, indicating his devotion to the Lord as his father Abraham's heir.

As he turned to look at me, a smile flashed across that sun-darkened face. My breath caught, and I was so overcome by the very sight of him that I fell right off my camel in my surprise and excitement! Oh what a sight I must have been, scrambling in the dirt in my travel robes, frantically trying to pull my maiden's veil over my face. But Isaac quickly came over to help me up. And from that very first moment his gentle eyes met mine, I knew this was a man I could love with my whole heart.

Still, in the end, I betrayed him. Despite my faith, despite my love— I put Jacob ahead of everything. Ahead of Esau, ahead of Isaac. I'm ashamed that I loved Jacob more than Esau. I'm ashamed that I let my faith waiver.

And now, here, at the end of my days, I know I will die without ever seeing my beloved son again. My Isaac has already passed on and I am left only with the other son to care for me. The one I betrayed as much as my Isaac. Still, he cares for me. After a time he was able to forgive me for my betrayal as we both grieved the loss of his father. Now, he is the one by my side caring for me in my old age, day after day. What an irony of fate!

Still, I know I will die with Jacob's names on my lips, wishing I had been able to see him just one last time. To see the man I know he must have become. I know should he and Esau ever reunite, Esau will forgive him as he has forgiven me. In many ways, he is better than both of us. He has provided me with the joy of grandchildren as I near the end. He has provided me with love, food, and shelter.

I hope Jacob has changed and grown and learned. I hope Laban did not make him worse. I know how Laban is.

I still cling to the promise God gave me. The promise that Jacob would be the one through whom God would build those promises. I realize I will never see that come to fruition.

Still, as I take my final breaths, I have hope.

Discussion Questions

1. If you're a parent, can you imagine so overtly and openly loving one child more than another? What do you think might drive that?

2. Consider the rivalry that also existed between Cain and Abel because God chose a favorite in terms of preferred offerings. How are sibling rivalries perhaps created/enhanced by outside forces?

3. If you have/had any siblings, what was/is your relationship with them like? Did your parents treat you the same or did you ever feel there was some sort of favoritism and how did that affect your relationship with both your parents and your sibling(s)?

4. If Rebekah and Jacob had not taken matters into their own hands, how might God have fulfilled this promise? Do we sometimes create "self-fulfilling prophecies" when we attempt to make things happen the way we think they should? What are the dangers in that?

5. Rebekah never saw Jacob again before her death. Do you think the price of her deception was worth it?

6. How might you imagine what the relationship between Isaac and Rebekah looked like after this incident?

Leah

———∽———

(Genesis 29:16—35:26; 46:15-18; 49:31)

THE FIRST TIME Leah saw Jacob, her breath caught. He strode into camp one day, moving his muscular build with an innate grace and confidence, standing nearly a head taller than most men. His shoulders were broad beneath his robes, his arms thick ropes of muscles earned from years of shepherding. Large, steady hands with long dexterous fingers spoke to both his strength and his talent for craftsmanship. He had a head full of dark curls that framed his rugged, chiseled face. His nose was straight and pronounced above lips that seemed locked in a roguish half smile. Those rich honey-colored eyes could pierce one's soul while simultaneously twinkling with mischief and charm.

For almost half a minute, she thought she was seeing the man of her dreams—until Rachel came tittering after him. Leah's heart sank as she recognized immediately the look Jacob was giving Rachel. A look no man had ever deigned to cast upon Leah. And who could blame them?

Leah had a humble, unremarkable appearance that failed to garner much notice. Her dark brown hair hung limp and straight to her shoulders, framing an oval face with prominent cheekbones and a long nose that protruded slightly. Her eyes were a dull mud-brown, with heavy brows accentuating her lackluster gaze. Though not ugly, Leah lacked any striking features. She was of average height and build, usually garbed in drab robes that did little to flatter her mousy looks. When she smiled, which was rare, it didn't quite reach her downcast eyes. Leah preferred to melt into the background rather than suffer the indignity of being measured against her dazzling sister.

In contrast, Rachel was endowed with graceful loveliness that drew all who beheld her. She had lustrous black hair that cascaded in gentle waves down her back. Her flawless bronzed skin glowed with a delicate blush upon her high cheekbones. Rachel had a small, straight nose perched above full lips that seemed always curved in an enchanting smile. Her large eyes were pools of liquid ebony, fringed with long dark lashes under delicate brows. Rachel moved with innate elegance, her lithe frame and height accentuated by the vibrant blue robes she favored. When she laughed, it was musical and layered, turning the heads of every man who heard it. Everything about Rachel radiated beauty, charm and vitality. No wonder she was treasured while Leah felt doomed to linger unwanted in her shadow. It was no surprise that despite Leah being the eldest, Jacob had asked for Rachel's hand in marriage and agreed to seven years of servitude for the honor. Men would literally agree to becoming slaves to possess her.

If Rachel had been humble, Leah might have been able to stomach it. But she wasn't. Rachel was beautiful and flaunted it. Regularly. Over time, Leah had grown to despise her sister.

But fate would play into Leah's hand, or so it seemed, for at least an instant.

As Leah lay in her bridal bed, it appeared too good to be true. Her father, at the last minute, had determined that they could not violate custom and let the younger daughter marry first. So he had come to her and told her that she would be marrying Jacob instead.

Rachel

Leah was stunned. Had Jacob actually agreed? Had he seen her and taken note of all the kind things she had done? She thought he hadn't noticed when she added extra meat to his stew, or made him a lovely coat for cold nights out with the sheep. He'd always given a perfunctory thank you and seemingly forgotten the gestures. But maybe he'd noticed.

And when she was brought to him as his bride, he had not objected! In fact, he immediately took her into his bed, made love to her, and quickly passed out from the wine with a slight snore. Maybe not the most romantic consummation of a marriage, but nonetheless…she now had what her sister desperately wanted! And she couldn't help but feel a little bit of glee.

Of course, she wasn't naïve enough to think that he wouldn't still have desires for Rachel. Maybe now that his seven years were over, they would return to Jacob's family down in the land of Canaan, and he would forget about Rachel and be content with a wife that loved and doted on him.

That dream died the moment Jacob awoke the next morning and gazed upon Leah first in horror, then in anger. He tossed her out of his bed and threw her clothes at her, growling at her to get dressed. Then he dragged her, barely clothed, out of their tent and in front of her father. Throwing her down before Laban, he demanded to know what happened.

Laban gazed up at him, nonplussed.

"Did you think I would let my youngest daughter marry first? Oh my no," Laban chuckled. "That is not our custom."

"The arrangement was for Rachel. Not…" he glanced with disgust at Leah. "Not *her!*"

Leah winced, fighting back tears as the words stung like the lash of a whip. She looked back and forth between her new husband and father in confusion.

"I served you faithfully for seven years for Rachel's hand," Jacob spat, fists clenched at his sides. "Yet on my wedding night you deceive me with...with *her* instead!" He couldn't even utter her name.

Laban leaned back against his cushions, nibbling on some bread as he regarded Jacob.

Leah gasped where she knelt trembling on the ground, her face burning with shame as she clutched her clothing tightly around herself. *He...he hadn't known?* Laban and Jacob argued heatedly above her as she lost the battle against the tears, and they flowed freely down her cheeks.

Neither man paid her any mind.

Laban finally held up a placating hand. "Calm yourself, Jacob. You had every opportunity to notice before you consummated the marriage. Is it on me you were too drunk to notice the wrong woman was in your bed?"

Jacob's jaw tightened. "I shouldn't have had to check to make sure it was the *right* woman!"

Laban sighed, picking up a piece of fruit and contemplating it as he continued. "Complete the bridal week with Leah first, as is custom. Then I shall also give you Rachel, in return for another seven years of service."

Jacob's chest heaved, his eyes blazing. Leah shuddered, a sob escaping her lips. This was not how this was supposed to be! She was a pawn in one of her father's tricks? Her marriage was a mere exchange for another seven years of Jacob's labor? Both men continued to ignore her.

She knew no man would ever look upon her with love when Rachel glowed temptingly nearby. And now he would make Rachel his other wife? She would be trapped. Trapped, not only in a loveless marriage, but forced to watch him love and marry another. And not just any woman, but her beautiful sister.

Still. She would be the *first* wife. Surely that would garner her some sort of preference in her new husband's eyes? But as he grudgingly dragged her back to the bridal bed, to satisfy his husbandly duties, she knew all he could think of was how at the end of the week, he could finally be with his beloved Rachel.

She tried to explain that she had known nothing about the treachery. Whether Jacob believed her or not, she couldn't tell.

Fresh tears spilled down Leah's face when he left at the end of the week, crumpling to the cushions as her slender frame shook with anguished sobs. She would never be anything more than a loathed obligation in Jacob's eyes. Her dream of love died the instant he gazed upon her face and saw she was not Rachel.

Leah flinched as no sooner had he left, than an enraged Rachel stormed into the tent, dark eyes flashing.

"How could you?" Rachel cried, standing over where Leah sat huddled on the cushions. Her long, slender arm lashed outward and Leah felt the sting of the other girls' hand slapping across her face before she had time to try and fend it off. "You knew how much I loved him! Yet you stole him from me without a second thought!"

Leah shook her head desperately, her trembling hand reaching up to nurse the reddening mark across her face. "No, sister, I only did as our father commanded..."

Rachel let out a bitter laugh. "Do not play the victim with me! You may pretend meekness, Leah, but I see through you. You think I never noticed how you looked at him? Looked at him with those soft, weak, weepy little eyes? Fawned over him? You aren't sorry. You aren't even remotely upset that you've caused me any pain! Admit it!"

Leah opened her mouth to protest, but then snapped it shut, realizing her sister would see through the lie that she let die on her lips. It was true. She had secretly hoped that her marriage to Jacob would elevate her for once. That she could throw the fact that Jacob was *her* husband in her sister's face.

"Well, you can rest assured," Leah finally said, sitting up and wiping at her tears, "whatever pain I might have desired to inflict upon you has backfired spectacularly."

Rachel's beautiful face turned into an ugly sneer. She leaned down and roughly grabbed Leah's chin, forcing their eyes to meet. "Jacob is mine in his heart. He will always see you as nothing but a loathsome obligation, while I remain his true bride and love."

Leah knocked her sister's hand away. "I'm painfully aware of that."

Rachel turned and stormed out of the tent and Leah sagged back against the cushions, sobbing.

She was now well and truly alone. Her husband would never love her.

Her sole comfort came in the fact that she was able to give Jacob what Rachel could not: children. Still, no matter how many sons and daughters she would provide for him, he would never look at her the way he looked at Rachel. Never would see her. So when Judah, her fourth son was born, she stopped seeking her husband's love and affection and simply praised God for the gift that had been given to her. At least in the eyes of God, the one who opened her womb to bear children, she was worthy.

Even into her old age, after Rachel had long since passed away giving birth to her second son, Benjamin, she was still there, existing between them. Jacob's heart never turned toward Leah; his passions never burned for her. Even her children were not as loved as the two Rachel bore, her death during childbirth seemingly leaving a permanent stamp of importance. When Jacob had given his beautiful robe, the one Leah had so painstakingly made for him, to Rachel's son, Joseph—it was almost more than Leah could bear.

So it was not without its irony that after Leah died and was buried, Jacob's bones were eventually laid to rest next to her, not Rachel. For in death she received the honor she had been denied in life.

Discussion Questions

1. Scripture says Leah had "weak eyes." What do you think that means?

2. Why do you think Laban tricked everyone this way?

3. Leah's story is seemingly tragic: locked in a loveless marriage while she has to watch her sister receive her husband's affections. How might you respond in a similar situation? What might it feel like to be trapped in a loveless marriage?

4. Leah winds up having more sons and is given the "final" honor of being buried next to her husband. Do you think the way God "made up" for her circumstances were satisfactory?

5. Leah eventually gives up trying to please her husband and gives her praise to God. Do you think you'd do the same in similar circumstances?

6. Do you think there's any connection between the fact that Judah, the son Leah gives praise to God for, winds up being the tribe through which David and Jesus are eventually descended from?

Dinah

(*Genesis 34*)

I AWAKE SLOWLY, feeling dazed and confused. My head hurts and my tongue feels thick from having drunk too much wine the night before. Blinking against the sunlight streaming into the lavish tent, I struggle to get my bearings. Where am I? This is not my family's tent, filled with the familiar smells of goats and freshly baked bread. No, I am in an ornate room with pillows and silks stacked high around me. I turn to see the form of a handsome young man in the bed next me. Fear and confusion flood my mind as the previous night's events come crashing back.

For years, I was not allowed to go to the Hivite festivals in the region, as they were cultic rituals that celebrated other gods that we were to have nothing to do with according to my father and mother. But what could it harm to go watch the dancing girls? I'd heard stories from the other women, leading my curiosity to get the better of me. So one evening, I snuck out from my tents and made my way to the center of the village.

Colorful banners fluttered from ropes strung between buildings. Vendors called out from stalls selling baked goods, jewelry, and rich fabrics. My heart beat faster taking in all the sights, sounds and smells. Then I noticed men stopping to stare as I passed, whispering to each other. I self-consciously pulled my cloak tighter, as I wasn't used to attention. Perhaps coming to the festival alone had not been wise.

In the town's center bonfires crackled, sending wisps of smoke into the cloudless sky. Women danced in a circle around a tall, stone pillar to the beat of a drum, ankle bells jingling with each graceful step. They seemed so uninhibited—laughing, their long black hair tossing as they moved. I yearned to join them, swaying to the beat of the drums as I too clapped and laughed, when suddenly I heard a voice behind me.

"You are far more beautiful than any of those dancers," a deep voice pronounced, the owner's breath brushing my ear.

I whirled around to see a handsome young man dressed in fine embroidered robes with a golden circlet on his brow. His black eyes regarded me warmly.

"But I'm afraid I do not recognize you, and I know most of the girls in my village," he continued.

"Your village?" I asked. He seemed rather full of himself, despite the good looks. Or perhaps on account of them.

He bowed low. "I am Prince Shechem, son of Hamor."

My breath caught. A prince? I'd heard of this Hivite prince. My eyes widened in awe, my cheeks flushing as I felt myself suddenly giggling. A prince was paying attention to me?

"Now might you do me the honor of telling me your name?"

"My, my…name?" I blinked in confusion, all thoughts having completely vacated my head. I stammered for a moment before I finally blurted out, "Oh, uh, I am Dinah. Daughter of Jacob and Leah."

His eyebrows ticked up in curiosity. "Jacob? The wealthy Aramean who has pitched his tents within our borders and pays us a tremendous amount of tribute?"

I nodded, unable to find my voice. "Oh, well, we should make sure nothing happens to Dinah, daughter of Jacob. My men can sometimes not always be gentlemen, so I fear it is not safe for you to wander alone. May I be your escort for the evening?"

I blinked rapidly, nodding again, still not trusting my voice as I took the arm he offered. I felt a thrill at the feel of his skin beneath my hands. Linked, arm in arm, we wandered the streets of the festival together as he handed me cup after cup of wine. Soon, my head was swimming and I was drunkenly giggling like a silly child as those handsome eyes bored into me. He traced a finger along the side of my face and I felt a thrill at his touch. I took a step and nearly lost my balance. His strong arms reached out to steady me. Suddenly, I felt dizzy and said I needed to lie down. Nodding in understanding, the prince led me away from the excitement of the center of the village toward what seemed a palace-like structure, constructed from thousands of sunbaked mud bricks. The exterior walls sloped slightly inwards, reaching about twenty feet high. Large wooden doors opened to a small courtyard.

It all felt hazy, like a strange dream as he helped me up the stone steps to what appeared to be his bedchamber. I paused, suddenly wary.

"I...I really ought to get back to my father's tents," I said nervously, my words slurring together.

"Oh, it's much too late and far too dangerous to take you out into the countryside now," Prince Shechem said, his voice sounding gentle as he put an arm around my shoulders to steady me. I allowed him to guide me toward the bed and sank down against the pile of pillows. The room seemed to spin and I tried to sit back up, but his hands firmly pressed against my shoulders, shoving me back against the cushions. Panic seized me as he pressed those lips, that only moments earlier I had found so soft and inviting, against me forcefully and painfully. I tried to squirm out from under him, but it was useless. He was too strong. I wanted to scream but my throat was constricted in fear and no sound emerged. Tears stung my eyes as he forced himself into me and I felt myself sink into unconsciousness.

Now, as I lie here, the memory of the night before flooding back, I try to quietly get out of the bed and find my clothing. But my tunic is torn and unwearable. Tears streaming down my cheeks, I desperately try to wrap myself in my cloak and sneak out of the room, but my movement has caused him to stir and I freeze as he rubs at his eyes and sits up on his elbows, glancing around the room sleepily before his gaze settles on me. He smiles.

Smiles!

And it's a kind, gentle smile like the one he wore before…before…I shake my head, unable to even name what happened, lest it become real.

It's then that I realize that I can't return to my father's tents. I've been…degraded. Defiled. Tears spring to my eyes as I frantically look around the room. Where can I go? Where do women like me go after no man will want them? I'm…ruined. I let out a strangled sob and then suddenly, he's standing next to me, holding me in his arms and at first I struggle against him, just wanting to run away, but then collapse against him, crying, knowing it's no use and I have nowhere to go anyway.

"Don't worry," he soothes. "This is okay among my people. I'll simply ask to marry you and it'll be fine."

I freeze. Marry him? I…I don't even know him! All I know is what he did to me.

I shudder, trying to block the memory. I cannot go home. Maybe if he marries me, the stain of my shame will be lessened. Surely my father will allow for this, even though it is not our way.

The prince leaves me alone in the room, saying he will work it out with my family. I do not feel any certainty. They will be angered at this violation against them. That this Prince just felt he could take what belonged to my father and my brothers. Marriage or not, what he had done would be unforgivable in their eyes. He took away their rights as much as he violated my body.

As I sit alone in the room, I soon hear the sound of light footsteps and I turn to see handmaidens crossing past the curtains to the room. They'd apparently been ordered to come bathe and perfume me. I stare numbly as they paint my face, arms and legs with henna in elaborate floral designs. They plait my hair with fragrant white blossoms and drape my limp frame in layers of finery. All evidence of what had occurred was concealed beneath silk and jewels.

"You shall be the envy of every maiden," one of the maids declares, though her smile does not reach her doleful eyes. "Try to be joyous, miss. This may yet surprise you."

I merely blink slowly in response, unable to shatter her futile hopes with the dark truth. There could be no happy ending to this woeful tale of mine. Confusion and worry gnaw at me as I began to wonder what fresh nightmare is about to unfold?

The maidens bring me food, but I shove it away. Oh how I wish I had simply stayed in my father's tents and not been so curious about the festival! If I'd have stayed home, I'd be safe amongst my family, doing my daily chores alongside my younger sisters rather than sitting here feeling trapped and knowing my life has now changed forever.

I am still trying to process everything. At least he is a prince, I tell myself. My life will not be all that terrible if I am married to a prince, right?

But once I'm his wife, he can do that to me anytime he wants, I think, shuddering.

The maidens finish dressing me and leave me alone with my uneaten plate of food.

The sun is nearly setting by the time I glance out the window and see him entering the courtyard. His gait now seems almost menacing. How had I thought he was so gallant?

I curl up protectively amongst the cushions as he enters the room and spies me.

"It's all arranged," he says quietly, leaning down to lift my chin with his hand so I am forced to look into the face that I briefly found so handsome. He leans in and kisses me and I cannot stop him. So I kiss him back, because what else am I to do? If he is to be my husband, I cannot deny him anything. I try not to shudder at the thought.

"The only stipulation your family had was that all of us must get circumcised like they are in order for me to marry you."

I frown. What's that about? "They cannot expect Hivites to follow Israelite customs, can they?" I say out loud. Circumcision is the sign of the covenant God made with our people. These Hivites did not follow the God of Abraham and Isaac. They are sons of Canaan. They follow the Canaanite deities. To circumcise not just Shechem, but the whole village, for their impending nuptials seems…strange. There has to be something more.

I don't try to consider what that might be as I feel him once again pressing against me, forcing himself upon me. This time I don't fight back and simply let him do as he wants, while he whispers words of love and endearment.

Eventually, I fall asleep and when I awake the next morning, Prince Shechem is gone. Breathing a sigh of relief, I crawl out of bed and begin to dress.

Then I hear it. A strange…moaning sound coming from the courtyard below. Walking over to the open window I look out and see men lying about the courtyard, groaning in pain as blood stains their hands and tunics from where they'd been circumcised. I see Shechem among his men, doubled over in pain as well, when suddenly, two of my brothers, Levi and Simeon, come bursting through the courtyard gates, swords in hand. They slash at the men and kill them while they are defenseless to do anything about it. I watch with mingled horror and relief as they slide a sword through Shechem's gut.

He glances up at the window where I am standing with a strange, sad look as he realizes my brothers' treachery. I gasp and suddenly feel pity for this man, despite what he has done to me. In moments, my brothers are in the room, gathering me up without a word and taking me back to our father's tents. I cover my mouth with disgust and horror as we make our way through the streets of the village where every man in sight has been slaughtered in the same way while they were defenseless.

But this really changes nothing, other than I am no longer going to be subjected to Shechem's whims. My father, upon learning of the slaughter, is enraged and immediately makes the entire encampment pack up our tents and move elsewhere. Jacob is fearful that others might look to attack us now for what Levi and Simeon have done.

Over the next few days and weeks, I keep to my mother's tent, too ashamed to face anyone else. My brothers and father act as if I am invisible, my existence ignored when they do accidentally catch a glimpse of me. My sisters-in-law whisper behind hands, glancing at me with a mixture of pity and disgust.

I still don't know how to feel about what my brothers have done. It isn't like they did it for my sake. The violation to me they had seen as an affront to their honor, not mine. My own mother finds it difficult to even provide me with more than perfunctory words of comfort. After all, she has her own bitter wounds to carry and her sons were all that mattered. Not me. Not to her.

I am ruined in their eyes. I cannot be suitably married off to anyone now to help solidify any sort of alliance.

I have become useless. No better than one of the slave girls except even the slave girls have more value than I do now.

So I stay huddled in my mother's tent, avoiding my family, avoiding our servants, dreading the summons I know is eventually coming.

At last my father, Jacob, calls my name, summoning me to his tent in a gruff voice. Taking a deep breath, I emerge hesitantly from my mother's tent and enter my father's. His face is hard and implacable; his expression grim as I approach on weak legs, palms sweating. Has he called me here to banish me?

My father regards me sternly. "I have found a man willing to take you as wife. You will marry in seven days' time."

I sway in shock. Marry? So soon? And to a stranger? I want to scream, plead, run away. But I know it is futile. I have no choice anymore. Not that I suppose I ever really did.

My father continues, "The man is Uri, a widower in his fifties. He has need of a woman to run his household and care for his three small sons." He waved a hand dismissively. "It is the best arrangement I could make for you under the circumstances."

I nod woodenly. Of course no young man of worth would consider me now. I must accept whatever dregs there may be, even given out of pity or desperation. My father and brothers will be relieved to wash their hands of me, too ashamed to keep me at home. While here, I am a constant reminder of how they were wronged. No one cares about my pain and suffering; that is moot .

At least if I must marry, a much older man might not force himself upon me too frequently. And a household of motherless boys needs someone to provide care. I cling to these bleak consolations. No matter how loveless or grim my future, at least I could serve some purpose.

I wipe at my unbidden tears. Tears that grieve the loss of a life and a future that might have been. A family that might have been mine. The children I might have birthed. The laughter I might have shared.

All because I'd wanted to see the dancing girls.

I want to scream. I want to run. I want to throw myself off a cliff rather than resign myself to this fate, this future.

Numbly, I turn away from my father and exit his tent. The sky is a dull gray, as though it feels my shame and sorrow. I see my mother huddled near one of the cook-fires. She glances my way—her dark, dull eyes only register a moment of sympathy before turning away from me. Do I remind her too much of her own misery and shame? Caught in her own loveless marriage?

I stare for a moment at my mother's fate. My father, tricked into marrying her, has left her with a life spent in misery, as she's tried desperately to win the affections of a man who will never love her.

I shrink away, panic seizing me as I realize my own fate will be likely worse than my mother's. At least my mother has the honor of being the first wife, of giving my father many children, many sons.

My mind races as I try to envision my future. I see myself as an even more broken version than my mother, with no children of my own to ever love me. No husband that will care for me beyond my ability to raise his motherless children. I'll be even less than the handmaidens, Bilah and Zilpah. I shudder in revulsion. I am lower than even a slave.

A shuddering sob escapes my lips as I press my hand to my mouth, as if to swallow it back. But the despair is too vast, the weight of it crushing. My future is set. I will linger in the background of my own life, a ghost among the living.

My gaze falls on the knife lying near the bread next to my mother, its blade glinting in the firelight. I slowly walk toward her and kneel down, my fingers trembling as they close around the handle. The cold steel feels solid; more real than my own body.

I need the emptiness to end.

My mother glances at me again, her lips pursed in a thin line as she gazes at me. She blames me. I can see it. She blames me for bringing even more dishonor on her than she already had.

Slowly I stand back up and make my way back to the tent, my hand still tightly gripping the knife hilt. Back inside I throw off the robe and I stare at the glinting steel. I remembered how easily my brothers had thrust their swords and knives into the throats and bellies of the Hivites. It didn't look too difficult.

Though their hands weren't shaking like mine. Surely they had been able to hold their knives steady as they pressed the cold steel against the skin of their victims.

I close my eyes, remembering the sharp, quick motion they had used across the necks of several of their victims, and I lift the knife, pressing it against the soft skin of my neck...and quickly slice through the flesh.

Discussion Questions

1. Dinah never speaks in the Biblical story. We never hear from her. Why do you think victims are so often silenced in scripture? Do you think that's reflected in how victims of sexual assault many times feel voiceless and powerless even today?

2. In ancient times, women were considered property, so the affront was considered an attack against Jacob, her father, not against Dinah herself. Who all do you think a sexual assault/rape like this affects?

3. Dinah disappears completely from the Biblical narrative after this incident. This story imagines that she was viewed as "damaged goods," so to speak, and therefore her "worth" is now almost meaningless in her society. Do you think given that context, Dinah's actions in the story are a likely outcome? If she continued to live, what might her life have looked like?

4. Dinah blames herself for not staying home like she should. How often do women blame themselves for the violence others do to them? How often do others blame the woman for what others do to them?

5. Jacob is angry that her brothers, Levi and Simeon, enact vengeance on his behalf. How does this story speak to cycles of violence?

6. What do you think God's view of all of this was? How do you think God might have viewed Dinah's decision to end her own life?

7. When women lose their virginity in some way, the social perception was/is that they are no longer "pure" and are viewed now as somehow "ruined" or "worthless." Why did, and does, that stigma apply to women, and not to men? Why is a woman's value wrapped up in her perceived "sexual purity," but a man's is not?

Tamar

(Genesis 38)

TAMAR SITS ALONG THE ROADSIDE, fidgeting with her veil and cloak to make sure she is covered enough that he will not recognize her. Nerves flutter like butterflies in her belly as she waits. It's a foolish plan, she knows, but what else is she to do? For years she has waited for Judah to marry her off to his youngest son as is her right. But Judah has delayed, believing her to be bad luck because his two elder sons she married both died.

Neither were her fault! Judah blaming her for their deaths was ridiculous. Her first husband, Er, died due to illness. Onan, Judah's middle son, died because he refused to impregnate her. According to levirate laws and customs, their first child would have been considered his deceased brother's, and would have inherited the eldest son's share of the inheritance. Onan, in his greed, had tried to deny any child Tamar would have had from inheriting half of Judah's inheritance.

Tamar sighs, her mind clouded with grief and uncertainty. She thinks back to when she first married into this family, full of hope for the future.

Since then, so much tragedy. So much heartache.

She still belongs to Judah's household yet has no husband, no children.

Year after lonely year passes as she lives in her father's home, anticipating the day she will finally belong to a household again, when Judah will marry her off to his third son when he comes of age. Occasionally news of Judah's family reaches her village. One day she is told Judah himself is now a widower—which means Judah himself could marry her if he chose to. Not long after, rumors spread that Shelah, the final son, has grown to manhood, yet still Tamar waits. Judah does not call for her.

Confusion gives way to smoldering anger as Tamar realizes Judah has deceived her. He has no intention of giving her to his youngest son, robbing her of security and lineage. She will be cast aside, her childless status a stain on her and her family. Judah has denied her what is rightfully hers according to custom. He broke his promise.

Tamar's indignation burns hot within her belly.

Now, as she sits by the side of the road, she is taking matters into her own hands to force Judah to do what is right. If custom will not protect her then she will choose to be cunning. She formulates a risky plan, one that could lead to her ruin. But she has run out of options and will not let Judah reject her so callously.

Having discarded her widow's garments and covering herself with a veil, disguising herself as a prostitute on the road to Timnah, she waits for him to pass. This deception goes against all she has been taught as righteous, but righteous men have failed her.

So be it.

As Judah approaches, she sees the familiar tall, muscular man with a full beard streaked with grey. His dark eyes are still keen under a furrowed brow. He wears the robes of a chieftain, with ornate embroidery at the hems. A sash is tied around his waist and his head is covered with a turban. Judah's stride is purposeful, his shoulders back. Age has weathered his face but not weakened his imposing frame. He walks with the confidence of a leader used to commanding respect. Tamar can see the family resemblance to her dead husbands in their father's craggy features and broad jaw. She steels herself, hoping the disguise of her veil will keep him from recognizing her as his twice-widowed daughter-in-law. She must play the part of seductress convincingly if she is to pull off her risky plan.

Judah's piercing eyes alight on her lurking form. Tamar's pulse quickens. It is too late for second thoughts now.

He pauses, his eyes combing over her. Her cloak does little to conceal her womanly shape beneath it. As he draws near, she takes a deep breath, gathers her courage and steps forward to meet his gaze briefly before glancing down demurely.

"Good day, my lord," she says softly. "Would you care to refresh yourself with me?"

He raises his eyebrows, looking both surprised and intrigued.

"You're bold to offer yourself so freely," he rumbles.

"A woman must make her way as best she can," she replies, shrugging slightly. She must play this role convincingly.

He harrumphs at this, skepticism in his tone. "And what is your price?"

"A young goat from your flock, my lord, to be delivered at a later time." She keeps her nerve steady as she names her price.

She sees the temptation flare in his eyes, yet he hesitates, clearly wary of her motives. Does he recognize her?

"I have no goat with me," he finally says, and begins to walk away.

Panicked, she reaches out and grabs his arm as she gently adds, "I only ask a fair wage for a weary traveler needing diversion. I will keep your signet, cord, and staff as pledge until the goat can be delivered."

Boldly she meets his penetrating gaze. Will he recognize her eyes? Call her out and have her stoned? She holds her breath as her hand still grips his arm.

At last she sees the desire in him overcome any doubts.

"Very well, you shall have your goat. But first I will have you. Come." He grasps her hand firmly and leads her away from the road. Her pulse races. Her risky plan is working.

But to keep her identity a secret when her clothes come off…that will be trickier.

Heart pounding in her ears, Tamar follows him to an isolated cave that serves as a stable. She must take care not to let her familiarity show, not to speak or move in a way that could make Judah suspect her. She knows it has been years since he has laid eyes on her. Surely he will not recognize her.

When they are hidden from view, Judah turns to her expectantly, and reaches for her veil. She grabs his hand and shakes her head. "That stays," she says breathlessly, moving his hand down toward her bosom. "You can see and have everything else, but that stays."

She turns her head to the side and remains silent as Judah embraces her, trusting the dim light, the passage of time, and his own desire will prevent him from recognizing her. She makes her responses minimal, uttering only what is needed to maintain the pretense.

Tamar has dreaded and despised the thought of being intimate with this man who has wronged her. Yet she lies still and pliant for his use. She bites her lip, holding back any cries that might reveal the sound of her voice.

When Judah finally leaves her, Tamar feels overwhelmed with turmoil. But her ruse has worked. Judah did not discern her identity. Her secret remains safe.

Quickly dressing herself, Tamar rises and returns to the road. She does not look back, does not dare to watch Judah walking away, oblivious that he has lain with the daughter-in-law he neglected.

Tamar must bury this knowledge deep within, along with the simmering rage and violation. She looks at the staff, cord and signet that she holds in her hands. If her reckless plan succeeds, it will be worth the cost.

Three months later it becomes evident that she has indeed conceived a child, and she is not surprised when one of Judah's servants arrives at her tent and seizes her. She grabs a small bundle as they drag her out into the central square of their encampment. Wood is being stacked against a pole that she is clearly to be tied to in order to be burned to death.

Swallowing hard, she turns to face Judah, whose face is twisted with rage.

"You prostituted yourself and brought disgrace upon this family. The penalty for that is death!"

Tamar raises her chin defiantly, tossing the bundle she has gripped tightly in her hand down at his feet. "You're right. I did prostitute myself," she hisses. The crowd around her lets out a gasp and angry murmurs begin to rise.

She raises her own voice as she continues. "I prostituted myself with the man this cord, staff and signet belong to."

His servants grab her arms and bind them behind her as they strip off her widow's garments. The pyre is lit as they stand there staring at one another, the bundle lying unopened between them.

Judah eyes her with confused ire as he finally, slowly, leans down and unties the bundle. Seeing his own staff, cord and signet he takes a shocked step back. Judah's roar of rage dies on his lips. His face grows pale, eyes fixed upon the tokens he thought lost months ago. He knows they are his.

A silence falls over everyone as he continues to stare at the items.

"Shall we get on with it?" the servant whispers.

Slowly, Judah shakes his head and lifts his gaze to meet Tamar's.

"No. Unbind her," he says at last.

The servant gasps. "But, my lord, she has prostituted herself. She has brought shame upon this family!"

Judah holds up a hand. "No. She is not the one who has brought shame to this family. I am."

The crowd collectively gasps. "She is more in the right than I am," he says, raising his voice for all to hear. "I did not give her to my son Shelah, as the law demanded," he admits hoarsely.

His gaze locks with hers. "I am to blame. For the shame I made her endure, and for the child she now carries, as it is mine."

Tamar breathes deep in relief as they unbind her, the threat of death receding.

Her ruse is vindicated. She has forced Judah's hand, her future now secure. She knows Judah will not cast her out. What began as trickery will end in redemption. Tamar rests her hand over her belly, praying for her child's safe arrival, not yet knowing she will be blessed with twins. Though far from ideal, these children are coming into being through resourcefulness, not wickedness. She broke the rules of society, but she will be scorned no longer.

Judah does not come near her again, yet still provides for her needs from afar. Her standing in the community is restored. After all, she bears the children of the chieftain now.

They are sweet fruit produced by bitter circumstances. Their eventual arrival proves that God can see beauty arise even from ashes.

Discussion Questions

1. In the ancient near east, Levirate marriage was the practice of marrying a widow off to the husband's younger brother, and the first male child she has would be considered her first husband's son and he would therefore inherit the elder brother's portion, usually half, of the inheritance, while the other half would be split between the remaining brothers. What do you think of this practice?

2. According to Near Eastern custom, known from Middle Assyrian laws, if a man has no son over ten years old, he could perform the Levirate marriage obligation himself; if he does not, the woman is declared a "widow," free to marry again. Judah could have set her free to marry someone else. But he does not—he sends her to live as "a widow" in her father's house. Unlike other widows, she cannot remarry and must stay chaste on pain of death. She is in limbo. Why do you think Judah does this to her?

3. Some believe the act of "spilling one's seed" in general is what angered God against Onan (Judah's second son), which leads to some beliefs that any sexual emission that is not done for the purposes of procreation is "sinful." Yet that is not what likely angers God in this story. The reason behind why Onan chose not to impregnate Tamar was driven out of a sense of greed—he wanted to inherit half his father's inheritance. That greed also leads to dishonoring Tamar. Which understanding do you think is most likely and why?

4. Tamar goes to extraordinary lengths to correct the abrogated justice against her. Why do you think this was so important to her? Would you ever go to such lengths to right an injustice that happened against you?

5. Twins were usually a sign of God's blessing and favor. Why do you think God rewarded Tamar for her deception?

6. Read the story of Shiphrah and Puah in Exodus 1. This is another example of God rewarding women for lying or deception. We typically think of deception as a bad thing, but in scripture, women use deception to either correct a wrong, or protect others. Does this suggest that there are times when it's okay to lie? How do we determine when those times are?

Miriam

(Exodus 2, 15:1-20; Numbers 12:1-15, 20:1)

MIRIAM STOOD on the crest of the hill, Moses and Aaron by her side, as she gazed down at the sea of people below. The Israelites filled the valley of Kadesh, camped in their multitudes as they had done for years now in the wilderness. Her aged eyes looked past them, to the horizon beyond. There, Miriam could see the Promised Land awaiting. The land of milk and honey which God had pledged to Abraham so long ago. A land they were still waiting to enter.

Though Miriam knew, she would not live to see the day.

Miriam's hair, once dark and curly, had turned to a shock of white. It framed her lined and weathered face like a shawl. Her back was bent from age and the many years of desert wanderings. She leaned on her staff, yet her eyes were still bright and keen as she gazed ahead.

Miriam's robes, once colored blue like the endless sky over the wilderness, had faded after years of sun and sand and the fabric seemed as fine and wispy as her hair. Her small frame had grown gaunt and fragile. Yet underneath, Miriam's spirit remained fiery and undimmed.

The wind on the hilltop tugged at Miriam's wrap, threatening to pull free her hair. But she stood steadfast, her gown billowing around her thin form. She was still steady on her feet, her stride sure and tireless from the long marches across unforgiving terrain.

Miriam's face was creased with lines that told of a lifetime of challenges and triumphs alike. The skin on her hands was parchment-thin, crisscrossed with remembrances of hardship and joy. She stood tall and solemn, gazing with clear eyes at the horizon.

After all the long years of slavery and then wilderness wandering, it was almost within reach. But Miriam knew she would not cross into that blessed land. Her time drew near. She could feel it. Somehow, she knew that her fate was tied to the wilderness. From the day the spies had come back and openly voiced their doubts about being able to take over the land, she had known they would not enter.

Because they had learned nothing from her mistakes. The spies had watched her being punished for openly criticizing and voicing her concerns to others about Moses's Cushite wife. Her sin had not been in the questioning. It had been in the open way in which she had cast doubt on her brother and his authority in front of everyone.

They too voiced their doubts openly to the point of instigating a rebellion. If they'd only have gone quietly to Moses or Miriam to express their fears and doubts, they might be within the borders of the Land of Canaan now instead of upon this hill on the outside looking in.

Every evening the three of them came up here to end their day gazing at the Promised Land. It's where God many times spoke to all three of them. Only Moses had seen God face to face, but Aaron and Miriam heard God's whispers at times in the wind.

Tonight, the winds were silent.

As Miriam turned from the vista, she looked upon the faces of her brothers who had been her faithful companions through the long years.

Moses, her younger brother, had also become grizzled with age. His beard was white now, though his eyes retained their intensity and focus. Years of leading the Israelites through the wilderness had left their mark on him. His face was furrowed but still emanated a sense of authority and wisdom. He leaned heavily on his staff. The staff that had parted the Red Sea and brought water from the rock. Like Miriam, Moses' body was weakened, though his spirit remained resolute.

Still, she remembered when he was a newborn, squirming and crying. How she'd carried him and placed him in a basket and set him in the Nile River to escape the decree from Pharoah. That all seemed like a lifetime ago. She supposed it was.

Still, her mother had been adamant that her son would not be killed. She'd grabbed Miriam's hands and stared into her eyes, tears glistening.

"You have to save him. He's important."

Miriam had listened, though she figured every mother thought her child was important. Yet, the cries of mourning echoed across the land of Goshen. Hebrew mothers wailed as Egyptian soldiers ripped baby boys from their arms. Miriam watched in horror as her neighbors tried fruitlessly to save their children.

Many mothers tried to hide their infant sons, stowing them away in baskets within their huts. But the Egyptians searched every home relentlessly. Just that morning, Miriam had watched in anguish from the shadows as her aunt begged the soldier not to take her newborn. Her pleas turned to screams as he kicked down her door and emerged with the crying baby, only to smash it against the ground, its cries abruptly ending as a small pool of blood formed around its tiny skull.

Her aunt threw herself to the ground, wailing and shrieking as the soldiers moved on to the next house.

Some Hebrew women snuck down to the Nile, placing their precious sons in reed baskets to float downstream. Soldiers in boats soon caught them, smashing the vessels and drowning the helpless infants. A few days earlier, Miriam had spotted a basket drifting peacefully as a mother watched and prayed from shore. But Miriam was not the only one to see it as it was soon spotted and overturned by Pharaoh's spearmen. She watched in abject horror as crocodiles swarmed and tore the bobbing, wailing infant limb from limb.

The mother let out a horrified wail, only to be silenced by a spear through her own throat as she pitched forward into the water, blood pooling around her as the crocodiles moved in.

A few mothers tried disguising their baby boys as girls, dressing them in their sisters' clothing. But it did not take long for the deception to be discovered. Miriam's heart broke as her neighbors' boys were discovered and killed without mercy.

Almost every home was shattered by wrenching grief.

Jochebed pressed a kiss to Moses' forehead. "May the God of Abraham, Isaac and Jacob protect this child," she whispered.

Why did their God not protect all the children, Miriam wondered silently as the cries of mourning still reverberated through the streets. In fact, why did this God her mother and father revered so fervently not free them from their bondage? Clearly, the Egyptian gods were more powerful, and she wondered, not for the first time, if they wouldn't be better off worshiping them. Maybe they would free them.

Miriam lifted the surprisingly light basket holding her precious cargo, looking down at tiny Moses sleeping in the basket, oblivious to the danger he was in.

Under cover of night, Miriam hurried from her family's dwelling in Goshen, placing the basket in the bottom of a wagon she then filled with bread. No one paid much attention to girls selling bread in the streets. She crept past the homes of neighbors, all locked in mournful silence. Her heart pounded as she reached the edge of the Hebrew quarter.

She scurried alongside mud brick walls, keeping to the shadows as she made her way toward the docks and fishing boats that had moored for the night at the river's edge.

Shivering from the cold, she waded out until the water lapped at her ankles and gently set the basket adrift. Miriam choked back tears as she watched the little vessel carried away by the current, her infant brother disappearing into darkness.

Miriam kept to the reeds along the shoreline, keeping pace with the basket as it floated downstream. She ducked behind boulders when Egyptian barges sailed by on patrol, their torches flickering. She held her breath, waiting for them to see the bundle in the water, but they sailed past. As the night wore on, Miriam was careful to stay hidden but keep her brother's basket in sight.

Just as the sky began to lighten, the river widened as it flowed past the great temples and palaces of the capital. Miriam's heart pounded as Moses' little basket bobbed ever closer to Pharaoh's mighty complex. That she hadn't intended. She glanced around and was about to wade across to where the basket had drifted toward a stone dock at the royal gardens, when she heard voices approach— the honeyed tones of royal women. Holding her breath, Miriam watched Pharaoh's daughter and one of her servants stroll to a little inlet of the river, clearly preparing to take a bath. Miriam sent up a silent prayer.

The Egyptian Princess swept down the palace steps toward the sun-dappled waters of the Nile. Her long, ebony hair was braided with gold and jewels that glittered in the morning light. She wore a fine, nearly sheer linen gown, the fabric clinging to her slender frame as she strode gracefully to the river's edge.

Her skin was smooth and olive-toned, her beauty etched in high cheekbones and a slender nose. An ornate collar of gold, lapis lazuli, and carnelian adorned her long, elegant neck. As a member of royalty, she held herself with perfect posture and poise.

The Princess paused at the riverbank as her servants rushed ahead, entering the shimmering water to ensure no crocodiles lurked in the reeds. As the other women drew near she held her breath and ducked beneath the surface of the water and stayed there as long as she could. When her lungs felt as though they might burst, she silently let her head emerge. The servants had already returned back to the palace steps. Satisfied, the Princess allowed her sheer garment to slide from her body and reveal a youthful, unblemished form underneath. With the grace of a goddess, she stepped into the life-giving Nile, its waters swirling around her toned legs and waist.

Moses' cries suddenly echoed off the palace walls. The women glanced around in surprise, and noticed the basket nudging against the dock.

The Princess paused, and looked around. Her eyes suddenly locked on Miriam and the girl held her breath as her heart began beating so fast, she was sure the Princess and her servant could hear it. Without taking her eyes off Miriam, she instructed one of her servants to fetch the unusual basket from amidst the reeds. Miriam clenched her fists as the Princess opened the lid and gazed down at the Hebrew infant inside.

"This must be one of the Hebrew boys," she murmured. Miriam did not move.

She turned to her servants, handing them the basket. "Take him inside, he's freezing. Warm him up."

One of the servant girls gave the Princess an odd look. "Aren't we supposed to call the guards to…you know?"

The Princess' face hardened. "You really believe that little child poses any sort of threat to Pharaoh? To the embodiment of Ra himself on earth? That's ridiculous!"

The servant opened her mouth to protest, but then snapped it shut as the Princess glared at her and instead hurried inside to find a blanket. The Princess shooed the other servant girls away before turning to face Miriam and motioned for her to come forward.

Miriam obliged, realizing it would do her no good to pretend she didn't see her. She waded out into the inlet and stood shaking before the Egyptian Princess.

"What's your name?" the woman asked.

"Miriam," she answered, casting her eyes downward. The other woman seemed completely unbothered that she was standing there naked still.

"Well, Miriam, you look too young to be the boy's mother."

Miriam shook her head. "No, your highness. I'm...I'm his sister."

"Well, your brother is going to need a nursemaid. I suggest you go find one for me. Oh, and you will now be in my personal service, is that understood?"

Miriam looked at the woman wide-eyed as she nodded in shock. "Yes...your highness."

"All right, well go find your mother and bring her to me."

Miriam turned to leave, then hesitated and turned back to face the Princess. "May...may I ask a question?" Miriam asked, her heart still pounding. She was daring to address a member of the royal family a question without first being addressed! That could mean death, she knew.

Instead the other woman nodded. "What is your question?"

"Why...why are you doing this? Why are you defying your father's decree and saving my brother?"

"Why did you defy Pharaoh's decree to save your brother?" the Princess asked.

"Because...he's my brother," Miriam said hesitantly. "And...I didn't want him to die."

"Well, Miriam, strangely enough, I don't want your brother to die either. In fact, if I could, I would save all the little brothers that are being thrown into the river or run through with a sword." Tears glis-

139

tened in the woman's eyes. For some reason, that surprised Miriam. She had always envisioned the entire Egyptian royal family as cold and heartless, out of touch with the realities of the commoners, especially the slaves.

"Yet," she continued, "as powerful as I am, I am not as powerful as Pharaoh. I cannot save them all, I cannot sway him to turn away from his horrifying decree. But, maybe I can save this one. Just this one. Maybe that will be enough."

Miriam stared at her quizzically. "Enough?"

"Do you believe in an afterlife, Miriam?"

Miriam frowned, shaking her head slowly. "I...I don't know. I've never thought about it."

"Well I do. When we descend to the dead we must meet Anubis, who will weigh our hearts against the feather of Maat, the goddess of wisdom and justice. If your heart balances with the feather, you will be deemed worthy to live forever in paradise with Osiris. I hope saving this one child will be enough to tip the scale of Anubis."

Miriam didn't know if any of that was true. Pharaoh's daughter had not lived to see her adopted son wield the power of his God. But Miriam silently wished that the story of the feather and the heart was somehow true and that the Princess was now in a place of paradise. She had been so instrumental in making this day, the Exodus, everything possible.

She turned to look at her elder brother, Aaron, who stood solemnly, his priestly robes hanging from his wiry frame. Age spots dotted his bald head and hands. As High Priest, the burdens of spiritual leadership had long weighed upon him. Miriam remembered Aaron's role in speaking for Moses before Pharaoh. His voice had echoed God's authority through plagues and miracles. Now it was hoarse with age as he recited priestly blessings over the people.

Like Miriam and Moses, Aaron bore the signs of their long and arduous journey. The golden vestments of his office still lent him an air of dignity and endurance.

Together, they had confronted Pharaoh with God's demand to free the Israelites from slavery. She had watched in awe as God worked wonders and miracles through Moses. At the shores of the Red Sea, she had danced and sung praises to God who had parted the waters to provide escape, closing them over Pharaoh's army.

Now here they stood, on the edge of Canaan. The generation Moses had led out of Egypt had perished, and a new nation stood in the valley below.

Miriam's heart ached knowing she would not join them in their new land. But she had faith that God would keep their vow to Abraham, and establish God's people in the Promised Land. She had played her part, helping guide the Israelites from slavery to freedom.

As the sun began to set over Canaan's hills, she said a silent good-bye. She had witnessed God's mighty deeds and led the people with unwavering faith. The story of the Exodus could not be told without her.

As the first stars appeared and a breeze cooled the hilltop, Miriam turned and descended with her brothers into the valley of Kadesh. She worried, though. The waters had begun to dry up. But somehow, God would provide.

Suddenly she turned to Moses and gave him a kiss on the cheek. He gazed at her in surprise.

"What was that for?"

"Don't lose your compassion when I'm gone, Moses," she said sadly. "When everyone is grieving, and the waters that I provided dry up, don't lose your compassion. Don't become overwhelmed with losing me."

He gave her a puzzled look and she smiled a little in pleasure that for once, she actually knew something he didn't. "Don't respond to the people in anger when my waters dry up," she repeated.

Crawling into her tent, she lay down and closed her tired eyes, knowing it was likely for the last time. The night air seemed to carry whispers from her past as she heard again the wailing of the grieving Hebrews over their children, mingled with the wailing of the Egyptians during the Passover and the violent roar as the Red Sea waters rushed back over Pharaoh's chariots. She tasted the manna from heaven and drank the gushing water from the rock. She saw the cloud and pillars of fire which led them by night and day.

Will my heart be weighed next to the feather? She suddenly wondered. Would she join Pharaoh's daughter in her paradise? A part of her hoped so.

Discussion Questions

1. While people regard Moses as the central figure of the Exodus story, it begins with five women whose daring and deceptive actions keep Moses alive (Shiphrah, Puah, Miriam, Pharaoh's daughter, and Jochebed). What would have happened to Moses had any of these five women not intervened when they did?

2. Why do you think we don't talk much about the roles the women played in this story and we focus so much on only Moses, Aaron and Pharaoh?

3. Miriam was also called a prophet of God alongside her brothers, Moses and Aaron. What do you think it means that Miriam was also a prophet?

4. In the Biblical account, Moses grows up knowing he's an Israelite. How do you think Pharaoh's daughter managed to keep him safe in the royal household where his adoptive grandfather had decreed his death?

5. In Numbers 12:1-10, Miriam gets in trouble with God for her anger at Moses' wife who was a Cushite. (This is likely a second marriage as Moses' first wife, Zipporah, was a Kenite). The land of "Cush" in modern geography would be Southern Egypt and northern Sudan. What do you think Miriam found objectionable about his wife? Why do you think God punishes Miriam for her objections? Why did only Miriam get punished, and not Aaron, who also voiced his objection?

Rahab

(Joshua 2 & 6)

THE SUN BEAT down on the city of Jericho, already shimmering with heat even though it was just past dawn. Rahab slowly opened her eyes, blinking against the bright beams coming through the open window of her home that lay inside the outer walls of the city. She could hear the sounds of the town coming to life outside—merchants calling out their wares, animals braying, carts rumbling over the packed dirt streets.

With a sigh, Rahab rose from her bed and began her morning routine. She carefully applied her makeup—the kohl lining her eyes, rouge on her cheeks and lips—transforming herself into someone desirable. Someone who could earn a living providing that which men demanded. She found it highly hypocritical that people judged her harshly for her profession, when she was only providing what was asked. Men wanted to have possession over their wives while simultaneously having sexual access to other women. *Those hypocrites should be angry with the men who make my profession necessary, not women like me for providing what they would take ruthlessly otherwise,* she thought.

After dressing in red flowing robes that concealed little and pinning golden ornaments into her long, flowing, black hair, Rahab made her way downstairs to the brothel she ran. She lived and worked within the walls of the great city of Jericho, her rooms affording a commanding view of the valley below and the hills beyond. As she looked out over the landscape, Rahab thought of her life here. It had not been easy growing up. Her father, one of the King's soldiers, was wounded in battle, making it impossible for him to work and earn a living. The King abandoned him, thus Rahab's mother was forced to work trying to sell bread at the market. But that hardly was able to sustain a family of five. Rahab's brother and sister were too young to work, but Rahab…well, Rahab knew she was a beautiful woman and men were constantly ogling her even when she was just a young teenage girl barely pubescent. One day, one of those men had offered her some money for sex. She'd been offended at first, but when she saw the coins and realized there was enough to pay for a week's worth of food, she accepted it and let him have her body.

She cried a little that first time, both from pain and the shame. She would never be an acceptable wife to any man now. This would be her future. Forever. Lying on her back, spreading her legs for whoever had the money to pay for it.

Over time, it grew easier. She cried less and less with each encounter. Soon she developed some regular clients and fell into a pattern. The money she was bringing home allowed her to care for her family. Eventually, she was able to purchase a little home within the wall of the city and her family all moved in with her. She used the bottom portion as a bar to feed and serve wine, the upper rooms were for her and some of the other women she hired. It had turned into a thriving business, which of course meant it had caught the attention of the King. He never allowed anything to thrive without his seal of approval. And a brothel was hardly going to have his blessing. But because of its location, he couldn't just set it on fire and burn it down, as that would weaken their defenses. Instead, he settled for strong men that came and demanded a tribute offering every few weeks. She paid it, but each time it was always for a little bit more and she began to feel the financial strain.

Prostitution offered a means of survival, though it came at a cost. She was shunned and looked down upon by proper society.

Still, it afforded her some freedoms other women didn't have. She answered to no man, for one. That made her dangerous.

A knock at her door interrupted Rahab's musings. It was early yet for most patrons, but she hardly had a sign that listed her hours of operation. Slipping into her professional demeanor, she opened the door with a smile and sultry voice. "Welcome, good sir. How may I be of service?"

Damar, a large, muscular man with tattoos and a large scar that ran down the side of his face, who happened to also be one of her regulars, came sweeping into the room and picked her up, kissing her.

"You're here early," she mused, toying playfully with his tunic.

"The King had us up early this morning searching for spies."

"Spies?" Rahab asked, curiously. "What kind of spies?"

"Israelites have been seen just beyond the Jordan," he said. "Scouts picked it up so we're scouring the city to see if any have infiltrated the area."

"Interesting," Rahab said thoughtfully, carefully digesting that information. "What worries you about them?"

"The Israelites?" Damar let out a laugh and set her back upon her feet. "They have been a marauding nation with no land for the past forty years, always just camped beyond our borders in the region of the Ammonites and the Moabites. But they have begun gathering their forces, clearly getting ready for some kind of invasion."

"Why don't you go attack them?"

"Attack a force of over two million people? They would overwhelm us. We do not possess those numbers. No, we are better off staying inside our walls and defending ourselves, but if there are spies here, they might learn of some of our weaknesses and breach those defenses."

Rahab let out a little laugh of her own. "I never thought I'd see the day you were afraid of anything, Damar."

"You don't understand," he said darkly. "This...God of theirs...it is said to have dried up the water of the Red Sea when they came out of Egypt. They utterly destroyed Kings Sihon and Og of the Amorites and took over the land of northern Moab from the River Arnon to the River Jabbok. They swept through and captured all the Amorite cities including Heshbon and Jazer. Then they moved north and defeated King Og of Bashan at Edrei, occupying all the land of Gilead and Bashan from the River Arnon to Mt Hermon."

Rahab's eyes widened in awe. "You...you sound afraid, Damar." She had never heard fear in his voice before, but it shook now. Despite it being early morning, he reached over and grabbed a goblet of wine and downed it nearly in a single gulp.

"They are really that powerful?" she asked.

He nodded grimly.

"Then, why do we not simply surrender to them and ask them to spare us if we have no chance of defeating them?" she asked.

Damar let out a bitter laugh. "You do not understand our King and the heart of a warrior. We will fight until the bitter end."

"Even if it is futile?" she asked.

He nodded.

"So," she continued, incredulous, "you and the King would let every person in this city perish for...what? Pride? Honor? You'd let your family die?"

His eyes narrowed. "What do you know of my family, whore?"

She blinked, taken aback by his sudden gruffness. He grabbed her by the throat and she clawed at it as he lifted her off the floor.

"Please," she choked out. "I...I meant no insult."

He gazed at her with hard eyes, his hand squeezing tighter until she began to see spots and just as she was about to pass out, he released her and she crumpled to the floor, choking and coughing. She had barely had a chance to recover before he was on top of her, ripping her sheer robe off and forcing himself into her. She bit back tears— tears she had not cried in years. It had been some time since a man forced himself on her like this. She'd nearly forgotten the difference between when she allowed it and when they simply…took it.

Afterwards, he threw some coins at her as she lay on the floor and stormed out of the room. Gingerly, she sat up, grateful that no one else in her family was up yet. She crawled back up the stairs to her private room and changed her clothes. There was nothing to do about it. She was honestly surprised it hadn't happened to her more often.

Still, she felt violated. Yes, even as a prostitute, as she hadn't consented, hadn't given her body to him willingly. She brushed away the tears. It was always a stark reminder that she had no control over anything and was small comfort knowing at least there was no honor to steal from her family.

As evening fell, the downstairs room filled, and several of her girls were already enticing their clients for the evening. She smiled a little, then glanced over at the door as it opened again.

The two men who walked in she immediately knew were strangers, dressed in dusty, travel-worn clothing. They were clearly not from Jericho.

She made her way over to where they were standing and smiled demurely. "Welcome, Gentlemen. You look like you've come a long way and are tired."

"We come seeking lodging for the night," the older of the two said. "We are willing to pay."

Rahab nodded knowingly. "Of course you are. Would you like some food and drink first?"

The men glanced around nervously and suddenly she realized: these were the Israelite spies Damar had been looking for earlier. Her mind remembered the violation that had followed and she set her jaw tightly.

"Would you prefer...a quieter, more private room?" she asked, lowering her voice. The elder of the two men nodded. She held out her palm and he dropped a bag of coins in them. She glanced inside at the silver and nodded appreciatively.

She turned to a younger girl, her sister, Pigat, who was working behind the bar. "Bring up some food for our special guests," she ordered, then turned back to the men. "Come. Follow me."

She led them up the stairs to her private rooms. Brightly colored tapestries and sheer curtains lined the walls, with incense burners filling the air with exotic fragrance. Plush cushions and low couches offered seating, alongside small tables bearing wine jugs and goblets.

The room held all manner of musical instruments—lyres, drums, and finger cymbals. Shelves displayed Rahab's collection of beauty products—pots of rouge and kohl, perfumes and oils. A tall bronze mirror stood in one corner, allowing her to artfully arrange her dark curled hair and apply dramatic cosmetics. The cushions lined up as beds when needed, with folding screens providing privacy. As a precaution, Rahab kept the heavy oak door barred, with only a small hole allowing her to identify visitors. She didn't need angry wives storming in on her.

Adjoining this reception area was Rahab's private inner sanctum. This smaller room held her personal items—clothing, jewelry, incense for offerings. Tapestries and gauzy fabrics in vibrant hues draped the walls and canopy bed, where she retreated alone to rest. A table displayed simple meals along with wineskins, kept cool in clay vessels.

As she discreetly slipped the latch shut to the larger room, she turned to her guests and motioned for them to have a seat. "So," she said, sliding herself down onto the cushions in a most provocative way. "Is this one at a time, or both together?" She let the sheer robe slip slightly, revealing one of her breasts.

The younger man stared at her and licked his lips nervously, but the older man seemed merely amused. "One at a time will be sufficient, I think," he said at last. "I'll let the youngster go first. He deserves the experience in case..." he let the insinuation die on his lips.

The young man's eyes widened and Rahab realized he had likely never been with a woman before. Oh, a virgin. They were always fun.

"Don't worry," she whispered as she crawled toward him on all fours, "I'll go easy on you."

Once she was finished with him, the older man took his turn. Afterward, as she was slipping her robes back on, she heard a faint knock on the door. She walked over and saw her sister with the plate of food she'd ordered brought up earlier. Unlocking the door, she let the girl in. The young boy scrambled to cover himself but the older man only laughed.

"You think she hasn't seen that before, boy?" he mused. The girl ignored the two men and set the tray down on a small table.

"Thank you, Pigat," Rahab said in a quiet voice and walked her toward the door. She glanced back at her guests then grabbed Pigat's arm and pulled her close and placed a bell in the other girl's hands. "If soldiers show up tonight, ring this bell so I will hear it," she said.

Pigat looked down at the bell in confusion. "We always have soldiers, sister..."

Rahab shook her head. "I mean on-duty soldiers who look like they're here on official business."

Pigat glanced over at the two men, then nodded.

The elder man frowned as she re-latched the door and turned back around. "What were you saying to her?" he asked warily.

"I told her to warn me if soldiers showed up. Something tells me, as my guests, you would not like such a visit."

The men quickly sat up and threw their clothes back on. "Why… why do you think they'd be here? Looking for us?" the younger asked.

"Because they were looking for you earlier. You're Israelite spies, are you not?" she asked matter-of-factly. "You don't exactly blend in," she continued as they looked at her in surprise. "It's very obvious those clothes are not yours, they fit you poorly, and your dialect is way off."

"Why…why aren't you turning us in, then, if you know who we are?"

She took a deep breath and was about to answer when she heard the distant tinkling of the chime she had given Pigat. She stood, alarmed, and glanced over at the men.

"Soldiers," she said. "Quickly, follow me. I'll hide you on the roof."

She pulled out a ladder and scaled up the wall toward the ceiling and pushed on a barely visible door that opened upward. The men scurried up after her and she lifted some flax for them to get underneath.

"Wait here," she whispered, and then scurried back down the ladder, closing the door and stashing the ladder just as she heard knocking on her door. Smoothing her robes and her hair, she plastered on her most inviting smile and opened the door.

Damar and another soldier shoved her aside as they walked in, and began looking around the room. They both wore stiff leather jerkins overlaid with bronze discs or scales, allowing flexibility while providing armor. Arm guards and greaves on their limbs offered protection as well. Circular bronze shields hung on their backs, and at their sides hung straight bronze swords with leaf-shaped blades designed for slashing rather than stabbing.

After a quick rummage through the room, Damar turned to her gruffly. "The King has received word that you are harboring two Israelite spies in your establishment, Rahab."

"Oh, you would have outdated information I'm afraid," she said, sighing heavily as she sat down nonchalantly against her cushions.

"You don't deny they are here?" he asked, stepping closer to her.

"Oh they're not here *now*...but they were."

Dark rage clouded the soldier's face and she swallowed hard, remembering how that rage had played out earlier that morning. She licked her lips nervously as she tried to not give into her fears.

"I mean," she continued, "It's true, the men came to me, and I... entertained them...but how was I to know where they came from? I had no idea they were the spies you were looking for. They were just paying customers to me."

Damar's eyes narrowed skeptically.

"And when it was time to close the gate at dark, the men left," she shrugged.

The soldier's jaw tightened with anger as his hand rested on the hilt of his sword, menacingly. "Where did they go?" he demanded."

"How should I know?" she asked innocently. "But I would imagine if you would pursue them quickly, you could still overtake them. They couldn't have gotten far."

Damar took a menacing step toward her and she stiffened, holding her breath. He paused, continued to stare at her for a long moment, before he made a gesture to the other soldier and they turned and left the room. She exhaled slowly and reached over to the table with a shaking hand, grabbed a goblet of wine, and downed it in one gulp.

Taking a deep breath, she stood and walked over to the window and watched as the city gates opened and a cohort of soldiers poured out, scouring the countryside.

Leaning the ladder up against the wall again, she climbed up to the roof to where the men were hiding.

"Why…why are you helping us?" the younger man asked.

"Those soldiers could have killed you," the elder added.

Rahab shrugged and glanced over the edge of the wall to where the cohort of soldiers was disappearing into the night.

"I have no love for our King," she said at last. "He is a cruel, brutal man who keeps the regular people in poverty. Plus, I've heard of what your people have done, how your God dried up the water of the Red Sea when you came out of Egypt. How you destroyed the kings of the Amorites beyond the Jordan."

She took a deep, shaking breath. "Our soldiers are terrified of you, and I've never seen them terrified. Your God is indeed God in heaven above and on earth below, and I know has the power to give and take life. I know when you invade, you will crush this city. But… if I deal kindly with you, swear to me by the Lord that you will in turn deal kindly with me and my family? I simply ask for a sign of good faith that you will spare my father and mother, my brothers and sisters, and all who belong to them and deliver our lives from death."

The two men glanced at each other as she stood.

"I could recall those soldiers and turn you over to them, but I would rather serve you and your God, than the Canaanites. They spurn me and shun me, steal my money. I have no love for them. Only for my family. Please."

She hated that she sounded like she was begging, but she was begging these strange men she knew almost nothing about. She was risking everything by helping them, and she didn't fully understand why. She was betraying her own people…granted, they were people who had done nothing but treat her horribly, but she still felt a twinge of loss at that reality.

The two men looked at each other for a long moment before they seemed to come to a silent consensus, the older man nodding and turning back to her.

"All right, our life for yours. If you don't betray us, then when the Lord gives us this land, we promise, we will deal kindly with you."

She breathed a sigh of relief and grabbed both their hands and kissed them. "I wish I could give you safe haven here, but if they came looking for you here once, they will likely return. I'm sure that my doors are being watched. Come."

She climbed back down off the roof and into her entertaining room again.

The men followed as she walked over to the window and looked out into the dark night and the sprawling landscape below. The soldiers that had once filled the area were nowhere to be seen.

"Have you gleaned all the information about the city that you need?" she asked absently.

"No, we haven't figured out how to breach these walls yet."

Rahab continued to stare out into the night. Damar was out there somewhere. "What if...there was a revolt inside the walls while you wait outside them?"

"Why...why would there be a revolt?" the elder man asked.

"Because the people of Jericho have never had the will to rise up against their King. But if they were to know you were coming, if they knew you were going to defeat them...the peasants might very well revolt."

"That would require you betraying your own people."

She shrugged. "They betrayed *me* long ago."

Glancing around her room, she grabbed a red sash that she used to tie up the tapestries and curtains and slowly lowered it out the window, tying it to a beam inside.

She turned to the men. "Go toward the hill country, so that they won't find you. Hide yourselves there three days, until the soldiers all return; then afterward you may go back to your people."

The younger man began down the rope, but the elder turned to her, serious. "If we see this red cord, and your family is here in this room with you, we will spare you as promised. But, if the cord is not there, if any of your family goes into the streets, they will be killed, we cannot protect them. And if you betray us to your people—we will be released from our oath. Do you understand?"

Rahab nodded. "I understand."

She watched as they descended the rope and disappeared into the night. Turning, she ran and unlocked the door, flying down the stairs to the main room. Her sister eyed her nervously as she approached.

"I need you to go find Avyukt. Tell him I need to see him, it's important."

Pigat nodded and ducked out of the brothel. Rahab glanced around the room, suddenly feeling very vulnerable, that any of these men might be the King's men in disguise. She fought the urge to kick everyone out and close up for the night. That would definitely draw attention and she didn't want to do that. Instead, she made her way back up to her private sitting room and waited for Avyukt to arrive.

The old man gave her an annoyed look as Pigat led him through the doorway to her private sitting area about fifteen minutes later. "This isn't exactly the kind of establishment I like to be seen at," the man stated in a gruff voice. A former soldier himself, Avyukt had been injured in the leg during a battle with some Jebusites and had been discarded and forgotten by the King's men—just like her father. Still, he possessed a wealth of tactical knowledge and leadership skills that had led to a rag tag group of underground dissidents within the walls of Jericho. They were small and not powerful, so they had waited, quietly, watching for an opportunity.

An opportunity like the one Rahab was about to present to them. She quickly told them about the Israelites' visit and said she had convinced them once they arrived in force, to wait outside the walls seven days before entering the city.

"If we attack the King's men internally, we will help weaken them and give the Israelites a better opportunity to easily overtake them when they enter the city. But after that, everyone who is left must gather here, in this room, or they will be slaughtered by the Israelites."

Avyukt leaned back against the cushions, stroking his beard thoughtfully. Rahab held her breath, hoping she was not making a grave mistake in telling the old man the Israelites' plans. She truly didn't think she was, and didn't believe this was betraying the spies, but would ultimately help.

God of the Israelites, I hope you are as powerful as you seem, she silently prayed.

At last Avyukt nodded and thanked her for the information before hobbling off back down the stairs. Rahab exhaled, wringing her hands and biting her lip. Hopefully she could save everyone she considered her family—all the poor and downtrodden in Jericho.

Over the next several days, there was a current of rebellion and excitement that coursed through the city of Jericho. From one of her windows overlooking the winding city streets, Rahab watched discreetly as Avyukt's followers prepared themselves for the coming uprising.

Under the cover of night, she watched as men and women slipped through the alleys, faces hidden by cloaks and hoods. Quietly they gathered bricks, clubs, and iron bars from the rubble of buildings damaged in past sieges. At the city blacksmith's forge, they traded stolen gold for daggers and spears forged of bronze. From the king's storehouses they snatched jars of oil, and made torches by soaking rags in the flammable liquid. They quietly brought their wares to Rahab's brothel for hiding.

Several days passed before the sound of the war horns and trumpets from outside the city walls could be heard. She glanced out her window to see the advancing army. True to their word, the army encircled the city...but did not try to enter. Breathing a sigh of relief, she ran downstairs to where Avyukt and his men were waiting.

There were two soldiers in the brothel that had come for their evening entertainment. Rahab nodded at her girls, and they quickly slid knives they had strapped to the underside of their wrists and soundlessly slit the men's throats. Rahab turned away as they stood desperately, but vainly, trying to staunch the flowing blood gurgling through their fingers, before collapsing on the floor.

"It has begun," she said to Avyukt, who gave an emotionless glance to the dying soldiers. He nodded gravely then motioned to his men, who grabbed their stashed weapons, and disappeared into the streets.

That first night, smoke rose over Jericho as the rebellion ignited. From her window, Rahab watched somberly as Avyukt's followers swarmed the streets with weapons raised. They stormed the armory, overpowering guards with raining bricks and clubs. Having armed themselves with swords and spears, they pressed on toward the main square.

Skirmishes broke out as rebels clashed with king's soldiers in the winding alleys. The night echoed with shouts and screams, the clang of bronze on bronze. By dawn, the rebels had taken control of the city's gates and lower quarters.

Outside, the sound of war horns and trumpets continued to sound. Soldiers didn't know what to do first—manage the rebels within or the invading army outside their walls. The end result was a disorganized military that was left only to fight in defense.

As the next few days commenced, Rahab saw fires blazing in the marketplace as rebels torched the tax collectors' offices. Arrows whistled from rooftops as rebels with bows ambushed soldiers in the streets below. The upper city remained under the king's control, but Avyukt's forces roamed the lower city at will.

The King struck back ruthlessly on the third day. Companies of soldiers burned homes and shops in areas sheltering the rebels. They cut down resistance fighters in broad daylight, leaving their bodies as bloody warnings in the street.

Yet the rebels would not relent. On the fourth night, they infiltrated the upper city disguised as merchants and servants. Then they emerged with weapons drawn, dragging nobles from their beds and burning the finery of the wealthy.

Day and night, Rahab watched the chaos swelling through Jericho like a tempest. Rebel and soldier alike fell by the dozens, their blood feeding the insatiable maw of civil war. As the sixth day neared its end, smoke hung like a perpetual pall over the ravaged city.

By the seventh day, Jericho's streets had become a maze of barricades. The rebels controlled the lower city, while the king's men still clung to the citadel in the upper city. The two sides exchanged volleys of arrows and hurled rocks back and forth. Both were weakened and wearied, yet neither would yield—until the morning of the seventh day.

At dawn, as the trumpets again began to sound outside the city, the rebels retreated, setting fire to everything they could, including their own homes. Thick smoke filled the air as the survivors made their way to Rahab's brothel.

She hurriedly brought in as many as the room could hold, and then she went upstairs where her family and many of the other women and children huddled together, their eyes wide with fear as she strode into the room and crossed over to the window that overlooked the sprawling countryside that was now filled with tents and soldiers. She lowered the crimson rope, and watched and waited as the Israelites paraded their priests and their ark around the city seven times, blasting their horns.

With determination, she walked across the room and lowered a second crimson cord out the window that faced the interior of the city.

Rahab's sister, Pigat, sidled up next to her, licking her lips nervously and coughing from the smoke that infiltrated the room. Rahab wrapped an arm around her reassuringly. "It'll be okay. They promised to spare us," she said—hoping and praying to that God of theirs that those men would be true to their oath.

As the priests and soldiers concluded their seventh trip around the city and their trumpets blasted one last time, a terrible groaning shook the walls of Rahab's chamber. She gasped in horror as the seemingly impregnable walls of Jericho were collapsing before her eyes.

Huge sections of stone that had been weakened by the fires were fracturing and falling away, leaving gaping breaches. Through the breaches marched rows of Israelite soldiers, their horn blasts proclaiming victory.

Rahab's family, still huddled in the corner of the room, gazed at her with faces white with terror. Her father trembled, muttering prayers. Her mother wept silently, clutching Rahab's young brothers to her breast.

"Do not fear," Rahab urged them, her own voice trembling slightly. "We will be saved. The spies...they'll keep their word."

But doubt gnawed at Rahab as the walls shuddered from the relentless Israelite assault. The once-invincible gates of Jericho had failed. Death now stalked every street and alley below.

A terrible crash split the air. Rahab turned to see a massive chunk of the citadel wall shear away and topple to the earth far below. The floor bucked under her feet, throwing her family to their knees. Outside, shouts and screams mixed with the unending blare of horns.

Where the north and west walls had stood, now there were only mountains of smoking rubble. Invading soldiers swarmed through the breaches even as the last of Jericho's defenses gave way.

Her eyes stung from the smoke and dust that filled the air, her lungs irritated as she coughed. But soon, she caught sight of them. The two men she had protected were slowly making their way toward her brothel, picking their way through the barricaded streets and piles of bodies. She felt a twinge of regret as she looked upon her fellow Canaanites that lay slaughtered on the streets below. She knew she was responsible for that, even if she hadn't been the one to strike them down, personally.

These were people who had ridiculed her, shunned her, chastised her. Still, the bloodshed was hard to take even though they were people she didn't care for.

Rahab led her family down the steps and into the room below where the remaining rebels stood huddled in fear, listening to the sounds of the invasion. Rahab pushed her way through the throng of people and opened the door as the two spies arrived. Their eyes widened when they saw the room full of people.

Before they could object, Rahab spoke quickly. "These are the people who have spent the past seven days weakening the King's forces from inside the city. They are…all my family."

The younger of the two looked ready to argue, but the elder held up a hand as he gave her a knowing, understanding nod. "Very well," he said gruffly. "Follow us."

They stepped out into the war-torn streets, the Israelite spies ahead to guide them. She winced at the sights and sounds assaulting her from all directions.

Soldiers were dragging young women by their hair, their screams rising above the din. The bodies of Jericho's fighters lay broken in the streets, set upon by dogs. The acrid smoke burning her throat could not mask the stench of death.

Rahab felt her mother and Pigat both trembling against her and squeezed their hands reassuringly. She could not show the fear gnawing at her own heart. The scarlet cord flapped in the wind above their heads—their only shield against the invaders' wrath.

Pressing on through the wreckage of the shattered gates, Rahab stepped over mangled corpses in Canaanite armor. She wondered if Avyukt lay among the dead. He had not returned to the brothel and had remained in the lower city, rallying the last of the rebels before the walls fell.

The open countryside beyond the walls offered a brief respite from the horrors. But Rahab knew a difficult journey lay ahead to reach safety in the hills. Glancing back at the still-burning city, she whispered a prayer for all who had perished.

Discussion Questions

1. In other places in scripture, prostitution is considered immoral (see Proverbs 23:27-28) and Paul even uses the term as a derogatory in 1 Corinthians 6:13 regarding how one uses one's body, which is a temple for the holy spirit. Why do you think this prostitute is given such high honor in scripture that she is included in the lineage of both David and Jesus? What do you think it means that someone of such low social status plays such an integral part in the Biblical narrative?

2. Rahab points out: *"She always found it highly hypocritical that people judged her so harshly for her profession, when she was only providing that which was demanded. Men who wanted to both have sole possession over their wives while simultaneously having access to other women sexually. Get angry with the men who made her profession necessary, not her for providing them with what they would take ruthlessly otherwise."* Which do you think is the bigger problem? Women providing what is demanded, or the men demanding such services be available to them?

3. Prostitutes fell into a unique category in society: they were the only women who technically were not owned by men, which means they in many ways had more freedoms than other women. How does that alter or inform your view of prostitutes/sex workers?

4. While brothels were likely good places to overhear local information, why do you think the spies went to visit Rahab in the first place?

5. Like Tamar, Shiphrah, and Puah, Rahab lies and uses deception to help the Israelites, and is rewarded for it. When faced with limited options, are such tactics considered okay? What might you have done in her place?

6. Do you think these stories, although they result in good things, have helped to contribute to stereotypical views of women being deceptive?

7. In this story, the city of Jericho is severely weakened due to an internal civil uprising. Archeologists have noted when studying Jericho, that the walls fell outward, rather than inward, meaning it looked more like a force from the inside pushed them down rather than a force from the outside. What do you think of this explanation for the Biblical account of how the walls simply "fell down" when the trumpets sounded the seventh day?

8. In James 2:25, the author calls Rahab "righteous" because she lies to the leader of her own country in order to save the lives of foreigners. Consider how such actions might be viewed in our modern context.

Deborah

(Judges 4)

DEBORAH STOOD atop the ridge on the slopes of Mount Tabor, overlooking the valley where the forces of Sisera were encamped for the night. A woman of regal bearing, her thick, black hair, which had just begun to see the first streaks of gray, was covered by a plain red headscarf. Barely visible lines creased the corners of her dark, insightful eyes that had seen forty years of Israel's troubles, though only twenty of them with her as their leader.

Her olive skin was weathered from years dispensing wisdom and justice from under the palm tree amidst the elements of the hill country of Ephraim. She stood taller than most women, her slender frame disguising the physical stamina required for her travels. Her steady hands, clasped now behind her, had soothed many who unburdened themselves before her. She moved with grace, yet with the energy of one who knew her purpose. Her face, resolute as she surveyed the valley below, was softened by the hint of a smile, reflecting her abiding trust in the God who spoke to her in the sacred fires. Though getting on in years, her vigor and vision proved she still had mighty work to do.

Torches flickered across the plain below as the Canaanites readied themselves for battle at dawn. Her own warriors were settled in around her, steeling their courage for the fight ahead. But sleep was elusive and Deborah was restless.

She'd coordinated many a battle before, drawn up plans and given orders for her generals to execute, but never had she led a battle that left her with such a need for solitude.

She snuck out of the camp quietly, picking her way up the rocky slope away from the sounds of the men. The stars glittered cold and bright in the moonless sky. Reaching a secluded overlook, Deborah sank down upon a boulder with a weary sigh as she wrapped her loose-fitting robes tightly around her. Thunder rumbled in the distance and Deborah shivered despite the warmth of the evening.

"I thought I might find you here." The gentle voice behind her was so familiar it seemed her own heart speaking. Deborah turned to see Talia approaching, her silhouette graceful as ever, fitting for one who knew these hills and valleys like the back of her hand from years growing up as a shepherdess. At the sight of the other woman, the knot in Deborah's chest loosened.

"You know me well," Deborah replied with a sad smile.

Talia took a seat next to her on the boulder, her chestnut braids swinging behind her, her grey eyes glimmering from the distant torchlight as she took Deborah's hand in her own. "I know you well enough to know that something is bothering you, which…" she paused a moment, glancing around, before continuing, "given the circumstances, I think anyone would understand why you are troubled."

Though spoken softly, the words pierced Deborah's soul.

She opened her mouth but could find no words. Tomorrow, if the Lord willed it, Sisera would fall. But the cost could not yet be reckoned. How many men would die under her command tomorrow? Oh, she knew they would be victorious, something deep within told her that, despite the odds, this was true—but every battle resulted in losses. There would be many a widow and orphan made tomorrow—on both sides of the battlefield.

Talia waited patiently until Deborah gathered herself enough to speak. "The Lord has called me to lead our people into battle. I have seen it in the flames of the sacred fire—He has spoken to me and promised me victory—but I am no warrior. For twenty years I have judged disputes and offered what wisdom I can. Now judgment of a different kind is at hand, and I fear..." She could not finish the thought.

Talia squeezed her hand reassuringly. "You did not seek this war. But the Lord knows your faithful heart and appointed you as judge over Israel. The same Spirit who gave you wisdom and vision will go with you tomorrow."

Deborah nodded. "I know. I don't doubt that. I just..." she shook her head and sighed heavily. "I'm so disappointed in the General, Barak," she said suddenly, her voice tinged with anger. "For all his valor, he refused to believe in my words enough to simply obey my command! Have I not proven myself a true prophetess on countless occasions? Have I not commanded them into battle before? Have they not trusted me these twenty-some-odd years to judge over them? Why the sudden distrust?"

Talia snorted with disgust. "Come on, Deborah. You know why."

Her mouth tightened. "Yes. Because I'm a woman. Always suspect, no matter how many years I have successfully and faithfully led my people."

Talia nodded and sighed deeply. "Still, you are their woman of fire."

Deborah smiled at that. Some would call her the "wife of Lappidoth," which also meant "woman of fire." Since she had never married, she had felt the title quite fitting. Married to the fires of God that revealed their visions to her and enabled her to lead with such unwavering justice and clarity had certainly consumed her life like a husband might have. The fires of God were indeed more of a husband to her than any man had been, or ever could be.

She still remembered the day she had been...anointed? Was that the right word?...as judge and leader over Israel.

It had been during the festival of weeks, or Pentecost—the spring harvest festival. It was also the commemoration of the giving of God's instructions to her people by Moses on Mount Sinai fifty days after they had fled Egypt.

As the evening grew late and the fires began to dim low, thirteen-year-old Deborah had remained sitting beside the pit, mesmerized by the flames and glowing coals. She couldn't explain it, but she always seemed to "see" things in the flames and the curls of smoke that would emerge. It was like they spoke to her and created images in her mind. Apparently this did not happen to everyone, and her mother would simply joke that it must be a gift from the Lord.

As she peered into the flames, she thought she could even hear a voice that night, hissing from the fiery sparks. As she leaned forward, hoping to hear them more clearly, a popping cinder leapt out and ignited her robes. Deborah staggered back in shock as the flames engulfed her. She collapsed screaming, certain death had come for her.

But her screams were born of fear, rather than pain, and they soon died off as she realized instead of searing pain, she felt only warmth envelop her. The fire, rather than burning her to a crisp, caressed her skin like a blanket. Opening her eyes, she saw tongues of flame dancing harmlessly around her body. She sat up, curious now more than afraid, as the fire spread around her in a ring, singing the bushes nearby.

Villagers had come rushing toward her at the commotion, then halted and gaped in awe at the miraculous spectacle. Fiery tongues leapt all around her as Deborah rose to her feet, unsinged. The flames formed a ring now around her and she took a few steps gingerly forward, into the very heart of the embers of the fire that had roared back to life, passing through them, unharmed. As she emerged, the inferno gently waned until she stood untouched, but naked as the fires had burned away her robes, in the smoldering pit.

A murmur rippled through the onlookers. Some whispered "Sorcery!" and made signs against evil. But her father, one of the elders of the tribe, stepped forward and reminded them of the bush that did not burn when Moses approached it on Mount Horeb.

"The girl is a prophetess," the elders had finally agreed. The fire, they determined, had revealed the girl's true calling.

In the months that followed, word spread of the miracle. She had become known as the "woman of fire," and the people began coming to Deborah, seeking wisdom and justice from one seemingly anointed by God. Her judgments carried such weight that all respected and obeyed them.

As she grew older, she realized her father was not trying to find her a husband, as once her calling had been revealed in the fires, no man wanted a wife to whom he'd be deemed inferior in status. So she had remained single.

Deborah hadn't really minded. From a young age, she had always known she had other proclivities. Deborah and Talia had known each other from before the fiery incident, and as they grew older both realized they didn't need a man in their lives. Talia quickly became her closest counselor and confidant, and eventually, as adults they would even share a tent together. Deborah never went anywhere without Talia by her side.

Deborah also quickly realized that the men accepted her rule grudgingly. They couldn't deny her abilities and that God's hand was clearly upon her as no prediction ever proved false, and no judgment of hers ever was deemed unfair or faulty. Still, men were scared of her and hesitant to obey her—for a multitude of reasons, she supposed.

Probably the same reason that Barak had refused to follow her orders and lead this battle unless she went with him. Well, that was all good. Victory was not her concern. Somehow, despite being overwhelmed by superior forces and their heavy iron chariots, she trusted they would be victorious. She had seen it in the flames.

Lightning flashed in the distance followed by a rumble of thunder a few moments later. Glancing up, she watched as the pinpricks of stars slowly winked out one by one with the advancing clouds.

Deborah smiled as she glanced out toward the approaching storm and began to laugh.

Talia gave her a confused look.

"Rain," Deborah laughed. "Rain is how we're going to win." She lifted her arms, closed her eyes and uttered her thanks to the living God who was providing the way forward.

Talia shook her head, still confused. Deborah grabbed the other woman's hand and stood up from the boulder, walked over to the edge of the overlook and pointed to the chariots that the torches illuminated far below them. Understanding slowly dawned on Talia's face as a wide grin replaced her confused scowl.

"They'll get stuck in the mud," they said together, almost in unison. They both laughed and wrapped their arms around each other once again.

Deborah fell silent, gazing at the woman who knew her best in this world. Talia brushed an errant strand of hair from Deborah's cheek, her touch igniting an ember of hope within.

"Do you recall when we were girls?" Talia asked tenderly. "We would sneak away to climb the hill overlooking our village and dream together of the futures unfolding before us."

Deborah allowed herself a bittersweet smile. "Such handsome husbands we imagined for ourselves. How naive we were then."

Talia shrugged. "Some dreams fade with time, but I also have no regrets on the journey we have gone on together. Or who you were born to be."

Deborah pulled her close until their foreheads touched. She had been called to this battle, but she was grateful she did not stand alone. The Lord had given her Talia's enduring love and companionship to lean upon for all these years. Tomorrow they would fight side by side, whatever that day held.

For this night, it was enough to sit silently beneath the watchful stars, drawing strength from one another for the battle to come. The battle she knew belonged to the Lord, but they belonged to each other.

After a while, as the thunder grew louder and the first heavy drops of rain began to fall, they both climbed back down the mountainside and returned to the encampment.

As lightning split the night and thunder boomed over the mountains, the downpour began. Deborah, standing just outside her tent, lifted her face to the drenching rain, tears mingling with the water running down her cheeks. The Lord always provided. Tomorrow Sisera's chariots would meet their end.

At dawn, the army broke camp and marched down the slopes of Mount Tabor. The muddy road slowed their pace as the rain continued to pour and create rivulets of water in the earth, but Deborah reveled in the knowledge that no matter how difficult it was for them to travel, it would be nearly impossible for the Canaanite army and their heavy chariots. She walked ahead of the supply carts, her robes sodden but her spirit soaring. She sang praise to the God of Sinai. Talia, beside her, lifted her lilting voice to join in the song. They were the only two women in the entire company of soldiers, but eventually the men began to join in, too.

By noon they reached the valley and arranged themselves in battle formation facing north. Scouts kept watch along the ridge line. As the hours passed, the storm subsided and the sun emerged. Deborah scanned the plain below for any sign of Sisera's approach. She knelt among the rocks and prayed. She felt it then…the warmth. The fiery spirit that felt the same as those flames had so many years ago against her skin. Only this was from the inside out.

A cry rang out from the lookouts. Far in the distance, a great host appeared where the trees gave way to the plain. At the sight, a shudder passed through the waiting warriors, but Deborah raised the spear she held in her hand above her head and shouted above the breeze, "Be strong! This very day the Lord will deliver Sisera into your hand!"

Barak strode among the men, steadying them for the charge. But they would hold fast here a little longer, giving the wadi time to ensnare Sisera's chariots.

Though no Israelite was of royal blood, Barak had the bearing of a king, commanding attention and obedience from his fellow warriors. He cut an imposing figure: powerfully built, with muscular limbs and a barrel chest, his typically olive complexion looked fierce and focused beneath his bronze helmet. His dark beard and long hair peeked out from under the helmet's edges.

Once again, she felt dismayed that the man had not trusted her, and by default, had not trusted God enough to have simply followed her orders. She wondered silently had she been a man giving the orders, would they have been followed without question?

She pressed her lips tightly together. She absolutely knew the answer and it only kindled a burning rage within her more. Woman of fire, indeed.

Deborah stood tall upon the heights, her blood pounding in her ears. She could feel a tingling, burning sensation in her veins as they prepared for battle. Deborah knew that feeling. It was like her blood was on fire, which meant the Lord of Hosts was present in Israel's ranks, his presence flowing through her, and she knew with unwavering doubt that the stars in their courses would now fight against Sisera.

Raising her spear above her head once again, her eyes blazing with the fire she felt inside, she shouted in a voice that reverberated off the rocky mountainside: "This day, the Lord will sell Sisera into the hands of a woman!"

Talia beside her lifted the war horn and blew, its blast echoing through the Israelite ranks. With a roar like thunder, ten thousand men charged down the mountainside. Deborah's heart pounded as she watched them descend into the fray.

The Canaanites rushed to meet them, and Deborah was able to identify Sisera's chariot leading the charge. But as the wheels churned the soft ground, they stuck fast in the mud as Deborah had predicted. Sisera cursed and lashed his horses furiously, but the wheels would not budge.

Deborah smiled with satisfaction as the Israelites fell upon the immobilized Canaanites with unchecked zeal. The clamor of battle engulfed the valley. From her vantage point, Deborah could not make out individuals anymore in the churning melee. But she marked the progress as the Canaanite lines collapsed inward.

When the arrows began flying, Deborah and Talia took cover behind a rocky outcropping. But she refused to take her eyes off the battlefield for long.

As the fighting raged, Sisera's distinctive chariot withdrew from the fray. Deborah watched as he abandoned his trapped forces and fled on foot. But even his retreat could not stop the Israelite onslaught. By midday, Sisera's mighty army lay decimated before them as Barak and the rest of the men pursued the remnants of the army to Harosheth-ha-goiim.

Deborah descended the last few feet, her robes stained with mud as she surveyed the killing field. Barak and his men returned and Deborah pointed in the opposite direction with her spear.

"Sisera went that way," she said. "Toward the clan tents of Heber the Kenite."

Barak shouted orders, rallying men to pursue. Deborah felt a flicker of disappointment once again that Barak had not trusted enough to win this battle without her. She liked Barak in general, so she supposed it was more hurt that she felt that he had chosen to not trust her. Now Sisera's end would come at another's hand, not his.

"Into the hand of a woman," Deborah remembered. Not just the army and the battle, but Sisera himself. She frowned. Would she be forced to run her spear through him? She supposed so. Death in battle would have been easier.

As Barak and his men took off in pursuit, Deborah gathered up her robes and followed behind him, picking her way across the ground that was wet no longer just from rain, but was now also slick with blood. For twenty years she had sat beneath her palm tree dispensing justice and wisdom, never doubting God was on Israel's side. But to behold God's wrath poured out like this troubled her.

She hadn't asked to be a military leader. She had never yearned to see and smell the death and destruction war wrought, though perhaps this was why she had been forced here: to see for herself the cost of war. It was one thing to give her commands and orders from beneath the relative safety and security from beneath her palm tree; it was something else to see it up close and personal like this. To hear it, see it, smell it. She supposed that was what angered her most about Barak's lack of trust: it had forced her to confront the realities of war, and she did not like them. How many of these men that lay dead in this valley was someone's husband, son or father? Granted, they were their enemies, but Deborah was wise enough to know that enemies today could wind up your allies and friends tomorrow. Though she doubted that with the Canaanites, she still questioned to some degree the need for such bloodshed.

As she walked past, one of the bodies suddenly reached a hand out and grabbed hold of her ankle. She let out a startled gasp but Talia lunged forward and quickly drove a spear through his throat, ending whatever danger he might have posed. Deborah gave the other woman a grateful smile as they continued across the battlefield.

Talia was truly one of her many gifts from God, and she didn't know what she would have done without her.

As they neared the tents of Heber, she saw Barak talking with one of the Kenite women. The Kenites were not enemies of Israel per say, as their great prophet, Moses, had been married to a Kenite woman named Zipporah, daughter to Jethro, a priest of Midian. Heber and his clan, however, had broken away from the rest of the Kenite tribes and made peace with King Jabin of Hazor, and that made them suspicious in Deborah's eyes.

As she approached, Barak turned and gave her a sour look. When she looked at him quizzically, he motioned toward the woman. "This is Jael, Heber the Kenite's wife."

Deborah eyed the other woman who bowed slightly in deference. Jael's slim frame belied her physical strength, honed from years pitching tents and tending flocks across the harsh landscape. Plain woolen robes disguised her womanly curves that were spattered, Deborah noted, with blood. Her tanned, calloused hands were gripped tightly together in front of her and told of a life spent living off the land. Dark, unruly curls were cut short around her face to keep them from her eyes.

Her lips did not smile in greeting, however, as she glanced warily between Deborah and Barak.

"Sisera came to Jael's tents seeking sanctuary and safety," Barak explained.

Deborah raised a curious eyebrow at that as she regarded the other woman. Men in battle frequently did not simply go into a woman's tent looking for shelter. They usually were after more...carnal desires.

Jael lifted her strong jaw defiantly. Her gaze locked with Deborah's. "I'm not a stupid woman, I know why he was here," she said, nodding toward Deborah.

"And?" Deborah continued.

The woman took a step back and lifted the tent flap. "See for yourself."

Barak wrinkled his nose in disgust and turned away as Deborah ducked down to peer into the tent.

Sisera lay there with an iron tent peg driven through his temple, nailing his head to the ground. His dead eyes still bulged from the shock. Deborah fought back the urge to sick up and quickly turned back around and straightened.

"You have done Israel a great service today, Jael, wife of Heber."

The other woman snorted a little at that. "Yeah, well, not much of a husband that leaves me here to fend for myself, and what did you think I would do? Sisera was defeated. Your armies are clearly the superior one and let's face it...we all know what he likely would have done when he awoke. I wasn't interested in any of that," she spat. Deborah nodded appreciatively and wondered if she'd have done the same given similar circumstances. She had never had a man try and force himself on her...yet. But if one ever did, she silently hoped she, too, would have a tent peg nearby.

As they turned away from the scene Deborah sighed heavily. "Make sure she and the rest of her clan are cared for," she said, turning to Talia, who nodded and rushed off to find supplies.

"We still have King Jabin to deal with," she said wearily to Barak, who nodded. The battle was won but the war still raged. There could be no rest yet.

"I'm...sorry," Barak said at last. Deborah's head snapped up in surprise as she regarded the man as he slowly removed his helmet.

"For?" she prodded. She wanted to make him say it.

"For...lacking faith in you."

Deborah shook her head. "No, it is not me you lacked faith in. You lacked faith in God. You know better than anyone that I am one of God's prophets, Barak, and yet you doubted the word I gave to you. To doubt me, was to doubt God."

He winced at that. It was easier to admit he had simply doubted the word of a woman. Yet she could tell from his dejected posture, that he understood all too well that what she said was true.

Much work remained to drive out the Canaanites and unify Israel's tribes. And much work remained to help her people see her as the authority figure she was. Though she figured that was a battle that would rage on long after she was dead and gone.

Deborah lifted her eyes to the hills surrounding them. Somewhere beyond lay her palm tree, beckoning her home. Home to where she and Talia might once again live their lives in peace.

Soon, she thought wearily as she turned and trudged back toward her troops with Barak.

Soon.

Discussion Questions

1. Other than Samuel, Deborah is the only Judge in all of scripture that is also considered a prophet. What do you think is the significance of that?

2. Many will say Deborah should not be viewed as a legitimate example of women in leadership because she was simply stepping in to do what the man, Barak, refused to do. The problem with this argument is that Deborah was already called a "leader, judge and prophet" over all of Israel prior to taking over as a military commander. Why do you think some even today refuse to acknowledge and legitimize her leadership role?

3. The Hebrew term "wife of Lappidoth" is used to describe Deborah in Judges 4:1. In Hebrew, this can also be translated as "woman of fire." Which do you think is the most accurate translation? Why?

4. Of all the Judges in the book of Judges, Deborah comes off as being one of the most successful and faithful. She never demands a sign from God or later constructs a golden calf (Gideon), doesn't make a hasty, reckless vow that brings about the death of her child (Jepthah) and doesn't enact her own personal vengeance (Samson), but simply does what she should. If Israel was at its best under the leadership of a woman, do you think had there been more women leaders things might have gone differently in the Book of Judges rather than ending in civil war?

5. While Deborah might have been thinking she was the woman who would bring an end to Sisera, it turns out another woman, Jael, is who finally takes Sisera out with the tent peg. Why do you think two women play such pivotal roles in early Israelite society?

6. The entire story is about the weak overpowering the strong: both from the perspective of the Israelites defeating the larger, better

equipped army of the Canaanites and that women, often deemed the weakest of society, are the major heroines. How does this square with later on in scripture when Paul states that God's power is made perfect in weakness? Do you really think what these women did would be considered "weak?"

The Levite's Concubine

(Judges 19)

ELEORA'S BODY had gone completely numb. It was like she was disconnected from whatever was now happening to it, floating above it as an observer rather than a participant.

She'd endured her husband's beatings for years, but never anything like this. Dozens of men, grabbing her body, smashing her face into the ground, twisting and breaking her arms as she'd tried to fight her way free.

Somewhere in the night she'd cried out to God. Where were the angels? Where were the men who would save her and rain fire and brimstone down upon her assailants? She'd heard of that happening once. The story was told among her people over and over again.

And yet, when it had happened here, in Gibeah, and her husband had thrown her out to the mob of men to have their way with her—no angels had come to the rescue. She'd had to endure every thrust, every ejaculation, every slamming of her body against the ground, every eruption of blood from her nose as it smashed into the paving stones over and over again, and every explosion of pain as they'd broken and dislocated her arms.

She wasn't sure who she hated more at the moment: her cowardly, brutal husband who had thrown her so mercilessly to these bastards; the mob of men doing this to her; her father who had so callously turned her back over to her husband; or God.

The God who had ignored her cries, ignored her pleas, ignored her anguish.

Not just today as these men ravaged and beat her body, but every time her husband, Abner, had hit her or abused her. Every time she cried out to God to save her.

And every time, there had been no answer.

Just like there was no answer now to her cries and screams. No one, man or deity, was going to save her.

Abner's beatings had been what had driven her away from him in the first place, when she had fled to her father's home. The journey had itself been dangerous, traveling by herself from the northern hill country of Ephraim to the southern region of Judah in Bethlehem. Still, she'd been willing to risk the dangers of traveling alone rather than staying another day with her husband.

If she could even really call him that. She was just a concubine, after all. Not quite a slave, but also not quite a wife. At any moment another woman of higher status could come in and supplant her place. All because her family had been too poor to negotiate a good bride price with someone else. All because…because Abner had ruined her for other men. She was no longer "wife" material. Abner's concubine was all she could aspire to now.

How was it she was punished for something Abner had done? How was she the one being punished because he had just taken what he wanted, and that made her of less value?

Legally, she wasn't even married to him, though she was still, somehow, his property and responsibility. It was unheard of for a concubine—or even a wife—to leave her husband, yet she had. She had fled, to escape the abuse and for four months, she thought she would be safe and free from him. When she'd arrived on her father's doorstep still bruised and battered, he hadn't hesitated to let her in and apologized profusely for having ever agreed to give her away to that man. Unfortunately, she was now legally his and had few rights. If she'd at least been a full wife, she could have demanded the council pressure him to divorce her for neglect and abuse. But then, if she were a full wife, he likely would not have neglected and abused her. Perhaps that is why he had targeted her—the poor daughter of a widower that no one would care anything about.

She'd been so smitten with him at first. He was a Levite, a member of the priestly class—a musician by trade. And he'd been so charming—oh so charming. She remembered that first day she'd met him as she'd made her daily trip to the well just outside the Bethlehem gate, jar balanced on her hip. She'd heard him before she even saw him, a sweet melody playing on a lyre had drifted through the air as she approached. Sitting beside the well had been a handsome young stranger plucking skillfully at the strings. He had been dressed in fine robes, with a neatly trimmed beard and chiseled features. Though he appeared to be a fellow Israelite, she hadn't recognized him as being from Bethlehem.

Eleora paused, not wanting to interrupt the lovely song. When the man noticed her, he ended the tune with a flourish and flashed a charming smile.

"I hope my playing isn't disturbing you," he said, politely moving aside.

"Please don't stop on my account," Eleora said quickly. "I was enjoying the melody."

"Were you now?" he asked, that charming smile broadening. "Well, when a beautiful lady makes such a request, who am I to deny her?" He lifted the lyre back up and began to play softly again, keeping his gaze riveted on her.

She blushed shyly as she came nearer to him in order to lower the bucket down into the well and pull it back up, filling her jar. Her cheeks continued to grow warm under his intense gaze, as she was unaccustomed to so much attention from any man.

Eleora knew he had just been kind by calling her beautiful, as that simply was not the case. She certainly wasn't ugly, but she knew the word beautiful would never be used to accurately describe her. Her dusty, worn tunic hung loosely on her too-slender, almost gangly frame. Wisps of brown hair peeked out from under her headscarf, which she wore wrapped simply with little adornment. Her plain face lacked the rosy glow of youth, making her appear older than her years. Still, there was a gentleness in her brown eyes that hinted at a kind soul underneath her humble exterior. Callused hands grasped the water jug, her tanned arms straining from its weight.

The man set the lyre aside and reached over to take the jug from her arms.

"Here, let me help you. I'll walk you back to your home."

"Oh!" Eleora said in surprise. He wanted to walk her home? She blinked in confusion as he handed her his lyre.

"Look, I'll let you carry this for me, and I'll carry the jug for you. Sound like a good trade?" he asked with a wink.

Eleora nodded dumbly and followed as he began making his way back through the city gate and into the town of Bethlehem. She hurried to keep up, once the shock had worn off.

He'd been such a chatty man as they walked back toward her father's house.

"I'm Abner, by the way," he said, glancing back at her over his shoulder as she scurried to catch up and match his stride side by side.

"Eleora," she managed to squeak out.

"What a pretty name," he said, his smile widening. "Pretty name for a pretty woman."

Eleora's flush deepened.

"Anyway, I'm a Levite musician, from the hill country of Ephraim."

"Like Deborah," Eleora murmured. She had heard Deborah, the prophet, judge, and leader, had also been a musician and she was from the hill country of Ephraim. Eleora admired the female leader turned general who had once led Israel to great victory. You didn't hear often of women in those roles, but God had chosen her to do just that. Eleora could only dream of being commissioned by God in such a way.

Abner's smile faltered slightly at the comparison and he gave her a sideways glance with narrowed eyes.

"Yes..." he said finally, slowly. "Like...Deborah." Clearing his throat, he quickly pivoted to talking about his travels and adventures. Eleora gave him her rapt attention.

Her father, Caleb, was home when they arrived. Caleb had been the only parent Eleora had even known, as her mother had died in childbirth. He'd been a blacksmith in his younger years, but the backbreaking work had nearly crippled him and now he worked as an assistant to a pottery maker, primarily running the store where the potter sold his wares. It was a measly income, but it kept food on the table and the tiny roof over their heads. Eleora had recently started as an apprentice to a dye-maker so she could learn to dye fabrics and also was able to bring in a little extra income to help out.

Like Eleora, Caleb was immediately taken in by Abner's charm and persuaded him to stay in their home while he was visiting. Abner agreed and stayed several nights.

And one of those nights, he charmed and coerced his way into Eleora's bed. He had told her it was all right, that he wanted to marry her, that he was madly in love with her. She'd succumbed to his kisses and allowed him to take her to bed.

The next morning it became clear it was all an awful trick. Abner arose early and confronted Caleb in the kitchen.

"Your daughter is now ruined for other men," Abner claimed. "But I'll take the little whore off your hands and take her as a concubine."

Caleb's jaw dropped. "A...concubine? Not a wife?"

"Did you not hear me?" Abner sneered. "She is no longer fit to be anyone's wife, but here..." he tossed some coins on the table. "I'll even pay something of a bride price for her. She didn't...displease me."

Eleora stood crying in the doorway. He had wooed her and seduced her, and now...she was ruined. Caleb turned to her and while there was a glint of anger and disappointment in his eyes, it was mostly resignation and sorrow. She had been all he had left to try and arrange for a bride price, and she'd betrayed that. Tears streamed down her cheeks as she tried to silently apologize to her father.

He reluctantly accepted the money and Eleora was packed up and sent on her way with Abner. The pretenses of his charm rapidly disappeared once they returned to Ephraim. He was verbally cruel and constantly told her how she didn't dress properly and wasn't as pretty as he had originally thought. The tiniest errors set him into a rage and she had learned to simply cower in silence rather than argue or fight back. Eventually the verbal abuse became physical, and after nearly a year of beatings, she left.

For four months she'd been able to stay with her father, but eventually, Abner came for her. She couldn't get a divorce, and her father had tried so hard to keep her with him as long as he could, convincing him to stay night after night. Of course, he had acted the perfect gentleman around her father. If she hadn't known better, she would have been tempted to believe herself that he loved her and wanted her home.

But once they started the journey back, his demeanor changed again and he became sullen and silent as they made their way to Gibeah.

"Your half-wit of a father delayed us so late in the day that this is all the farther we're getting tonight," he grumbled. Eleora said nothing.

"Of course," he continued, "had you not run off to begin with, I wouldn't have had to come here and retrieve you."

Eleora looked off into the distance as the city gates to Gibeah loomed ahead. "I don't suppose you know anyone in Gibeah?" he asked.

She shook her head. They were Benjamite, she was Judean. Why would she know any of them?

As evening fell, they sat in the gate waiting, as was custom, for someone to invite them into their home. Most people just gave them suspicious looks and kept walking.

"If we have to wind up spending the night out here in the gate," he started to growl under his breath when an elderly man walked up to them.

"Gibeah is no place for a young woman—or man for that matter— to be out at night," the man said. "Where are you travelers from?"

"Ephraim," Abner said. "I don't have a lot of cash but I have my lyre, I can play in exchange for some room and board. My concubine here, she…can sort of sing, too."

The elderly man's eyes lit up. "Ephraim you say? I, too, am from the hill country. Come, stay with me tonight. I'm sure we might know some of the same people."

They had followed the man to his home and while they were eating, there was a knock at the door. Outside a pack of men stood demanding that Abner be given to them, and Abner, instead, grabbed a hold of Eleora and tossed her out the door, muttering, "stupid whore bitch, you did this to yourself."

Now, she was only vaguely aware as it shifted from night to morning as slivers of sunlight nudged their way through her swollen and bruised eyelids.

She was alone now, exposed in the street for all to gawk at. Those who saw her simply walked around and tried to avoid the pools of blood that had formed around her. With some effort, she rolled over on her stomach. Burning shards of pain shot throughout her entire abdominal section. Scraping her already broken and bloodied fingers against the ground, she tried to claw her way back to the door that had slammed in her face the night before.

The door where the men still sat safely behind. The door that had not opened all night long to check on her or rescue her from her assailants.

The door that had sealed her fate.

With a final gasp, she collapsed on the threshold, her hand scraping against the door.

She was only dimly aware of her husband's voice shouting at her to get up, his toe nudging her side before she sank into the deep, blissful embrace of death.

Discussion Questions

1. The story of the Levite's concubine is probably one of the most disturbing incidents and scenes in the entire Bible. Why do you think this story was included in scripture?

2. Compare this story to the incident of Sodom and Gomorrah in Genesis 19:1-14 with the three men and the village demanding they be released into their care. Why do you think God intervened in that case but not with the Levite's concubine?

3. If you continue reading beyond this story in the book of Judges, the Levite uses his concubine's death to start a civil war within Israel, but fails to recognize his own complicity with what happened to her. He threw a vulnerable woman out to be abused to save himself. How often do you think those of us with some semblance of power sometimes sacrifice vulnerable people to save ourselves rather than standing up for them? How often do we use the tragedy that befalls vulnerable people as an opportunity to further our own agendas, rather than take the time to recognize our own complicity with what led to it in the first place?

4. Read Ezekiel 16:49—after reading Ezekiel and this story, how does this reframe the sins committed in Sodom and Gomorrah?

5. In this story that gives us more background into their relationship, can you identify the signs of an abuser early on? The love-bombing, charismatic personality, etc.?

6. It was virtually unheard of for a woman to run away from her husband in the ancient world. What kind of courage do you think it took for her to do this? What kind of betrayal must she have felt when her father handed her back over to the man who was abusing her?

7. Some English translations say the concubine was guilty of adultery. It is disputed whether the first word of Judges 19:2 is derived from זנה zaná ("to commit fornication/adultery/harlotry, to be a harlot, to play the harlot, to prostitute"), or זנח zanákh ("to reject, spurn, be angry with/at, cast away, remove far away, desert.") Despite the obvious direction this retelling has opted to pursue, what do you think is the most likely understanding? Given how other stories of prostitution have been handled thus far (Tamar, Rahab), would this have been a sin worthy of what happened to her?

Ruth

(Ruth 1-4)

THE HOT MIDDAY sun beat down on Ruth's head and shoulders as she bent to gather the stray heads of barley left behind by the harvesters. Her back ached from stooping repeatedly, her hands were stiff and sore from grasping the shafts of grain. But Ruth persisted, driven by the gnawing hunger in her belly and the greater need to provide for her mother-in-law, Naomi.

Her slender, willowy frame that reflected the hunger she had known since leaving her homeland, bent over the stalks of wheat. Her dark, wavy hair had been plaited to keep the strands from her eyes while she worked. Her skin was golden-brown from the desert sun, smooth across her high cheekbones but crinkled at the corners of her large, expressive brown eyes. Eyes that had seen sorrow and loss, but still shone with curiosity and ready laughter.

Her clothing was simple—she wore the plain garments of a field worker rather than a fine mantle or jewels as she did in her former life. Her dress was cinched at the waist by a braided cord, the fabric faded and worn from her journey. Any beauty she possessed came not from ornamentation but from her innate grace and spirit. Some might consider her mouth too wide, her frame too slender, but to those who knew her, Ruth's kindness and courage lent her real beauty that came from within.

Still, this was her life now, scavenging in the fields of Bethlehem like a beggar. Such indignity for the former wife of a respectable man. But Mahlon was gone, taken by the same bitter famine that had brought his family to her homeland of Moab in search of food.

She fought back the tears that threatened to overwhelm her. The day Mahlon breathed his last, Ruth felt something inside her collapse and go numb. She'd had to bury her own parents only weeks earlier as they'd died from the famine as well. It had been torture to stare into his gaunt face, so terribly still, as she wept in utter despair. Where was she to go? What was she to do? She had never even had the chance to have children with him—not that they could have fed them had she had them. She'd likely have had to bury them as well, like Naomi burying both her sons.

Ruth drifted through her days like a ghost. Simple tasks became impossibly heavy, and at night she lay sleepless. Curling into Mahlon's absence each evening, loneliness overwhelmed her. Day brought no relief, just endless labor to distract her from the cavernous loss.

Friends urged her to accept another suitor, have children to chase away the shadows. But the thought only brought fresh waves of sorrow. She could not picture looking into another man's eyes, holding any child but Mahlon's son in her empty arms.

When Naomi announced she was returning to Bethlehem, Ruth insisted she go with her. What did it matter where she dwelled, now that her home had died? At least in Judah she might keep busy providing for Naomi, ignoring the hollow ache within herself. Work and time—those were the only remedies Ruth knew to treat such wounds. She clung to the hope that one day, if she kept putting one foot before the other, the pain might begin to ease.

Now, as she labored under the hot sun, Ruth had no choice but to swallow her pride along with the meager gleanings she could scrape together.

As she wiped sweat from her brow, Ruth surveyed the field, making sure to keep her distance from the land owner, Boaz's, hired men. She watched them joking, and laughing as they swung their sickles, harvesting barley for the owner's profit. She had seen how they treated some of the other women, however, and had seen them leering at her as well from time to time and tried to steer clear. Ruth harbored no resentment. It simply was the way it was. Occasionally she felt pangs of longing where she missed her own people, though she knew returning to Moab was impossible now.

A murmur passed through the field hands, pulling Ruth's attention to the far edge where a tall, middle-aged man was striding through the field. He had the sturdy build of a man clearly accustomed to physical labor. Years of working the fields had left his tall frame tanned and muscular. His arms were corded with sinew and his hands calloused from harvesting grain. Though in later middle age, he still moved with vigor and alertness. His face was open and honest, weathered from long days under the hot sun. He had a scruffy beard beginning to show touches of grey that matched the hair on his head. Hazel eyes radiated kindness and wisdom gained from a lifetime of hard work as they gazed out over the field.

Ruth lowered her eyes, not wishing to attract notice. Surely this must be Boaz, the landowner, and if she kept her head down, he would not bother himself over one insignificant gleaner. She must be diligent, make haste to gather all she could before the day's end. She hurriedly began pulling at the stalks of wheat around the edges of the field—according to Israelite law, farmers were to leave the edges unharvested so the poor, like her, could gather their own wheat and not starve.

"Stay close to my servant girls," a male voice suddenly said. "The men have been instructed not to harass you."

Ruth's head jerked up in surprise to see the man standing over her, offering a skin of water. Flustered, she stood and bowed low in thanks, stammering praise for his generosity, though inside frustration simmered over his assumption she needed protection. She quickly stamped it down.

He was showing her a kindness, she knew. Still, she had traveled the dangerous roads from Moab to Judah alone with only Naomi, and had been the protector! But outwardly Ruth showed only humble gratitude. Maybe this man would prove kinder than most.

His eyes crinkled into a smile. "You're Naomi's daughter-in-law, are you not?"

Ruth nodded dumbly.

"From Moab?"

Ruth winced. "Yes," she squeaked out. She knew that her people were hated and despised enemies of the Israelites because they had attacked and tried to hinder Boaz's people from entering into the Promised Land. Well, that and their religious practices. But Ruth had abandoned those in favor of the God Naomi and her family worshiped.

Rather than judgment, however, Boaz eyed her curiously. "I've never been to Moab. I've only gone as far as this side of the Dead Sea."

Ruth's eyes suddenly lit up despite herself and found herself gushing, having an opportunity to speak of her homeland. "Oh, we lived at the base of the mountains just along the sea, so I used to gaze out over the Dead Sea at sunset, its fiery orange light glistening off the water. And every morning the mountains glowed red in the dawn light. Back when we had plenty of food, we would gather around fires to share meals and stories under endless stars. Every spring wildflowers would burst from the cracks between rocks. Palm groves would rustle and whisper in the breeze." Her face suddenly fell as she remembered those things which were no more. Her husband, who was no more. Her father-in-law, her own parents. "We used to celebrate with feasts lasting late into the night. Music, laughter and joy filled those warm evenings. I...I miss those times," she said sadly, then glanced up at him, startled that she had shared so much.

He was watching her with interest, however, rather than judgment.

"I'm sorry for all that you've lost," he said so gently it brought tears to Ruth's eyes. Just that little token of compassion in this strange and hostile land seemed so rare and foreign to her. She sniffed and wiped quickly at her eyes, blinking them away.

"Well, those times are gone and things are different now."

"Why did you come back with Naomi?" he asked suddenly. "Why not stay in Moab, marry one of your own people? You're still young and beautiful. Surely you would have had no problem."

Ruth found herself blushing slightly at the compliment, and bit her lip nervously. How did she explain that she was too heartbroken back then to even consider another suitor? The pain of losing Mahlon had been too fresh, too real, that all she wanted to do was run away and Naomi had given her that opportunity.

"I loved my husband dearly," she said at last, "and Naomi was as close to me as my own mother. I couldn't let her come back here alone. I couldn't...I couldn't lose her, too."

For a long moment, Boaz simply stared at her, holding her gaze. Not in an unkind way, not even really in a curious way anymore, but more in a sorrowful and compassionate way. She almost felt he understood her pain to some degree, though she knew that was impossible. No one could know what she felt.

She lowered her eyes, not wanting his to bore into hers so intensely anymore.

"Well," he said finally, clearing his throat. "If you run into any trouble, tell them that Boaz will have their hides if they bother you." He gently patted her shoulder before moving off, leaving Ruth staring after him, suddenly feeling confused.

At day's end, Ruth made her way home heavy-laden, the bulk of grain upon her back drawing curious glances from passersby. Naomi would be thrilled, she knew, but more importantly, their bellies would be filled tonight. A rare feeling of satisfaction moved through Ruth as she pushed open the door.

"Look, Mother!" she cried, letting the grain spill onto the floor before Naomi. The older woman wept and held Ruth's face as she kissed it. As they prepared their meager dinner, Ruth recounted her encounter with the man in the field.

Naomi's eyes grew wide with excitement.

"Boaz you say? He is a kinsman, my dear one. And he clearly favors you." Naomi pressed Ruth's hand, a matchmaking glint in her eye that Ruth found both amusing and annoying. Could she not simply enjoy a full stomach without thoughts of more?

But Naomi was determined in her strategy. She instructed Ruth on how to approach Boaz at the threshing floor that night, when his defenses would be lowered from drink and food, and satisfaction at the harvest's bounty.

Ruth balked. "You...you want me to...prostitute myself?" she asked in horror.

Naomi let out a disgusted "Bah!" and waved her hand. "You're not prostituting yourself. You're simply...making yourself available for his needs."

"That sounds like prostituting myself," Ruth grumbled.

Naomi's jaw set with determination as she looked at her daughter-in-law. "Have you forgotten our situation, Ruth? You did not have to return here with me, but since you did, we must do what's needed to survive. You won't last long in those fields day after day trying to keep us fed. I know of Boaz. He is a good man. And unmarried."

Ruth frowned thoughtfully. "Why is that? Why hasn't he married?"

Naomi shrugged. "I believe he was once. But...she died, if I remember correctly. In childbirth. Both perished so he has no children."

Ruth felt a pang of sympathy for the man. He too knew sorrow like hers. That explained the look he had given her. That look of... understanding.

Ruth lay uneasy through the night, nervous anticipation mingling with resignation. She hadn't disliked the man, but this wasn't really how she would have wanted to go about garnering his attention. Still, if this was what she must do to secure their future, then so be it.

When at last the household slumbered, Ruth rose, washed, anointed herself, and made her way quietly to the threshing floor on the edge of town.

The moon cast a soft glow on the threshing room floor as Ruth peered from the shadows. The men were toiling tirelessly, separating grain from chaff under the night sky. The air was filled with the rhythmic sounds of threshing tools and the occasional laughter of tired laborers taking brief breaks as they drank wine and shouted to one another. The swinging wooden flails struck the wheat heads and loosened the wheat from their husks in a steady, almost musical rhythm—a *whap* against the golden stems. Oxen were dragging a wooden sled across the pile, its sharp edges crushing the stalks and releasing the grains. The sound of rushing straw and the murmurs of the workers created a quiet hum that filled the air and rose above the noise of the threshing.

Another group of men held the winnowing forks, long wooden tools with prongs that fanned out at the end. They dug the forks into the mixture and flung it high into the air. The breeze took over, carrying the lighter chaff away in soft swirling clouds, while the heavier grains fell straight back down to the ground like a clean rain. The process was repeated, forkful after forkful, as the farmers worked in unison.

The lighter chaff and straw fluttered off to the side, forming a growing mound of debris downwind. It wasn't long before the floor was divided into golden piles of wheat on one side, and heaps of dry, brittle chaff on the other.

In a corner, a fire flickered, providing warmth against the cool night. The flames leapt and crackled whenever someone would shovel some of the chaff into it. At last the grain was all that was left, ready to be bagged. But that could wait until morning.

They stopped working and sat down, exchanging cups of wine, savoring the fruit of their labors. She soon saw Boaz's form as it stood and wandered over toward a quiet corner, collapsing near a heap of grain. For a long while she sat unmoving, waiting for the rest of the men to fall asleep as well. When the fire had burned down to mere embers, and the only sound she could hear was the deep breathing and snoring of the men, she quietly crept around the outer edge until she was close enough to his sleeping form she could hear him snoring.

Slipping over to him, her heart pounded loud in her ears.

Silently she gathered his cloak around herself and lay down next to him, reaching under his tunic. She'd been married once, she knew how this worked, and yet, she felt like a novice virgin as she awaited his waking with mingled dread and hope.

He moaned slightly in his sleep, before suddenly jerking awake. Ruth shrank back as he sat up with a start. "Who are you?" Boaz demanded in confused alarm. Ruth sat up slowly, willing courage she did not completely feel into her voice.

"I am Ruth, your servant," she said softly. "Naomi's daughter-in-law. I've been working with your servant girls in the field."

He blinked in confusion before the name registered.

"Spread your protection over me, for Naomi says you are a kinsman and redeemer. And I…" she swallowed hard as he stared intently at her. "And I…desire your protection and blessing." Ruth held her breath, watching the comprehension dawn on his face. *Please let this be enough*, she prayed. For herself, for Naomi, and for the fragile hope they nurtured of a new life.

Boaz glanced around nervously. Seeing everyone else had fallen asleep across the threshing room floor as well, he turned back to Ruth, motioning for her to curl up closer to him as he did indeed cover her with his cloak.

"You know you're not permitted here," he whispered hoarsely.

She nodded. "Yes. I know. But…I didn't know how else to approach you."

"And…I believe there's one who is a closer relative than I am that could lay claim to you."

Ruth's eyes widened in surprise. Naomi had not mentioned that, and she wondered why. "Oh," was all Ruth managed to say.

"I'll meet with him tomorrow and see if he wants to lay that claim."

"I see," Ruth said, her heart falling. She at least had known Boaz was a kind man. She knew nothing about this other.

Seeing the look on her face, he smiled and touched her face gently. "Do not worry. He's selfish and will not want your firstborn child to carry the name of your previous husband. But I am curious, why have you not gone after someone…younger?"

The blush in her cheeks deepened. "You…you were kind to me. I'm a stranger in these lands. Finding kindness among strangers is not always easy."

"Well," he said at last, enfolding her under his cloak, "you shall be a stranger to these lands no more."

For the first time, in a long time, Ruth felt hope.

Discussion Questions

1. In this retelling, Ruth describes her "seduction" of Boaz as "prostituting herself." Some scholars contend that "feet" is a euphemism for male genitals. This clearly alters how one views what Ruth was doing when she "uncovered his feet" and lay down beside him. Given the threshing floor was known for where "illicit" sexual encounters happened (see Hosea 9:1, *"Do not rejoice, O Israel, with joy like other peoples, For you have played the harlot against your God. You have made love for hire on every threshing floor."*), what do you think really happened? (Consider that Boaz thinks he needs to marry her.)

2. Consider the fact that Ruth is a widow, a foreigner (from a country that the book of Deuteronomy strictly forbids from participating in the assembly of worship), extremely poor as she's having to pick grain from the fields of the wealthy to survive, and is probably engaging in some form of "illicit" sexual behavior. She winds up in Jesus' lineage along with Tamar, Rahab and "Uriah's wife" (Bathsheba). What are at least three things these women all have in common?

3. The book of Ruth is often seen as a rebuke of the book of Judges —the story of the righteous foreigner compared to how Israel descended into depravity and civil war. Considering this story follows on the heels of the story of the Levite's concubine, where do you see the differences in terms of how women are treated/portrayed?

4. Ruth is looking for a husband for the sake of safety and security, not necessarily love. Consider for a moment the dichotomy between men being a means of safety and security, but also the potential to trap them in an abusive situation.

Michal

(1 Samuel 18:20-19:17, 25:44; 2 Samuel 3:13-14, 6:16-23)

SOUNDS OF REVELRY, music and cheering drifted through the open window. With a sigh, Michal stood and pushed the curtains aside so she could look down to the streets below where she caught sight of her husband, David, dancing with complete abandon—and without clothing—in the streets below. She wrinkled her nose in irritation and disgust as the adulation of the crowd seemed to only feed his antics more. There was a time, she noted, when she would have thought nothing of this. A time when she would have laughed and giggled at his care-free attitude, but maturity and heartache had altered her perspectives. Having spent the past ten years abandoned by David, wedded to another, and time spent learning the games played in the royal court, such conduct was simply unbecoming of a king. Her father, Saul, would have never debased himself in such a way in front of his subjects.

Her father.

There was a topic that was just as complicated and difficult for her to wrap her head around as David. Saul had by no means been perfect. If she was honest with herself, she knew he had not even been a good man—or king—treating her like a common whore that he simply married off like she was a broodmare.

Still, she had not minded when he married her off to David. She had, after all, loved David from the moment he had stepped foot in her father's court with his lyre, soothing her father's headaches. Michal was immediately drawn to the handsome young shepherd musician, enraptured by the sweet melodies he plucked skillfully on the strings. Though just a lowly shepherd, David seemed to possess an inner light and confidence that immediately attracted her.

When her father would fly into one of his violent rages, only David's gentle playing could calm him. Michal marveled at how David tamed her father's frenzy with his peaceful hymns. In quiet moments, Michal would steal away to watch David play, admiring his seeming humility and courage. Their different stations notwithstanding, Michal longed for David to notice her as more than just the king's daughter, to see her as the woman she was becoming. She was not ugly by any means, but she knew she did not possess the immediately striking beauty that turned heads whenever she entered a room. She had a pleasant, agreeable face —some might even call her looks plain. Her dark, wavy hair framed generic brown eyes and modest features. She was neither statuesque nor petite in build, simply average in height and weight.

Still, despite her best attempts, he seemed uninterested, his eyes only lighting up when her brother Jonathan entered his presence.

She knew it was ridiculous to be jealous of her brother, yet she hated to admit she had been. Now, of course, she'd give anything to have any of her brothers back in her life. David had in many ways utterly destroyed her entire family.

She wiped angrily at the unbidden tears that sprang to her eyes as she thought about the massive amount of grief and loss she had undergone these past few months. Her entire family was gone. She was ripped from the arms of a loving husband, whom she had spent the last decade with only to now be imprisoned in her childhood home by a man she had once loved to the point she had betrayed her own family—but now resented with every fiber of her being.

She knew it wasn't fair to solely blame David for the fact that he and her father had become enemies. Much of that was Saul's own doing. He had become obsessed with the idea that the young shepherd boy was trying to usurp his throne. At the time, she had dismissed his rantings as those of a paranoid madman. Her father had always been an eccentric man, prone to wild superstitions, refusing to even go into battle unless he'd received what he felt were the proper omens and signs to do so. She had always found it highly ironic that he tended to consult with mediums, while simultaneously outlawing their use and existence within his fledgling kingdom.

Being the first king of a developing nation came with stressors, and aside from being a brilliant military leader, Saul really had no skill in the political realm—and he knew it. He was no statesman. He was a leader who simply used brute force to get his way. He was insecure when it came to his tenuous hold on the Tribes of Israel and his inability to fully unite all the tribes only added to his insecurities. So it was no wonder when this young, handsome, charismatic shepherd boy was brought to court by the prophet Samuel, and quickly began to win the hearts and minds of the people with his military genius, that her father had begun to feel threatened. David excelled in not only the areas Saul himself was good at, but had a charm that Saul would never possess. Michal knew that charm all too well, having succumbed to it herself for a time.

That lopsided grin in a handsomely ruddy face, dark eyes that twinkled with mischief when he spoke, and the hard muscular frame from years as a shepherd warding off wild animals. Her father should have known better than to try and send a teenage shepherd boy out against the Philistine giant Goliath if his aim was to see David killed in battle. The young boy had spent a lifetime honing his skills slinging rocks at wolves and bears that threatened his sheep.

If he could bring a bear down, a man—even an abnormally large one—would have been nothing. But one of her father's many weaknesses was he never thought his plans through well enough to see how they could potentially backfire. The incident, rather than removing David as some imagined rival, had done the opposite: it had catapulted him into fame and the hearts of the people to the point her father had been forced into letting him become a leader in his army.

Despite herself, she smiled somewhat at the memory of the first time she had seen David atop that military horse, those handsome locks of curly hair falling so innocently across his forehead and eyes as he seemed to naturally fit the role he'd been thrust into.

Saul really had no one to blame but himself for David's rise to power, she mused reticently.

And that was where her father's paranoia and games had really affected her life. Those rash decisions that he didn't think through in terms of the ramifications thrust her front and center into his schemes when he offered her up to become David's wife. At that young age, Michal failed to understand what her father was doing, despite the fact that it elated her to no end. To finally have and possess David all to herself!

Of course, she was naïve in thinking any woman would ever hold David's heart exclusively.

David, for his part, had seemed equally dumbfounded, stammering that he was a poor man that could never afford the bride price of a King's daughter. So her father had named a price.

A ridiculous price. She had run to her room sobbing as Saul sent David on a virtual suicide mission. He could marry her only if he returned with a thousand Philistine foreskins.

Yet once again, her father had failed to consider what might happen if David actually succeeded.

When he had returned, riding his horse triumphantly toward the palace and dumping the cart full of Philistine foreskins before her father's throne—not one thousand but two thousand—her heart had swelled. He loved her! He had killed two thousand Philistines to earn her hand in marriage!

Of course, it had not been the marriage he had desired. It had been the power and admittance to the royal family David had craved. She still wondered at times if that ambition hadn't been there all along. If David's presence at court hadn't been all a strategic calculation— just as her father had claimed.

After all, David had once boasted in their marriage bed while drunk that God had anointed him King long before he ever entered Saul's courts. He'd been trying to explain to her that his marriage to her had been "in the stars from the beginning." He'd almost sounded as bad as her father—a warning sign she should have heeded. What nonsense that had seemed—God anointing a rival king to her father when God had also anointed Saul. If that had been true…

She gritted her teeth once again thinking of those implications. Of a God who purposely pitted these two men against each other. Two men she had loved…and lost. Oh, make no mistake, she knew she had lost David some time ago—in fact she wasn't sure she had ever really had him to begin with. Not his heart, anyway. His demands that she be returned to him as part of a farcical treaty agreement were not born out of love for her. She may have once been that naïve, but no more. No, she knew she was nothing more than a legitimacy claim to the throne that he was using to shore up his power and allegiances.

And poor Palti. She could still hear his wails of grief as she'd been carted off by Abner, David's general. A lower court official, he had, unlike David, loved and adored her. While yes, she had still elevated his station, he had also treated her with more love and kindness than she felt she deserved, especially given she had never been able to fully reciprocate that same love and devotion. It wasn't his fault her heart had belonged to another.

In retrospect, as she surveyed her current situation, he had deserved much more from her. He had been a good husband, unlike the one that now held her prisoner.

What an absolute fool I've been, she thought again bitterly, shaking her head and turning away from the spectacle below. *He may be the one dancing like a fool in the streets below, but I was the one who was truly foolish. I had once taken his side over my father's. Lied to my father. Helped him escape. And now? Now my life, my family, all lie in ruins. He was no different from my father. I was just a pawn in their games.*

Her brother Jonathan had shared her allegiance to David, however. He too had been caught up in the young man's charms, acting as a liaison between him and their father when he was on the run. Only to die on the battlefield—David nowhere near his side to protect him.

David cared about only one thing...David. Those whom he professed to love—they were just a means to an end. That realization had come far too late.

As she glanced around her room, she mused sadly that her father's paranoia had clearly not been quite so ridiculous as she now stood here, a prisoner in her own home with her entire family, excepting her sister, Merab, and her mother, dead. Protecting David all those years ago had cost her everything. Every hope of happiness. Every hope of love.

A goblet of wine sat on the small table in her sitting room. With an angry shriek, she grabbed the goblet and flung it against the wall, watching the red liquid drip like blood down the limestone wall.

The door to her room swung open as a serving girl and guard both stepped in, glancing around anxiously.

"Are you all right, your highness?" the girl asked cautiously, spying the goblet that now lay discarded on the floor with the wine spattered across the wall. The girl frowned, her shoulders relaxing slightly as she quickly deduced the cause of the commotion.

Michal did not answer initially. She merely stared with a detached curiosity at the red stain oozing down the wall. Finally she turned to look at the two standing in the doorway, catching sight of Abigail, one of David's other wives, scurrying down the corridor. No doubt to greet David when he arrived at the palace with all sorts of fawning and affection.

Well not her. She would not lower herself to that level. King or not, she was the daughter of a former king, and first wife of the current king. Someone had to conduct themselves with some semblance of dignity.

"No, I'm not alright," she said at last. "But I do not believe that it matters much to any of you, as I doubt you'll allow me to leave this room and return to my other husband. The one who actually cared for and loved me."

She let out a heavy sigh as the girl and the guard gave each other a wary glance before the guard retreated from the room and shut the door. Sitting down in the chair near the table from where she had grabbed the goblet as the serving girl began to clean up the wine mess, Michal felt her shoulders slump, suddenly weary and tired.

"I'm not even thirty years old, and already I'm a bitter old woman," Michal stated sadly. The serving girl glanced up at her worriedly, but said nothing. Michal knew the girl would never speak ill of the King.

King. It still sounded strange to refer to that young, ruddy little shepherd boy who sang sweet songs and ran around the countryside with a band of outlaw thugs, king.

"I could have made him respectable," she mused, shaking her head sadly. "I could have guided him, taught him." She grabbed another goblet and held it out as the serving girl scrambled to her feet and filled it with wine. This time Michal chose to drink its contents rather than spraying them across the wall. Finishing off the wine she stood and walked over to the door, knocking loudly for the guard.

He opened the door and gave her a skeptical look. "Take me now to see my husband," she said, her back straight and voice firm.

Come what may, she was going to let the King know what she thought of his display.

Discussion Questions

1. Michal usually gets a bad rap for showing disdain for David's dancing before the ark and the maidens. After all, David was just trying to show his exuberance and love for God, correct? Given what David has done to Michal—used her simply as a pawn in securing his claim to the throne—do you think Michal is justified in her disdain? Do you think this display is really what caused her to "despise him in her heart" (2 Sam. 6:16)?

2. Michal once lied to her own father to save David's life because she loved him. Can you see anything in David's actions that would suggest he ever reciprocated that love and affection?

3. Michal remains childless—despite the fact that she held disdain for David, how do you think Michal felt about that reality given the importance put on providing an heir?

4. Michal would have been the only wife to continue the line of the previous king. Not having children thus ends Saul's bloodline on the throne. How might that knowledge have affected her?

5. How does the Bible portray the power dynamics in their marriage, and how did Michal's position as a princess influence her relationship with David?

6. The Bible tells us that David "loved" Michal's brother Jonathan, and he deeply laments and mourns Jonathan's death. But the word "love" is never used to describe his relationship with Michal. What do you think is the significance of that?

Maacah

——— ⌒ ———

(2 Samuel 3:3, 13:1-19:10)

ABSALOM IS DEAD.

My beloved eldest son. My heart wrenches and shatters into a thousand pieces as I collapse to the floor, weeping bitterly.

Absalom, my brave warrior. So determined to right the wrongs of his father, to bring justice for what was done to his sister, my only daughter, Tamar. But his rebellion has failed, and he is now lost to me forever.

I immediately know my life is now forfeit as the mother of a usurper. I cannot feign ignorance of my son's rebellion, David knows me too well. He knew the anger I harbored when he had refused…refused!... to punish Amnon for what he had done to my sweet, innocent Tamar.

Dark thoughts swirl through my mind as the tears stain my face and I await what will happen to me. For I know I am not innocent. I never attempted to quell my son's anger at his half-brother. I had not admonished him for killing Amnon in retribution, and in fact had fled with him to my father's kingdom in Geshur to protect him from whatever punishment might befall him.

So much changed that awful and terrible day when Amnon chose to violate my daughter. Absalom and I both had plead with the King to punish him for his sin.

But we should have known better. How could David punish his own son for doing that which he had done himself? Everyone knew how David had simply taken Bathsheba from her husband, then had her husband, Uriah, killed. I'm not sure why any of us should have ever expected any sort of justice from him.

Because he is still the King, I hear the little niggling voice in my head say.

Absalom might have rightfully become the king one day had it not been for that incident. Sure, Amnon was the eldest, but everyone knew my Absalom was well-qualified by birth and temperament to be a leader, and I had every right to hope that he would one day succeed David. He was certainly idolized by all, of high and low status, and would have been a popular leader, as was evidenced by the many who flocked to his side in rebellion against the King.

Some days I wonder what happened to David. If you ask Michal, she would say nothing, that he was always this way. But even she hesitates slightly when she considers the man he was in his youth.

Tears stream down my face as I consider what might have been. All my hopes and dreams for my children lie in shambles. My daughter shamed and disgraced, my eldest son dead.

But there will be no sanctuary for me anymore. I am disgraced. Daughter of a king who participated in a failed coup attempt.

Still, I regret nothing. I do not regret siding with my son against my husband. Ours was a marriage of political convenience, not love.

The heavy tread of footsteps echoes down the corridor. My heart pounds, but I stand tall as the guards arrive. Their grim faces tell me all—they are here for me.

Roughly they seize my arms, dragging me from my chambers. I do not resist. They pull me through the palace halls, the walls and stone floors blurring past. Courtiers and servants pause to stare, then quickly avert their eyes. None will speak for me now.

At last, we reach the dungeons, dark and damp beneath the earth. They thrust me into a cell and slam the barred door. The cold of the stone seeps through my robes as I sink to the floor. So this is to be my new home, until David decides my punishment.

My heart aches for my fallen son. I see his face, remember his youthful smile. He was so determined to right wrongs, to be a greater king than his father. But it was not meant to be.

I mourn too for my sweet grandchildren. Absalom's daughters, Tamar and Maacah—named after his sister and me. They will grow up without a father now. And likely without a grandmother too, once David passes judgment.

But I remain defiant. I lift my head high. Let David enact his punishment. I will not cower or beg for mercy. I am still a princess, daughter of the King of Geshur. If my life is required for Absalom's rebellion, then so be it.

But as night falls, I fall into a restless, exhausted sleep, only to be awakened by the creak of the dungeon door piercing the silence. I sit up straight, assuming it will likely be my jailor coming to drag me before the court and have me executed. To my surprise, I look up to see a lithe figure entering, covered in a dark cloak. As she pushes back the hood, I let out a sharp gasp.

"Bathsheba!" I exclaim in astonishment. Though I suppose I should not totally be surprised. It was her grandfather, after all, who advised my son and had he continued listening to Ahitophel, Absalom might very well be sitting on the throne right now instead of rotting in a grave somewhere.

Whatever I might think of Bathsheba, I know she is not actually my enemy. Not anymore, at least. Whatever threat I posed to her sons' claims to the throne is now dead.

There can be no denying the woman's beauty and grace as she seemingly glides into the cell. While I was raised at court and taught all the proper ways to hold myself, that same grace comes naturally to Bathsheba. Her face is perfectly oval, with smooth olive skin that glows with vitality. She has large, almond-shaped eyes fringed by long dark lashes. Their deep brown hue contains glints of gold that flash enticingly when she laughs or smiles. Her nose is elegantly straight and her lips full and ruby-red.

Framing her lovely face are cascading locks of raven black hair that shine like silk. The dark waves that frequently tumble freely down her back are today artfully braided and pinned, complementing her graceful swan-like neck.

She has a slender, yet womanly, figure. Her arms are sculpted with delicate hands and long, tapering fingers. Her waist is tiny but flares into gently rounded hips. Her legs are shapely and toned.

She moves with feline grace, holding her head high. The fine linens and jeweled robes she wears only enhance her natural radiance. The glittering gems at her throat and in her ears cannot compare to the light in her eyes. No one questions why David was drawn to her.

I sit silently in the dark cell, back straight, hands folded as I watch her approach me. But I will not rise. Despite my current circumstances, I am still both the daughter and wife of a king. If she notices the slight, she does not let on.

"Tamar is safe in Geshur," she whispers in a voice too low for the guards to overhear. I let out a sigh of relief and she smiles as she sees me visibly relax.

"And Absalom's children?" I ask.

"They are safe as well. David has promised there will be no retribution against them, as they cannot be held accountable for their father's actions."

I close my eyes and say a silent prayer to the God of Israel. It's been a while since I prayed, as everyone has always known that God stood on the side of David. At least, that's what the prophet Nathan continued to declare, despite all the king's bad antics. God was faithful, Nathan insisted, even when the King was not. I had never known exactly how to feel about that. Grace and mercy were all well and good, but justice at times seemed to be abrogated when it came to his beloved David.

"Then I can die in peace," I breathe. "Thank you, Bathsheba."

The other woman gives me a quizzical look and sits down next to me, taking my hand in hers. "You think David is going to execute you?"

"Of course," I say. "What choice does he have?"

"Maacah, David went up in the chamber above the city gate and wept and cried that he wished he had died in Absalom's stead when he found out that Joab had killed your son."

I blink in astonishment. "He...did what?"

Bathsheba nods. "And then Joab rebuked him for turning what should have been a day of celebration for David's forces into a day of mourning and forced him to stand up and address the people with a speech of victory. But believe me when I say, he wishes you no ill will, despite what Joab may want."

"Joab," I spit in disgust. David's commander of the army was a loathsome, power-hungry individual.

Bathsheba again pats my hand. "Oh, Joab will get his due one of these days should my son Solomon ever ascend the throne," she promises me. "That wretched snake," she adds under her breath. I fight back a giggle.

I feel a slight wave of guilt wash over me for all the times I resented and spoke badly of Bathsheba. Of all people, we wives should know better than to judge another woman's addition to David's harem. Still, Bathsheba tended to catch all of our ire as we labeled her "the hussy." Truth was, we were simply jealous of her beauty and of the favored status she held amongst all the wives. David made no secret about which of us he preferred. While I certainly wasn't as low in status as Michal, no one held a candle to Bathsheba. Yet how could we blame a woman who, like most of us, had very little say in how we were taken as his wives. Mine was an arranged marriage—an alliance between Judah and Geshur. Abigail was probably the only one among us who had conspired in some way to win over his affections. But even she was ultimately cast aside once Bathsheba entered the picture.

Yes, we wanted to instinctively blame Bathsheba for something she had no control over. We all knew when David wanted something—David got it. And he had seen and wanted Bathsheba, despite her marriage to another man. For when the king summoned you, married or not, you didn't say no.

I had never really paid the woman much mind. She was beneath my station as far as I'd been concerned. A Hittite. Wife to a warrior in the army. A commoner. The means through which she had become a king's wife had never been what annoyed me. We women had few options in that realm. It was that she always held a higher status in David's eyes than me, a princess and king's daughter.

Within the palace hallways, we wives tend to avoid each other, as we are always scheming and jockeying for favor. It now occurs to me how ridiculous this is. We are more powerful if we join together. If we had all gone to him, demanding something be done about Amnon when Tamar was raped…surely even Ahinoam would have had to agree that what her son had done was terrible and wrong.

But I also realize that Bathsheba is already angling to ensure it is her son who will succeed David as king rather than any of the other sons. It's not entirely shocking, however, as Solomon, compared to his elder brothers, was like her Absalom—a natural leader. Just as Absalom would have made a better king than Amnon, Solomon would likely make a better king than any of the older boys.

"So what is to become of me, then?" I ask finally. "Clearly I cannot stay at court. Even if David does not wish me dead, Joab will surely see to it I am removed one way or another."

Bathsheba nods her head in agreement and I suddenly realize there are tears in her eyes. Then it occurs to me.

"Your grandfather?" I ask softly.

She shakes her head and wipes the tears away before they have a chance to slide down her cheeks. "He took his own life once he realized Absalom had followed the advice of that spy, Hushai. He knew he was doomed. Joab would have never let him live."

I squeeze her hand in solidarity as I slowly begin to realize I may not die after all. At least, not by David's decree. Perhaps I have been too harsh in my judgment against him. He truly did love his sons. After all it was his love for Amnon that stayed his hand and denied my Tamar justice. It was his love for Absalom that did not seek retribution when he killed Amnon, and in fact, allowed Absalom back into Hebron, if not Jerusalem. I was so blinded by my anger over Tamar I had been unable to see the grace he had repeatedly extended to his sons, even if it was to a fault.

David had never learned the happy medium of bestowing grace and mercy, while still enacting some form of justice. Neither Absalom nor I had ever desired Amnon's death. Not at first. Just some form of punishment. His removal from the line of succession would have been a good start.

But his refusal to enact any form of justice had led us all to these tragic ends.

Bathsheba stood and let out a heavy sigh. "I will arrange transportation for you and send you north to Anatolia. I have family there. They will care for you."

"Anatolia," I say absently. Of course, Bathsheba was a Hittite, the empire that still reigned to the north of Israel, even if she was a mere commoner by Israelite standards.

She leaves me, and it is the next day when a guard removes me from my cell. Instead of being escorted to the King's Court, a covered wagon laden with wares awaits me. I huddle beneath the contents of the wagon as it slowly rattles out of Jerusalem. I am completely disoriented and unable to get my bearings on where I might be headed, but the next day I can smell the salty sea air and I know we have likely arrived in the port city of Jaffa.

As the wagon comes to a halt and the driver grunts at me to get moving, I blink in astonishment as my sandaled feet hit the docks of the bustling city. Criers hawk fresh fish, fruit, and livestock in a cacophony of different tongues. Dockworkers shout and sing sea shanties as they haul amphorae of olive oil, wine, and grain. The din of the market mixes with the slap of waves against weathered piers.

My eyes dart about, wary of danger, as I spy a variety of different ships that line the harbor. I recognize Egyptian, Aramean, and, at last, Hittite. My eyes widen as I approach the Hittite ship and I see my daughter, Tamar, standing on the deck. I rush forward and cling to my remaining child, weeping with relief and, dare I say, even joy. I had feared I would never see her again.

I turn around to thank the driver, but the only one still standing there is Bathsheba, wearing a tired and sad smile. I blink in astonishment. She must have brought my child here herself. I move to thank her but she shakes her head and raises a hand in farewell. I raise mine back.

And then she is gone. I turn back to my daughter. We will forge a new life as we sail north toward Tarsus. In a strange way I feel a sense of relief that we will no longer be caught in the web of intrigue and deceit that still awaits Bathsheba and her children in David's court.

As we set sail, I turn my face upward and feel the sun warming my skin. Maybe there truly is a God after all who sees more than just the king. Maybe there is a God that actually cares about the rest of us.

Discussion Questions

1. We know virtually nothing about Maacah from scripture, other than she was Absalom and Tamar's mother, and was a princess—the daughter of Talmai, King of Geshur (located in the Golan Heights, which is in the southwest corner of modern Syria). Given David's love for Absalom, and the reality that Absalom had attempted a coup against him, what do you think really might have happened to Absalom's mother?

2. The rape of Tamar by David's eldest son, Amnon (2 Samuel 13) is what sets the events in motion for Absalom's eventual rebellion. David chooses not to do anything in response to Tamar's rape, which infuriates Absalom and so he takes matters into his own hands (compare with the story of Dinah in Genesis 34) and kills Amnon. Absalom never forgives David for his lack of justice toward Tamar and eventually leads the coup attempt. How much of all of this might have been avoided had David simply acted in some way to give Tamar justice? What might he have done? Would anything short of killing Amnon have satisfied Absalom?

3. Do you think Maacah supported her son in his coup against David?

4. Bathsheba's grandfather is an advisor to Absalom in his coup attempt—and is only thwarted when Absalom chooses to listen to a mole in his ranks rather than Bathsheba's grandfather. To what degree do you think Bathsheba's grandfather's involvement is related to what happened to Bathsheba?

5. Amnon and Absalom both grew up likely knowing about the incident between David and Bathsheba. How do you think that might have informed Amnon's actions, thinking he could just take a woman without consequence?

6. Like Dinah, we never hear from Tamar again after Amnon rapes her. We are simply told Tamar was left "a desolate woman in her brother's house." What are some of the lasting effects of these moments of violence against women when they receive no true justice?

7. If you were in Maacah's shoes, and one of your husband's sons from another wife had raped your daughter, how might you behave toward that husband if he did nothing?

Bathsheba

(2 Samuel 11-12; 1 Kings 1-2)

THE MOMENT NATHAN entered my chambers, I knew something was wrong. His wrinkled face bore the weight of grave tidings. I had spent years learning to read the expressions of men who moved within David's court. They rarely approached me without an agenda, whether hidden or plain. But Nathan—Nathan was different. He had always been a man of truth, a prophet whose words carried the breath of the Almighty. Even so, trust did not come easily to me anymore. Not after all I had endured.

The past still clung to me, though I rarely spoke of it. There were nights I could still hear my dead husband, Uriah's, voice in my dreams, his laughter lost to the winds of time. He had been an honorable man, and he had died because of the man I was now married to. I had belonged to Uriah in a way that I would never belong to David. Our relationship had been built on love, not lust; on trust and companionship, not violence and deception.

That resentment would never leave me. The other wives always looked upon me with scorn, as though I had wanted any of this. All I had ever wanted was a simple life with Uriah where we would grow old watching our children and grandchildren play in the court-yard of the house we shared.

But what was I to do when the King's men showed up at my door? How did he even know me? Who was I to refuse the King? I remember feeling panicked, wondering if it had anything to do with Uriah. Was I being summoned to be told that my husband had died in battle? Except, it made no sense that the King himself would deliver such news. Uriah was not high enough in the military ranks to warrant such an honor.

I would soon find out what he wanted.

When I returned home, my body no longer felt like my own. I had been taken into the king's private chambers, made to submit to his desires, and then sent away as though I were nothing more than a passing pleasure. I remember kneeling in my home, staring at the walls Uriah had built with his own hands, feeling defiled.

What would I tell Uriah? Would I even tell Uriah? Could I hide such a horrible secret from my husband?

And then, as the weeks passed, I knew there would be no hiding what had happened.

I had not seen my husband in months, and yet...I was with child. So I sent word to the King.

Oh what regrets I have from that moment of desperation, that moment of self-preservation! I thought only of my own life at that moment, not considering what might happen to my husband as a result of my telling the King.

I had no idea that action was going to seal my husband's fate. That King David would call him back from the battlefield in an attempt to have him have sex with me so the illegitimate pregnancy would be hidden.

But Uriah knew me too well. He knew the moment he saw me; he could see it in my face. He was a smart man, so he knew the fact that the King had ordered him back, that the King was somehow involved meant the King was also responsible for my condition.

"I will not let him simply hide what he has done," Uriah said, his anger simmering beneath a controlled voice. So he had slept outdoors for the neighbors to see—that he would not lay in bed with his wife while his men were still in the thick of battle. As punishment, David sent him back to the front lines, with his own death orders in his hands.

He couldn't just kill him. He had to add insult to injury, as though my husband had done anything to the King other than be a faithful soldier.

That act in and of itself was so cold, so cruel, so utterly despicable that there was no possibility I could ever feel any affection for him. He was a dangerous man that I dared not cross.

At first, I blamed myself. Had I never sent word to the King, Uriah might still be alive. Though the reality was, I likely would not. I would have been accused of adultery and presumably killed. Still, I found myself questioning: Was it my fault? Could I have resisted David more? Or was I merely swept away by the will of a man who had never been denied anything he desired?

The child we had conceived out of that moment of violation was taken. I had not even a child to console me in my insurmountable grief. I'd lost my husband, I'd lost my child, and was forced to live with the man responsible for it all.

But what good were these thoughts now? My life was no longer my own to shape—it belonged to the next son I birthed, Solomon. He was my purpose, my duty, my redemption. I'd had three other sons, but Solomon—Solomon was the one that captured David's heart after the death of Absalom. And now, as Nathan stood before me, I knew that purpose was threatened.

Nathan bowed slightly before speaking. "My lady, have you heard? Adonijah, son of Haggith, has declared himself king. He has gathered Joab and Abiathar the priest. They feast even now, proclaiming him as David's heir."

His words struck like an arrow to the chest. I straightened, gripping the arms of my chair. "How is this possible? Does the king know?"

Nathan's lips pressed into a firm line. "David does not realize what is happening. He is old and weak, and those who serve him have allowed him to drift into silence. Adonijah acts boldly, as though he is already king. If this is not stopped, he will seal his claim—and when David passes, Solomon will be in grave danger." He hesitated before adding, "And so will you."

I exhaled sharply. I had long known this to be true. My son was a direct challenge to Adonijah, who stood next in line after the deaths of Amnon and Absalom. Everyone knew that Abigail's son, Daniel, was too feeble-minded to ever be made king.

While Solomon was not the next in line, it was no secret he was David's favorite and in a moment of remorse for what he had done to Uriah, David had promised to make Solomon king.

But if Adonijah gained the throne, he would not be merciful. Solomon would not live to see the sunrise of a new reign, and I would not live long after him.

I met Nathan's gaze. "What do you propose?"

"You must go to the king, my lady. Remind him of his oath to you. The Lord has willed that Solomon shall reign after David, not Adonijah. But David must be awakened to this treachery before it is too late."

David's oath. It was the promise I had clung to all these years. Still, David could be treacherous. Had that promise been spoken only in private, meant to soothe my heart but never to stand as law? Or did David truly intend to uphold it? If he did not act now, Solomon would be lost.

And yet...I could not ignore a deeper question. Why did Nathan care so much? He was a man who moved in shadows, who spoke on behalf of God Himself. Why should he entangle himself in this matter?

"Why do you do this, Nathan?" I asked. "What does it matter to you who sits on David's throne?"

Nathan's eyes darkened with meaning. "Because the Lord has chosen Solomon. And because justice must be done."

"Justice," I murmured, the word tasting bitter on my lips.

Nathan exhaled. "Do you not see, Bathsheba? The way of kings has never been kind to women. The Lord and I both watched what David did to you. We saw how you were taken from your husband, how your life was reshaped without your consent. And when Uriah was sent to his death, I was the one God sent to rebuke David for his sin." His expression grew heavier. "But even as I delivered that judgment, I saw your suffering. I saw how you were given to the king, made his wife, and forced to bear the weight of his actions. Forced to bear the loss of your first son for actions over which you had no control."

I swallowed hard. I had never spoken of these things aloud, not even to myself.

Nathan continued, his voice softer now. "The Lord did not forget you, Bathsheba. He saw what was done to you. And now, justice must be done—not just for your sake, but for the sake of Israel. If Adonijah takes the throne, he will rule as his pride dictates, not as the Lord commands. But Solomon...Solomon is chosen. For your sake."

I looked away, my hands trembling in my lap. How strange that Nathan, a prophet of God, would be the one to acknowledge what I had endured. No one else ever had. David had taken me, then taken my husband's life, and the world had moved on. I had accepted my fate in silence, pushing forward because I had no other choice. But now, here was Nathan, offering a different path —a chance to claim not only my son's future but my own vindication.

I rose. "I will go to the king."

Nathan nodded. "And I will come after you, to confirm your words."

As I left my chambers, my thoughts churned like a restless sea. I had always been careful, always measured. But now I would have to speak boldly. I would have to remind David of the promise he had made—and demand that he uphold it.

I would have to finally, at last, find my voice that had been silent for so long.

When I entered the king's chamber, the sight of him shook me. David, once so strong, now lay in his bed, his body thin, his eyes dim. He was the man who had taken me into his household, the man who had ordered my husband's death. He was also the man who had fathered my children and promised my son a kingdom. I had never loved him, at least not the way I had loved Uriah. Yet he *had* treated me tenderly, raised me up as the favored wife above all the other wives. I held a place of honor none of the others held, not even his first wife who was the daughter of the former king.

But I knew better than most the cold, calculating heart that he possessed at times. Only Michal probably knew it as well as I did. It was probably for the best I had never loved him. Michal had made that mistake once. Love had little place in politics. For now I had to think as a queen and a mother, not as a wife.

I nodded toward Abishag, the young girl that had been given to David to warm him in his old age. A duty I was strangely grateful I had not been forced to fulfill. As I looked upon the young woman, I felt no animosity. If there was any jealousy, it was only for her youthfulness that she still possessed. A youthfulness that had been stolen from me.

Despite my indifference toward the woman, I also did not view her as worthy to listen in on such discussions. She was a concubine. Not a wife.

My words were not required. The girl merely met my gaze and immediately rose from her place beside him in his bed, quickly robed and left the chamber.

I knelt before him. "My lord," I said, my voice steady despite the storm in my heart. "You swore by the Lord your God that my son, Solomon, would reign after you. But now, Adonijah has declared himself king. He feasts with Joab and Abiathar even now, while you remain unaware."

David blinked, slow and tired. "Adonijah?" His voice was weak, but I saw the flicker of realization in his eyes.

"Yes, my lord. And if you do nothing, all Israel will believe he is king. But where are Solomon, your servant Zadok, and your faithful warriors? They were not invited. He does not see them as allies, but as threats." I took a steadying breath. "And when you sleep with your fathers, my lord, what will become of me? Of Solomon? We will be counted as traitors to Adonijah's reign. He will not spare us."

David's expression darkened. He might have been old and failing, but he understood the game of kings. He had played it too well for too long. His gaze sharpened, and I knew he was listening.

Now, I told myself. *Use the affection you know he still has for you. For once, you use that for something good.*

I reached forward and grasped his cold, skeletal hand, and looked deep into those eyes with as much tenderness as I could muster for the man. "He would kill me, my lord. You know he would. Would you leave me to endure such a fate after...everything?"

For the briefest moment, I believed I saw tears welling in his eyes.

As I opened my mouth to speak again, Nathan entered, bowing low. "My king, did you declare Adonijah as your heir? For he claims to rule already. If this is not your will, you must act now."

A silence stretched in the chamber, thick with the weight of decision. And then, with great effort, David pushed himself up.

"No," he said, his voice low but firm. "Solomon will reign."

Relief coursed through me, but I dared not exhale yet. Not until action was taken.

David called for Zadok, for Benaiah, for Nathan. He commanded that Solomon be anointed at Gihon, that the people proclaim him as king before the Lord. And in that moment, I knew—I had won.

No. Not I. Justice. Justice had won. Justice for me, at any rate.

There would never, truly, be justice for Uriah.

When I left David's chamber, I held my head high. For the first time I felt the burden I had carried for so many years lift, ever so slightly. I had fought not just for my son, but for myself. For my place. For the justice that had long eluded me.

Nathan had seen it. The Lord had seen it.

And now, all of Israel would see it too.

Discussion Questions

1. Much debate has surrounded Bathsheba's role with David. Some claim she was a temptress. But consider this: David was a powerful king who remained home when he should have been with his troops (2 Samuel 11:1). The storyteller signals that David shouldn't have been there to see Bathsheba's ritual bath, which was required by custom/law after her menstrual cycle. The king's palace stood at the highest point of the city, allowing him to view anyone's home—and baths weren't taken indoors then. What do you think? What power dynamics were at play? What realistic options did Bathsheba have when summoned by the King?

2. Unlike Tamar and Dinah, while Bathsheba is a victim of David, we do hear from her again and she goes on to have a son who becomes the next king. Do you think the small semblance of acknowledgement and justice she receives when Nathan confronts David on his sinful actions (referring to Bathsheba as an innocent lamb) against both her and her husband impacted the way in which she was able to move forward? What might this tell us about how we should care for victims even today?

3. Why do you think scripture states that their first son was killed by God as punishment for what David had done, but then turns around makes his second son with Bathsheba, Solomon, the next king, even though he wasn't next in line? How does this interpretation of the story portray it?

4. Why do you think Nathan goes to Bathsheba to try and have her persuade David to name Solomon the heir rather than simply going to David directly himself?

5. How do you think Bathsheba truly felt about David—the man who had taken her from and killed her husband, but then made her a favored wife within his court?

Jezebel

———— ⌒ ————

(1 Kings 16-21; 2 Kings 9)

THE AIR in the palace was thick with the heavy scent of cedar and frankincense, an aroma that masked the underlying decay of a kingdom in turmoil. Queen Jezebel sat on her gilded throne, her posture regal despite the undercurrent of tension coursing through the palace. She idly twirled a strand of her dark, perfumed hair between her fingers, her sharp, painted eyes scanning the columns of the hall where her attendants and eunuchs stood in silent vigil. Her other hand lazily toyed with a golden goblet filled with pomegranate wine as she tapped a lacquered nail against its side; the only sign that something had disturbed the Queen's calm.

The sound of hurried footsteps echoed in the chamber, breaking the stillness. A eunuch, his face pale and glistening with sweat, approached and fell to his knees before her. His trembling form did not escape Jezebel's notice.

"What is this urgency?" she demanded, her voice cool and commanding as she brought the goblet near her lips. "You burst into my presence unbidden. Speak, and let it be worth my time."

The eunuch's head remained bowed, his voice barely above a whisper. "My Queen... I bring grave news from Jezreel."

Jezebel's eyes narrowed, and her fingers froze mid-motion, the goblet poised at her lips. A faint frown marred the perfection of her painted mouth. Jezreel was where her son, King Joram, had gone to recover following his defeat at the battle of Ramoth-Gilead. Word had reached her that the King of Judah, Ahaziah—who was also her grandson through her daughter's marriage to the late King of Judah—was attending to his wounds and caring for him.

"Grave news?" She set down the goblet of wine in her hand with a deliberate clang against the stone table beside her. "Do not stammer. Say what you came to say."

The eunuch swallowed hard and raised his head slightly, his voice faltering as he spoke. "It is your son, Joram, the King. He…he has fallen, my Queen. Slain by Jehu."

For a moment, Jezebel did not move; silence enveloped the room, thick and suffocating. The hall seemed to hold its breath as her piercing gaze locked onto the eunuch. "Slain?" she repeated, her voice deceptively soft, like the hiss of a viper before it strikes. "Slain by Jehu? That…military commander? Explain yourself. Now."

"Jehu claims that a student of the prophet Elisha…"

"ELISHA!?!?" Jezebel momentarily lost her composure, her face twisting into a visage of rage and fury as she stood, knocking her goblet of wine off the table at the mention of the prophet's name. "*Elisha*?!" she repeated. "The successor to that traitorous usurper of Israel, Elijah?!"

Her vision swam with rage as the eunuch nodded. Taking a deep breath, her nostrils flaring, she regained her composure, smoothed out her robes and sat back down. "What did…Elisha…have to do with this?"

The eunuch's voice quivered as he continued. "He apparently anointed Jehu to be the King of Israel."

Jezebel's steely gaze bore into the eunuch as she said, very quietly and controlled, but the dangerous hiss in her voice unmistakable, "Oh did he now?"

The eunuch nodded and continued, swallowing hard. "Jehu came to Jezreel with his men, claiming vengeance. King Joram rode out to meet him, trusting in peace. But Jehu raised his bow and struck him through the heart. His body...was cast into Naboth's vineyard, as Jehu declared it the will of the gods."

At the mention of Naboth's vineyard, Jezebel's expression again hardened. A flicker of something dark crossed her face—anger, grief, or perhaps both.

"The will of the gods?" she repeated, her voice rising with each word. "And who is Jehu to claim the authority of the heavens? A usurper. A murderer. A jackal feeding on the carcass of lions."

Her hands gripped the armrests of her throne, her knuckles white as the delicate gold filigree bit into her palms. "And Ahaziah? My grandson and King of Judah, son of my daughter, Queen Athaliah?" she demanded sharply. "Was he not with Joram?"

The eunuch hesitated, then lowered his head further as the Queen rose with an eerie calm, this time slowly, from her throne; her movements deliberate, the heavy folds of her embroidered robe brushing against the cold stone floor. She now towered over his trembling figure.

"Ahaziah fled to Megiddo, but Jehu pursued him. He, too, is dead, my Queen."

For a moment, Jezebel's lips pressed together and the weight of the news settled over her like a storm cloud. Her fingers gripped the folds of her robes tightly, her chest rising and falling. For a moment, she said nothing. There were no tears, no signs of collapse. Instead, she straightened her back, lifting her chin as if daring the heavens themselves to strike her down.

Wordlessly, she stepped down from the dais, her robes flowing around her like storm clouds as she moved to the window, gazing out at the horizon.

"So," she said, her voice a dangerous whisper, "the lioness has lost her cubs, and a jackal prowls in their place. The blood of kings has been spilled, and this traitor Jehu parades as the hand of judgment." She let out a sharp, bitter laugh that echoed through the chamber. "Judgment, he says. He thinks himself righteous, yet he is but a tool, wielded by powers he does not understand."

Turning back to the eunuch, her eyes burned with a fierce intensity. "Summon my attendants. If this…Jehu…comes for Queen Jezebel, let him find her prepared. I shall not cower in shadow. Let him see me, a queen to the end. Let him face the wrath of a mother whose sons he has slain. He thinks he can snuff out the flame of Jezebel so easily? Let us see who burns whom."

She swept out of the throne room, leaving a silent and stunned court staring as her form receded out of sight.

The air in the hallway seemed to tremble with the weight of her presence as the dim light of flickering torches cast her figure into sharp relief. She walked with deliberate, unyielding steps, the soft click of her jeweled sandals against the stone floor echoing like a war drum; her bracelets jingling faintly with each step, like the warning of a serpent coiling to strike. Her heavy, embroidered robes flowed behind her, a cascade of deep crimson and gold that caught the light, transforming her into a figure both regal and menacing.

Her attendants and guards shrank back as she passed, their eyes lowered in deference. Jezebel's face was a mask of cold determination, her pursed painted lips dared any to question her resolve. Her eyes, sharp and defiant, stared straight ahead, the smoldering embers of her fury and grief barely contained.

The queen's mind churned with thoughts of revenge, dignity, and power. Jehu's name burned in her mind like a brand, but she would not meet him as a grieving mother or a defeated ruler. No—if

Jezebel were to fall, she would do so as a queen, a force of defiance etched into the memory of her enemies.

Still, she had no intention of falling.

Reaching her chambers, she pushed open the heavy wooden doors with a strength that belied her slender frame. The room was bathed in the warm glow of oil lamps, their light glinting off gold-framed mirrors and jeweled ornaments. The scent of myrrh and rosewater filled the air, a stark contrast to the tension simmering within her.

"Bring my finest garments," she commanded her attendants without turning to look at them. Her voice was low but edged with iron, leaving no room for hesitation. "The black and gold robe, and the crown of Tyre. And fetch the cosmetics."

Her maids scurried to obey, their hands trembling as they gathered the items she had named. Jezebel strode to a gilded vanity, gazing into the polished surface. Her reflection stared back, unbroken and unbowed. She reached for the kohl, her fingers steadying themselves as she applied the dark pigment around her eyes, accentuating their intensity. The act was methodical, as if she were a warrior preparing their face for battle.

Grief, sharp and unyielding, pierced her heart, however. As she stared at her reflection, she noted the once-vibrant colors of her royal robes seemed muted, a stark contrast to the fiery spirit that burned within her. This was her second son to die due to that horrible so-called prophet Elijah, that troubler of Israel...and troubler of her family. Her first son, who had also been named Ahaziah, had fallen out a window and Elijah had stated that he would die from his injuries because he had sent messengers to inquire of his fate from her gods, not his desert God.

Her anger mingled with her deep grief. Even as tears threatened to spill from her eyes, Jezebel steeled herself. She was a queen, a daughter of Phoenicia, raised to be a pillar of strength in the face of adversity. She straightened her back and fought back tears. With a deep breath, Jezebel thrust back her shoulders, her gaze hardening with determination. She would mourn her son and grandson later, away from prying eyes and judgmental whispers. But when the time came to face Jehu and his men, she would do so with the regal bearing that had defined her as a queen. No one would dare question a *king* for not indulging in public mourning when faced with an enemy at the gates. Therefore, they should not question a queen for not indulging it, either.

Her thoughts momentarily veered toward ruminations of her daughter who now reigned as Queen regent in Judah. That had been a stroke of political genius, marrying Athaliah off to King Jehoram of Judah, who had died only a few years earlier of some disgusting disease that caused his bowels to fall out.

News of Ahaziah's death, Athaliah's son, surely had also reached her.

Be strong, my daughter, she thought bitterly. *Be strong as they come for you too. As they try to destroy our entire lineage.*

Athaliah was her mother's daughter, though. Jezebel knew Athaliah would not go down without a fight. Just like she would not go down without a fight.

Her attendants returned, draping the robe over her shoulders and adjusting the golden crown atop her intricately braided hair. As her handmaidens scurried about, arranging her elaborate headdress and adjusting the folds of her gown, Jezebel's mind wandered briefly back to the days of her youth in Phoenicia. She had been a princess, raised with the belief that kings and queens held absolute power, their whims subject to no one's approval. Adjusting to the Israelite laws and customs had been difficult and a constant source of frustration for her, a constraint upon her regal authority.

Her lips curved into a bitter smile as she recalled the incident with Naboth's vineyard. Ahab, her weak-willed husband, had been prepared to accept the man's refusal to sell his inherited land. In Jezebel's eyes, such an act of defiance against the crown was unthinkable. Had she been born a son instead of a daughter, she would have seized the vineyard without hesitation, for did not all lands rightfully belong to the sovereign? Instead, she'd been forced to pen a letter in her husband's name, ordering the death of the man who dared say no to a king!

And again, that wretched Elijah had meddled in her business. The memory of him caused her jaw to clench. How dare he challenge the might of not just the King and Queen of Israel, but of Baal, the god she had worshiped since childhood? His slaughter of her prophets had been a personal affront, a stain upon her honor that could never be washed away.

She had clearly won that battle in the end, as Elijah hadn't been seen in years, succeeded by an equally offensive prophet known as Elisha.

Through the open balcony doors rose the sound of the distant clash of metal and the echoing cries of battle. Jezebel could hear the grinding of iron against iron, the panicked shouts of her guards, and the heavy boom of the outer gates succumbing to Jehu's relentless assault.

As the handmaidens finished their ministrations, the sounds grew louder, closer, like the tide rising to consume her palace.

Jezebel rose, the full weight of her presence filling the room with her back straight and her chin held high. Her expression remained calm and composed even as a deep rumble shook the walls, and dust drifted from the ceiling. Her painted lips curled into a sharp and mocking smile. She would face this usurper, Jehu, with the same regal bearing that had marked her reign. Fear flickered within her, a momentary shadow that she swiftly banished. She was a queen, and queens did not cower before lesser men. She was a vision of defiance, her beauty sharpened into a weapon, her sorrow transformed into an unyielding armor.

"Let Jehu see what a queen looks like," she murmured, more to herself than anyone in the room. "Let him know that even as he spills my blood, he cannot extinguish my fire. They will see that they have entered the den of a lioness."

The attendants hesitated at her words, glancing at one another in nervous silence. She caught their reflections in the mirror and turned her head sharply. "Are you so afraid of the men with swords?" she snapped, her voice cutting through the air like a blade. "Stand up straight. If this is the end, then we meet it as women of the palace, not as frightened mice."

As one final touch, she reached for a string of pearls interwoven with blood-red rubies, which she draped around her neck. The weight of it was familiar, comforting even, as if it were a reminder of the power she had wielded, the kingdoms she had commanded.

Another roar of battle sounded, closer now, shaking the foundations of her chambers. The flickering light of torches outside cast chaotic shadows on the walls.

With one final glance at her reflection, she turned to leave, the light catching on her crown and casting faint rays against those same walls.

With purposeful strides, her steps steady and unhurried, as though she were walking to greet a guest rather than a usurper who had taken everything from her, she made her way to the balcony, her gaze sweeping over the scene below. Jehu's forces had already breached the palace gates, their triumphant cries echoing through the corridors. Her son, her beloved prince, had fallen at their hands, a sacrifice to this man's ambition.

Jezebel's lips curled into a defiant sneer as Jehu's figure came into view.

His horse, a great black stallion with flared nostrils and foam-flecked flanks, moved with a violent grace, its hooves striking the stone with a sharp, rhythmic finality.

Jehu himself was a figure carved from the chaos of war. His armor, dented and stained with dirt and crimson, bore the scars of countless battles. The bronze plates glinted menacingly in the flickering light of the fires now devouring Jezreel, though soot dulled their luster. A thick leather belt cinched a sword at his side, its blade streaked with blood as though freshly drawn from the flesh of his enemies—the blood no doubt of her family.

She bared her teeth in a growling hiss as he approached. His face was a mask of hardened determination; his beard rough and unkempt. There was something wolfish about his expression—hungry, relentless, and utterly without mercy.

As he entered the city square, he slowed his mount and raised his hand, signaling his men to fan out. The dust stirred by the hooves of his horse swirled around him, creating a haze that only amplified his ominous presence.

As his eyes scanned the palace ahead of him, his gaze locked onto the balcony where Jezebel stood in the doorway—their eyes meeting in cold hatred for one another.

She would not go gently into the night, like some meek lamb led to slaughter. If this was to be her end, she would face it head-on, her regal countenance unwavering.

As she stepped onto the balcony, her voice rang out, clear and commanding, "Is it peace, Zimri, murderer of your master?" Zimri, that commander who had turned on his king and killed him. Oh, she knew Jehu did not come in peace.

The words hung in the air, a challenge hurled at the man who dared to usurp her throne. For a fleeting moment, Jezebel allowed herself to savor the thrill of defiance, the exhilaration of standing tall in the face of adversity.

Jehu's reply was swift and cutting, his gaze fixed upon her with contempt. "Who is on my side? Who?"

The answering cries from his men echoed like a death knell, and Jezebel felt a sudden chill run down her spine.

Some of the yells had come from within the room behind her. As Jehu's words rang out, ordering her eunuchs to cast her down, Jezebel's mask of arrogance faltered. A flicker of fear ignited within her, a primal instinct for survival that warred with her regal pride.

She whirled around to face her betrayers, knowing already that she was alone, abandoned by those who had once sworn fealty to her crown.

The eunuchs, once her loyal servants, now turned against her at Jehu's command. Their hands seized her, dragging her towards the edge of the balcony with brutal force.

In those final moments, as her body tumbled towards the unforgiving ground, Jezebel's mind whirled with a torrent of emotions. Regret for the lives lost in her pursuit of power, anger at the injustice of her fall, and a fleeting sense of relief that her suffering and grief would soon be over.

As the impact shattered her bones and stole the breath from her lungs, she was only vaguely aware of the ravenous wild dogs that sank their teeth in her flesh.

Jezebel's last thoughts were not of her lost kingdom or her shattered dreams, but of the defiant spirit that had burned within her until the very end.

For she was Jezebel, the Phoenician Princess, and even in death, she would not bow before the whims of lesser men.

Discussion Questions

1. Jezebel has been viewed as one of the Bible's worst villains, next to Herod and Pilate. What do you think?

2. As a Phoenician princess, Jezebel believed in absolute monarchical power. How did this clash with Israelite traditions (like in Naboth's vineyard case where kings couldn't seize tribal land), and possibly lead to her downfall? How was Naboth's vineyard a turning point in her story?

3. How do Jezebel's final moments reflect her character throughout her reign? Do you think her defiance in the face of death was admirable or foolish? Why?

4. Discuss whether you think Jezebel was purely a villain, or was she also a victim of political and religious forces beyond her control?

5. Jezebel was a powerful woman in a male-dominated society. How do you think her story has influenced the way history and literature portray strong women?

6. Jezebel stands out as both a powerful female leader and a foreigner. Scripture consistently portrays powerful foreign women (like Jezebel and Potiphar's wife) as villains, while depicting marginalized foreign women (Ruth, Rahab) more favorably. What underlying fears or concerns might explain this biblical pattern of suspicion toward influential foreign women?

7. Jehu justified his actions as divine judgment. Do you think his rebellion and violence were truly an act of divine justice, or a convenient excuse for a power grab?

8. How do you think Jezebel's influence shaped King Ahab's reign? Do you think she was the true power behind the throne, or was Ahab just as responsible for their actions?

Athaliah

(2 Kings 8:26; 11:1-20)

As QUEEN ATHALIAH navigated her way through the corridors of power within the royal palace, her day was consumed by the weight of governance and the machinations of politics. Dressed in opulent robes adorned with jewels, she strode toward the throne room—a throne she had seized by force seven years earlier when her son, Ahaziah, had been slaughtered with his uncle, King Joram of the Northern Kingdom, Athaliah's brother, followed by word that her mother, Queen Jezebel, had also been killed by that usurper Jehu.

Correction: a throne she had been forced to seize, but a throne she felt was rightfully hers. The fact that she had to fight ruthlessly for it was just a technicality in her mind.

If living under Jezebel's roof for her entire childhood had taught her anything—it was how to survive. And survive she would. Even if it meant doing the unthinkable. She would not suffer her mother's fate, nor make her mother's mistakes. Her mother, Queen Jezebel, always still had a soft spot for her children. Athaliah realized she was included in that soft spot, but to her that softness was exactly that: soft. A weakness. And weakness needed to be rooted out at all cost if you intended to rule and hold a throne.

Especially as a woman.

No, instead, she set about killing her own children and grandchildren to ensure she held the reigns of power and no one, not even her own offspring, would challenge that power.

That was how you stayed alive. You trusted no one. Loved no one.

The memories of those dark deeds should have haunted her, she supposed, creeping into her thoughts like shadows in the night. The faces of her children and grandchildren, once filled with innocence and love, had become twisted in agony as she snuffed out their lives one by one. Each death should have been a dagger to her soul, a sacrifice made in the name of ambition and self-preservation.

Yet she had discovered she felt very little remorse and guilt at their deaths. They were, like everyone else in her life, merely a means to an end. Her mother had always played the dutiful wife and mother as Queen, always playing the puppeteer from behind the scenes, never boldly able to act with true authority of her own. It was authority only granted to her from either her husband or her sons.

Athaliah refused to live in the shadows of the men that had always sought to dismiss her. No one was more qualified to run the country than she was. Certainly she was more qualified than some sniveling little child, which would have been the only option if she had followed the traditional means of succession.

But Athaliah was not interested in following rules. She was a queen. That meant she got to make the rules that others would be forced to follow. Her mother had never fully understood that. Athaliah had spent years gathering her allies and paying for their loyalties. In a world ruled by treachery and deceit, there was no room for sentimentality, love, or weakness.

As she strode down the corridors, servants scuttled out of her way, bowing low in reverence as she passed by them. She heeded them not, paying little attention to those whose station was so far beneath her they were not worthy of notice. Unless, of course, one of them failed to offer her the proper respect. Then they would feel the full brunt of her wrath.

It was important to make sure they respected her at all levels. Even a single slight would grow out of control.

Ruling with fear was the only way to keep her subjects in line. And she would be the most feared queen—indeed she was the only queen—to ever rule the Kingdom of Judah.

Athaliah exuded an aura of regal authority as she swept past, every step a testament to her unyielding resolve.

She took her position on the throne as her guards surrounded her. They were formidable in their appearance, clad in armor adorned with the emblem of the royal house. Their stern expressions and seemingly unwavering loyalty spoke volumes of their dedication to Athaliah and her regime.

Her councilors and advisors scurried past the guards, lining up to eagerly discuss the pressing matters of the day with her.

Eliam, she believed that was his name, was her economic advisor. Short but thin, he reminded Athaliah very much of a little weasel as he slicked his dark hair back away from his face. He licked his lips nervously as he brought forth a papyrus scroll that served as the ledger for keeping track of the royal treasury.

"Your Majesty," he began, bowing deeply, "as I have been warning for some time, we have now reached the difficult reality that..." he gulped before continuing, "the treasury is depleted."

His voice shook only slightly as he continued to intone gravely. "The coffers are running dry, and the people grow restless."

Athaliah's lips curled into a cold smile. "Then we must find a solution," she declared, her voice ringing with authority. "Increase the taxes," she offered, waving her hand dismissively. "Problem solved."

"Uh, yes, of course, Your Highness," Eliam said nervously, clearing his throat. "But the people are already being squeezed beyond that which they are able to bear financially."

Her eyes flashed with anger and Eliam took a slight step back. "King Solomon. You remember him?"

"Mmmm...yes, your Highness."

"King Solomon knew how to get things done, did he not? Taxed the people so he could build these testaments to his legacy that we now all enjoy. If he had not increased the taxes and labors of the people, we would not have this beautiful palace, would we?"

"No, Your Highness," Eliam squeaked out meekly.

"We would not have the beautiful temple..." she motioned toward the window in the direction of the Temple...and let her words trail off as she frowned. A loud clanging of what sounded like swords and shields, and even...were those trumpets sounding?

"What's that noise?" she demanded of her economic advisor.

"I...I do not know, Your Highness," he stammered. Glaring at him and muttering about how worthless he was, she stood and strode over to the window. A large crowd was streaming toward the Temple as people shouted and ran.

A strange, cold knot of dread formed in the pit of her stomach. Whatever was happening, some instinct told her it did not bode well for her.

As Athaliah observed the chaotic scene unfolding outside the window, her mind raced with possibilities. Beneath her otherwise composed façade, lurked a paranoia born of ambition and insecurity. She knew that her grip on power was tenuous, with rivals and enemies lurking in the shadows, waiting for an opportunity to strike.

What could be causing such a disturbance at the temple? Had her enemies finally gathered enough courage to challenge her rule?

The Temple...that would mean...the priest, Jehoida. A hot flash of anger burned where that cold knot had been. She knew she should have done away with him. He was never loyal to her. He had openly opposed her rule over and over again. She'd told herself that the backlash of killing the High Priest of the Temple would incite its own rebellion among the people. But perhaps she should have risked it.

Turning away from the window, she faced her councilors and guards, her expression a mask of steely determination. "Prepare the royal guard," she commanded, her voice cutting through the air like a whip. "There are the sounds of rebellion at the Temple."

No sooner had she gotten the words out of her mouth when a messenger came bursting into the throne room, his breathless voice carrying the weight of revelation. "Your Majesty," he gasped, "it is Jehoiada the priest. He has incited a rebellion against you! The Captain of the Guard says you must come quick to put an end to it!"

A surge of fury swept through Athaliah's veins as she processed the news. So, it was the priest Jehoiada after all. Indeed, letting him live had been a grave mistake. Well, she would take care of that in short order.

"Sound the alarm," she ordered, her voice cutting through the air like a blade. "Gather the royal army. We march toward the temple at once."

Her guards sprang into action, their movements precise and coordinated as they surrounded her and readied themselves for battle. Athaliah's heart pounded with anticipation, her senses heightened as the clamor outside grew louder. But her resolve remained unshaken. She was a queen after all—the rightful ruler of Judah— and she would not allow anyone to usurp her throne.

With a resolute expression, Athaliah led her forces out of the palace and toward the Temple proper, her heart ablaze with righteous fury. For in that moment, she knew that she would stop at nothing to retain her throne—even if it meant wading through rivers of blood.

They marched up the steps of the outer court, through the women's court, and past the altar. The sight that met her at the doorway to the Holy Place made her blood run cold.

The priest Jehoida stood tall and imposing with a countenance weathered by years of devotion to the temple. And there, next to him, by the copper pillar of Boaz that stood at the top of the final staircase, amidst a throng of jubilant voices and triumphant cheers, stood a young boy now crowned king in defiance of her rule. The seven-year-old boy's eyes met hers and she gasped in recognition, as the unmistakable resemblance to her son, Ahaziah, stared back at her.

Joash! Her grandson who had only been and infant the last time she saw him.

Her mind raced.

No, this wasn't possible! She'd had him killed! He'd been the youngest, an infant at the time. She'd ordered his death. They'd assured her he had been killed!

Her mind reeled at the betrayal. Who would have…Her thoughts were cut short as another figure stepped into view beside Joash.

Jehosheba! She nearly hissed the name of her son Ahaziah's half-sister by another of her husband's wives, who emerged and stood at Joash's other side. She stood tall and willowy, but her eyes blazed with defiance.

Another crucial error, Athaliah thought in fury. She'd made the mistake men had made for eons before her: she'd underestimated another woman. Jehosheba had been one of the first to declare her allegiance to Athaliah and so she had spared the other woman the same fate as the other children and grandchildren.

But Athaliah had not followed her one rule: no soft spots. Soft spots were weaknesses.

And Jehosheba had been a weakness. Having had no daughters of her own, Jehosheba's mother had died in childbirth and Athaliah took the girl under her tutelage, raising her as though she'd been her own flesh and blood. A girl she had never seen as a threat. A girl, now a woman, she had thought was truly loyal to the woman who had cared for and raised her.

But like Athaliah had learned from Jezebel, Jehosheba had learned from Athaliah.

A stupid, incalculable blunder. Jehosheba almost seemed to smile as she observed the realization of who had bested her dawn across Athaliah's face, enraging Athaliah further.

"Treason! Treason!" Athaliah at last screamed at the top of her lungs. "Seize them!" she screamed at her guards.

Only her guards didn't move. Instead, they turned their swords and spears at her and before Athaliah even realized what was happening, they had grabbed her by the arms and held a sword to her throat.

"Not in the Temple!" the old priest's voice rang out as the crowd fell silent.

"Do not shed blood in the House of the Lord," he continued. "Take her outside the Temple proper."

As they began to shove her forward another voice sounded across the crowd.

"Wait! One moment."

The guards paused as Jehosheba made her way forward, contempt for the woman that stood before her written plainly across her face. She stopped when she was within arm's length of the Queen.

"I should have known never to trust you," Athaliah spat.

"You're right," Jehosheba said with equal venom in her voice. She reached out and slapped the other woman before continuing with a hiss. "Did you really think I was just going to sit back and let you slaughter my entire family? Our entire family? That any sane woman—or man for that matter—would simply accept what you'd done?"

She took another step closer, so her nose was nearly touching the Queen's. "But I wanted you to know, before you died, before you met the same end as the rest of our family that you slaughtered at your command—that it was me. I was the one who bested you. I was the one who raised your grandson here in the Temple. Right under your nose. And you know how I did it?"

Athaliah didn't answer, anger simply seething from her flaring nostrils.

"Because I knew you were a Baal-worshiper like your whore of a mother, Jezebel, and wouldn't step foot in the sacred Temple of Solomon. I knew that this was the one place he'd be safe from you once you'd finished your rampage."

"Every day you looked me in the eye and lied to me," Athaliah said with cold fury.

"Every day you looked me in the eye and pretended like you hadn't made me watch as you slaughtered my brothers and their children," she said, choking back a sob. Athaliah might have been tempted to roll her eyes if her situation hadn't been so incredibly dire. But in that moment of reckoning, Athaliah laughed instead.

"The mistake every ruler eventually makes. Underestimating the determination and survival instinct of a woman. I spent too much time around men. I made their same grave error." She leaned toward the other woman as best as the guards would let her. "Make no mistake, Jehosheba. Your day of reckoning will come soon enough."

Jehosheba smiled. "Perhaps, but you'll never live to see it." With that, she motioned the guards as they shoved her roughly forward and out of the Temple proper and into the street. The crowd made way as they watched in hushed silence as she was forced to her knees.

So, she thought to herself, this was how her rule was going to end—in bitter betrayal. It almost made her laugh. Her own guards turning on her, exactly as her mother's guards had done. In the end, she supposed, it all came down to one thing: they were never going to accept a woman as ruler. Jezebel knew that. She had tried to teach that to her daughter to no avail. She had believed that if she wielded enough power through fear, they would not betray her.

As the sword fell, sealing her fate, Athaliah had one last thought: they may not accept the rule of a woman, but if it weren't for a woman, they'd have no king now. She smiled at the bitter irony as the sword cut deep through her neck, severing her head from the rest of her body and she thought no more bitter thoughts.

Discussion Questions

1. Athaliah justifies her brutal actions as necessary for survival and rule. Do you think power always requires ruthlessness, or could she have ruled differently and still maintained control, considering she was a woman? How different are the standards between women and men in leadership?

2. Athaliah dismisses her mother, Jezebel, as weak because of her love for her children. Do you think love/compassion and power can coexist in leadership, or does one have to be sacrificed for the other?

3. While Athaliah underestimates Jehosheba, was this really her greatest mistake, or were there likely other critical miscalculations that led to her downfall?

4. The High Priest Jehoiada plays a key role in overthrowing Athaliah. How did religious authority impact political power in this story and how does this compare to the intersection of religion and politics today?

5. Do you think Jehosheba's satisfaction at Athaliah's downfall was about justice being served, or was it simply revenge? What is the difference?

6. What might the irony of a story about a woman tearing down another woman in power reveal about women in power, both in the story and historically?

7. Athaliah is portrayed as a villain. Considering she was the daughter of Jezebel and was raised in the brutal politics of the time, could she be seen as a tragic figure as much as she is an evil one?

8. Athaliah believed that killing her family was necessary to secure her rule. Can an immoral act ever be justified for the sake of governance? How do we reconcile morality with perceived political necessity?

Huldah

———— ⟨∞⟩ ————

(2 Kings 22:14-20)

HULDAH SAT in her humble dwelling, the warmth of the morning sun streaming through the window, casting a golden glow upon the earthen floors. Her aging hands were busy with the task of grinding grain, a daily chore that brought a sense of rhythm and purpose to her life. Every day as she walked among the people, a growing sense of unease niggled at the edges of her mind. It was almost like a curse, that when she walked among them, she'd get flashes of the streets being in turmoil and upheaval.

Something was coming. She just hadn't figured out what.

It had been that way her whole life. Images. Flashes of insight. Knowing things she shouldn't. Sometimes seeing flashes of an event, only to have her vision happen days, weeks, months, or, even sometimes, years later.

When she was younger, it scared her. She thought maybe she had been touched by evil forces. But soon, she began to realize that her visions and dreams were like those of Joseph—they were warnings. Which meant, they came from the Most High God that her people had abandoned worshiping some time ago. She avoided the Temple, even though it was supposed to be the place the Most High God dwelt. God had not dwelt there in some time. Other forces had taken it over. She felt a dark shadow that hovered over its magnificent stones.

But she gained a reputation in Jerusalem over the years. Her visions refused to let her stay quiet in the midst of so much corruption and suffering among her people. It was like a fire that burned within her. When she would see injustice, she would address it. They had begun to revere her as a prophetess, as one who spoke the word of the Lord.

She had balked at such a title initially. A prophetess? Surely not!

Yet, she could not deny her own visions and dreams, her own flashes of insight and words that were given to her to speak that seemed to almost take over her body like a consuming fire.

But she was a woman. She had so little power aside from those who respected her ability to tell the truth about any given situation and lay it out for them. It had made her popular among the poor and powerless…not quite so popular among the ruling class. Her husband, an artisan, was working on renovating the Temple that she so carefully avoided. He told stories of how the king would come in almost daily to see how things were going. As though something troubled him as much as it troubled her.

The only reason she believed she had been kept out of prison was this new king, Josiah, seemed to actually have some reverence and fear of the Lord. She wasn't sure what that stemmed from but it was a welcome change. Still, a sense of foreboding and destruction weighed heavily on her heart and mind.

A sudden knock at her door shattered the stillness of the morning. She jumped slightly, and laughed at herself. *Some prophetess,* she thought wryly. Didn't see that coming. With a groan, she stood. The years were not being kind to her and her back felt stiff as she made her way to the door.

Swinging it open, she was met not by the familiar faces of neighbors or acquaintances, but by the imposing figure of Hilkiah, the high priest of the temple, accompanied by a retinue of solemn-faced messengers. Their presence sent a ripple of unease through her, for she knew that their visit heralded nothing good.

Hilkiah simply stood there a moment, his attire, resplendent in richly embroidered robes of ceremonial significance, marked him as a man set apart. At the heart of his ensemble lay the ephod, a sleeveless vestment crafted from fine linen adorned with threads of gold, blue, purple and scarlet. Woven into its fabric were images of pomegranates and bells, symbolizing fertility and the call to worship. It rested on his shoulders, its weight a tangible reminder of the solemn responsibilities entrusted to him. Beneath the ephod was a tunic of pure white linen, its hem mirroring the motifs from the ephod. Around his waist was the sash, dyed in shades of blue, purple and scarlet, which served as a symbol of his authority.

A turban of fine linen wrapped carefully around his brow and adorned with a golden crown-like plate sat atop his head. Hilkiah was nearly the same age as she was, standing tall and poised. An imposing figure that demanded respect from all who crossed his path.

Huldah couldn't help but glance down at her own modest robe of undyed linen and the simple linen headscarf, its edges frayed with age yet meticulously arranged to frame her face with care. Her shoulders were stooped with age, though in her own way exuded an air of regal dignity and an aura of authority that also commanded respect.

For a moment, the two just stared at one another, not speaking. Who was, after all, the true representative of God in this moment?

At long last, knowing the High Priest would never defer to a woman, she gave a slight bow of recognition and motioned for him and his retinue to enter her humble abode.

"How may I serve the Kohen Gadol?" she asked, not lowering her eyes as she bowed. She would give him some deference, but not everything his station might have otherwise deserved. He had allowed far too many abominations in the Temple for her to even use the honorific Kohen Mashiah, or anointed priest. Simply gadol, "high priest," would have to suffice.

He stiffened slightly at the slight, his lips pressing into a thin line, his eyes narrowing as he regarded her. Clearly the man was visibly uncomfortable coming to her home. He glanced around her humble house and asked absently, "Is your husband at home?"

She shook her head. "Shallum? No. He is actually at the Temple today working on the King's renovations."

"Ah, yes. Of course," he said absently. "Shallum. Yes, Shallum is responsible for why I am here today, I understand."

She felt a knot of fear. What had happened to her husband?

The priest turned to his attendants and extended his hand. One of them produced a papyrus scroll and handed it over to him. It was worn and weathered, covered with what looked like ages of dust. He grudgingly then held the scroll out to her.

"We found this in the Temple and were unsure of its origins. We thought...the King thought...you might be able to tell us."

Huldah hesitated, eyeing the scroll skeptically before glancing back up warily at Hilkiah, folding her arms across her chest. "Why come to me? You are the high priest. Are you not the one trained in such matters?"

Both Hilkiah and his men glanced at each other uncomfortably. Finally, the priest cleared his throat and thrust the scroll forward. "We were...unable to determine its true origins."

Huldah raised a surprised eyebrow as she reached out to take the scroll from his hand.

She felt a slight jolt of something like lightning travel up her arm as she took hold of it and let out a nearly imperceptible gasp. She walked the scroll over to her table and sat down, carefully unrolling it, her hands smoothing over the rough papyrus with reverence and care as the ancient Hebrew script revealed itself before her.

It was a very old dialect. So old, she could barely make heads or tails out of it.

Still, the words rushed at her like a torrent of divine knowledge, the letters themselves seeming to glow on the page for her. Her hands began to tremble slightly as she finished.

"You already know what this is," she said almost in a whisper.

"Yes," Hilkiah said solemnly. "I knew it the moment I saw it, but the King...the King wants to know what sort of wrath we will incur for having ignored it all these many years. He told me to inquire of the Lord and...well..."

"Your own oracle fails to tell you the true word of God?" Huldah asked, already knowing the answer before he gave a resigned nod.

So, she thought. *You came to me. Because you believe I am a true and trusted oracle of the Most High God.*

But she kept the thought to herself. What was God going to do? How was she supposed to know what God was going to do...

The air around her suddenly seemed to dance and swim, crackling with energy as a faint shimmer danced just at the edges of her vision and consciousness, growing brighter and more insistent with each passing moment.

Hilkiah and her home before her darkened and seemed to give way to the brilliant light, which in turn disappeared in a brilliant flash, and she found herself standing in the middle of Jerusalem, on the steps of the Temple. Only it was not the city she saw every day. The once glorious city was engulfed in flames, its streets littered with the rubble of fallen buildings and the cries of the wounded and bereaved echoing through the air. The sights and sounds of unimaginable suffering washed over her like a tidal wave, threatening to engulf her in a sea of despair.

Chariots roared past her as flames licked hungrily at the sky, casting an eerie glow over the crumbling walls and shattered buildings. The air was thick with the acrid stench of smoke and ash, mingling with the anguished cries of the city's inhabitants as they fled in terror from the advancing horde. The conical helmets with pointed tops hammered out from a single piece of iron and decorated with bronze inlay in the form of parallel lines around the base bore the distinctive markings of the Babylonian soldiers. Between the two upper lines was a procession of officials or attendants which ran around the entire head piece. A further panel of bronze inlay at the front showed the king with the crown prince and an attendant framed by a bud-and-garland border.

Homes lay in ruins, their timbers reduced to charred remnants of their former glory, while the once bustling marketplaces were reduced to smoldering heaps of rubble and debris.

Amidst the chaos and destruction, the Temple stood as a beacon of defiance, its majestic façade marred by the ravages of war. The sacred halls, once filled with the sweet fragrance of incense and the reverent murmurs of worship, now echoed with the sounds of battle as desperate defenders fought to protect its sanctity from desecration.

But not even the Temple could withstand the relentless onslaught of the Babylonian forces. With a deafening crash, its mighty gates were breached, and the invaders poured inside like a flood, their weapons gleaming in the flickering light of the flames.

Within the Temple's hallowed precincts, the air was thick with the smell of blood and death as the defenders waged a desperate last stand against the tide of invaders. But their efforts were in vain, for the Babylonians showed no mercy to those who stood in their path. Huldah did not recognize the bodies of the priests that lined the inner sanctum of the Temple as the soldiers showed no reverence, no regard for the Holy of Holies that lay behind where the curtain, now burned away, had once hung. The gold of the ark gleamed in the firelight. She felt a wave of sorrow emanating from the golden box that had served as the footstool of the Most High God.

As the first echoes of battle faded into the night, the Temple lay silent and desolate, its sacred halls defiled by the blood of the slain and the ashes of the fallen. The once glorious Temple now smoldered like a funeral pyre.

Huldah continued to stare at the Ark of the Covenant. Never before had she laid eyes on this holiest of artifacts—a sight reserved for only the High Priest of the Temple. She knew better than to approach it or to touch it as it contained the very power of God, and she knew the stories of those who touched it and died.

Still, something in it called to her, summoning her as the lone witness to this devastation.

Then a voice boomed in her ears, shattering the hushed silence as it reverberated off the crumbling walls: "Tell them!"

With a blinding flash of light that erupted from the top of the ark, she straddled two worlds. She could both still see the devastation before her, as well as the hazy figure of Hilkiah standing in her home. Reaching out, she grabbed hold of Hilkiah's arm—something that was typically forbidden. Her voice took on an ethereal, unearthly quality as she spoke to him, her eyes rolling back in her head so only the whites were visible.

"Thus says the Lord, the God of Israel: Tell the man who sent you to me: 'Thus says the Lord: I will indeed bring disaster on this place and on its inhabitants—all the words of the book that the King of Judah has read. Because they have abandoned me and have made offerings to other gods, so that they have provoked me to anger with all the work of their hands, therefore my wrath will be kindled against this place, and it will not be quenched.' But as to the King of Judah who sent you to inquire of the Lord, thus shall you say to him: 'Thus says the Lord, the God of Israel: Regarding the words that you have heard, because your heart was penitent and you humbled yourself before the Lord, when you heard how I spoke against this place and against its inhabitants, that they should become a desolation and a curse, and because you have torn your clothes and wept before me, I also have heard you, says the Lord. Therefore, I will gather you to your ancestors, and you shall be gathered to your grave in peace; your eyes shall not see all the disaster that I will bring on this place.'"

The vision suddenly vanished from her sight, and she let go of the priest and collapsed, gasping on the floor. Hilkiah took an alarmed step back, whatever anger he might have had initially at her grabbing hold of his arm replaced by shock and horror at her words.

"Witch!" one of the attendants with Hilkiah hissed.

But Hilkiah raised a hand, silencing him. "No, what she speaks is truth," he said slowly. "We have brought this upon ourselves."

Without another word, he turned and exited the house. The other attendants followed him out, leaving Huldah lying on the floor, shaking.

She'd experienced visions before, but nothing like that. Nothing so vivid, so real. She could still smell the acrid smoke and her eyes still burned. With trembling legs, she stood and walked to the door, squinting into the bright sunlight.

The sight outside was completely the opposite of what she'd just experienced. The buildings she'd seen in ruins only moments earlier were still standing in all their splendor. Rather than anguished cries, she could hear the happy chattering of passersby, talking about the mundane moments of their lives. She raced as quickly as her short legs would take her toward the center of the city, where the Temple stood with its golden doors gleaming like the sun atop the hill it sat upon.

With trepidation, she made her way to the steps of the Temple. The workers were busy and ignored her as she climbed up the stairs into the outer court. She knew she was forbidden from entering beyond the women's court but still…she could feel it beckoning and calling to her. Pulling her as though unseen hands were shoving against her back. But she gritted her teeth and refused to move any further.

It was forbidden. She would not go beyond the threshold of the women's court. But even from where she was standing, she could see across the men's court and through the open doors of the sanctuary. The long, heavy, purple curtain stood toward the back of the holy place. She could feel the energy pulsating from behind it. It thrummed in unison with her heartbeat. Closing her eyes she felt the rhythmic pulsing.

When she closed her eyes, she saw the exact same Temple she was standing in, only it was devastated once again. She could smell the smoke, feel the heat of the fire. See the Ark pulsating with white hot energy. Then suddenly, there was a little boy standing right in front of her with a bloodied lamb held in his arms. He eyed her curiously, then smiled and seemed to evaporate in a wisp of smoke.

I will no longer dwell here, the voice seemed to whisper. *My dwelling place shall not be contained by these walls any longer. My people will scatter. But they will know my voice one day when I call them back to me.*

Then suddenly…it stopped. The pulsating ended. The vision evaporated. The voice fell silent. Opening her eyes, she took a deep breath and turned her back on the Holy of Holies and slowly walked back out to the outer court and stood atop the steps that led to the street below where people were bustling about their daily lives.

They have no idea, she thought sadly. *They have no idea what is coming. Maybe not for several years. Not until Josiah is dead…but it is coming.*

She shivered and hoped she would not be around to witness her vision become reality.

Discussion Questions

1. Scholars believe the scroll found in the Temple during Josiah's renovations was the Book of Deuteronomy. Consider the implications that were it not for a woman prophetess, the Book of Deuteronomy might not be in the Biblical canon.

2. What does Huldah's interaction with Hilkiah suggest about the role of women in spiritual leadership during that time?

3. Why do you think King Josiah and Hilkiah were inclined to defer to the spiritual leadership of Huldah rather than trying to find a male prophet?

4. How does Huldah's vision of Jerusalem's destruction inform the theme of divine judgment on the city?

5. What does Huldah's final vision at the Temple suggest about the shifting nature of God's presence among God's people?

6. How does Huldah's prophecy compare to other prophetic warnings in the Bible?

7. What role does King Josiah's humility and repentance play in delaying God's judgment and how does it reflect on leadership and responsibility?

Esther

(Esther 1-9)

THE MIRROR STOOD BEFORE ME, its polished surface reflecting a woman I barely recognized. The Queen's crown sat waiting on a velvet cushion beside me, a weighty reminder of who I had become. My maids worked silently, their hands deftly braiding my hair into an intricate design and smoothing the folds of my royal gown. The deep purple silk, woven with threads of gold, shimmered with each movement.

I should have been focused on the task ahead—approaching the King unbidden, knowing the risk it carried, knowing the fate of my people rested on my shoulders.

While my hair and my attire all reflected back the image of royalty, my eyes still revealed who I truly was—Hadassah, an orphan girl from a quiet corner of Susa, swept into a world of palace intrigue and schemes I never sought.

I had been fifteen, a simple Jewish girl, when I was dragged away to become part of King Xerxes harem. We were herded like cattle into carriages and taken to the royal palace, where the other girls and I were separated into chambers. Some cried openly, while others stared blankly at the walls, their spirits broken before the competition even began. I felt like a lamb led to the slaughter, powerless and terrified.

Life in the harem was surreal. The air was thick with the scent of perfumes, and the walls were adorned with luxurious tapestries. The other women—some as young as me, others older and more confident—were subjected to rigorous beauty treatments. For twelve months, we were groomed, perfumed, and prepared for one purpose: to be presented to the King and then taken to his bedchamber.

Presented. Trotted out like a brood mare to be ogled and studied seemed more like it. At least, that's how I imagined it.

The chief eunuch, Hegai, oversaw the harem with an air of authority. He was not an imposing figure, being of average height with a wiry build that suggested efficiency rather than strength. His complexion was a warm olive tone, his face lined with the marks of experience rather than age. Though his exact age was difficult to guess, he bore the look of someone who had long since learned how to navigate the treacherous waters of royal life. His dark, almond shaped eyes were sharp and calculating, always observing, always measuring. It was said he could discern a woman's worth to the King with a single glance. His head was shaved, as was the custom and tradition among palace eunuchs, accentuating his high cheekbones and a mouth that rarely smiled but often pressed into a knowing smirk. He dressed simply, but impeccably, in robes of deep blue and gray, the subtle patterns of his garments hinting at his high station without being ostentatious. A gold medallion, engraved with the emblem of the royal household, hung around his neck—a symbol of his trusted position in the king's inner circle.

Hegai noticed me early on, though I did not know why. Perhaps it was my quiet demeanor, or perhaps it was something else. Whatever the reason, he favored me, offering advice and ensuring I received the finest oils and ointments. "There is something different about you," he said one day, his eyes narrowing as he studied me. "I think the King will see it, too."

I wasn't sure whether his words comforted or terrified me.

As we all waited for our turn, the women within the harem moved like shadows, speaking in soft murmurs or not at all, each one of us locked in our own thoughts about the future. The competition between us was unspoken, but ever present; an invisible thread that both bound us together and kept us apart. The nights were the hardest, when the silence settled in, heavy and suffocating as we waited for the king's summons. The other girls all hoped to be chosen, yet most feared what awaited when that moment came.

After our year of preparation, as the lamps burned low and most of the girls had retired to their chambers, Hegai would come for us— one by one.

When they returned, I could see the strain in their faces, the redness around their eyes as they would silently slip into their chambers.

One evening, while the others slept, I found one of the other girls sitting in the corner of the chamber, clutching a pendant her mother had given her. She was crying quietly, her tears falling onto the polished floor.

When I approached, she looked up at me, her dark eyes now hollow and haunted.

"I did not please him," she said at last and lowered her head again.

I stared at her confused. What did that mean exactly?

"What happened?" I asked gently.

She shook her head but did not answer. Her shoulders shook with sobs as I wrapped my arms around her, holding her tightly.

"I'm nothing now," she sniffled bitterly. "Just another girl in the harem. Ruined for other men. I'll never leave this place. I'll never see my family again."

I wanted to tell her that wasn't true, that she of course would go home...but the lie died on my lips before the words could form.

"Trust in God," I heard my cousin Mordecai's frequent words to me before I'd been taken echo through my mind.

The problem was…God was not here in these chambers beneath the palace. We had been abandoned and were on our own if we had any hope of getting out of this.

Eventually, the other girl fell into a fitful sleep, and I stole away into the courtyard, the soft glow of moonlight illuminating the gardens. The air was cool, carrying the faint scent of jasmine.

Hegai appeared from a nearby corridor, his presence as steady as ever. He had become a quiet ally to me over the past months, though his motives for favoring me were still unclear. He paused when he saw me, then approached, his expression unreadable.

"You should rest, Esther," he said, his voice low and firm. "You'll need your strength for the days ahead."

Esther. The name still sounded strange to my ears, but I had taken my cousin Mordecai's advice and used a Persian name rather than Haddassah to hide my Jewish identity.

"I will rest soon," I replied. "I had hoped for some guidance."

He raised an eyebrow, folding his hands behind his back. "Guidance? From me?"

"Yes," I said, looking directly at him. "You know more about the King than anyone here. And I believe you also understand the dangers that come with this place."

He hesitated, studying me closely. "You think too much. It's dangerous," he said at last.

"Then perhaps you can help me stop thinking," I said with a faint smile. "Tell me something I've been wondering about since I arrived. What was the real reason behind why Vashti was banished?"

His face darkened instantly. "You already know the reason. She disobeyed the King."

"Indeed," I said. "But something tells me there's more to that story than we have been told."

"You're too inquisitive for your own good, Esther," Hegai grumbled and started to turn away. I reached out and grabbed his arm. He stared at it, his eyes narrowing in irritation. It was forbidden for us to touch any of the royal household in such a way, even the servants, but somehow, I knew he would not punish me for it; though I did immediately drop my hand now that I'd stopped him.

"If I'm to understand the King—if I'm to survive him—I need to understand why the last queen fell from his favor. So I..." I paused. I couldn't let him know what my real plan was. "So I don't repeat those mistakes."

"Don't disobey him," Hegai grunted.

"Vashti had to have known the cost—so why did she risk it then? If all the King did was demand she join him for dinner with his friends..."

Hegai's mouth pursed in anger, his cheek twitching slightly. My instincts were right. There was more to the story and the public version caused Hegai to chafe. I kept pushing.

"Why would she risk it just to be stubborn?"

Hegai sighed, his shoulders suddenly slumping slightly. He looked at me, his expression conflicted, as though weighing the risk of speaking the truth. He glanced around, making sure no one else was within earshot. Finally, he motioned for me to sit on a nearby bench. He remained standing, his arms crossed, his voice low and cautious.

"The King had been drinking heavily," he began, "as had his advisors and nobles. They were celebrating one of his victories—an extravagant affair, as most of his gatherings are. Xerxes, in his drunken state, decided he wanted to display Queen Vashti before his guests."

"Display her?" I asked, frowning.

Hegai's lips pressed into a thin line. "He ordered her to come wearing her crown," he said carefully. "And that was all he wanted her to wear."

My stomach turned in revulsion at the unspoken implication. "And that's why she refused," I said softly.

"She did," Hegai confirmed. "She was proud, and rightly so. She had dignity and wouldn't allow herself to be humiliated, even by the King. But Xerxes...he doesn't take defiance lightly, especially not in front of an audience. His advisors stoked his anger, telling him that Vashti's disobedience would set a dangerous example for all the women in Persia. They said it would make men weak in their own homes."

"And so he banished her," I said, piecing it together.

Hegai nodded. "To save face."

I sat quietly for a moment, absorbing his words. It was a sobering story, but it told me much about the man I would soon face. Xerxes was ruled by pride and easily swayed by those around him. His power was absolute, but his ego was fragile.

"Thank you for telling me," I said finally, looking up at Hegai.

"I'm not sure I should have," he said, shaking his head. "Be careful, Esther. The king's temper is unpredictable. If you make him feel slighted, you'll meet the same fate as Vashti—or worse."

"I understand," I said, standing. "But sometimes, the only way to stand before a storm is to know where its winds are weakest."

Hegai frowned, clearly unsettled by my words. "Don't play games with him," he warned. "You're clever, but cleverness won't save you if the King turns against you."

"Perhaps not," I said, meeting his gaze. "But knowing what makes him weak might."

What I kept to myself was that I had no intention of winning over the King and ultimately winding up in that bedchamber. If defiance

was what he despised, then defiance would be what he would get...
in public. Like Vashti, I would force his hand.

That night, as I prepared to meet the King, I held Hegai's words
close. Xerxes was a man who needed to be seen as powerful, even if
it meant silencing those who opposed him. But his need for approval
—his desperate desire to save face—was also a crack in his armor.

I didn't know if I would succeed. But I knew one thing for certain: I
would not lose myself, no matter the cost.

When the time came for me to be presented to the King, I felt as
though I were walking to my execution—and I very well might have
been. My heart pounded as the attendants dressed me in a shimmering gown and adorned me with jewels. They brushed fragrant
oils into my skin and arranged my hair into an elaborate style. My
stomach churned with a mix of fear and disbelief. What would the
King think of me? Would he dismiss me as quickly as he had
dismissed Vashti? Or possibly even worse—would he choose me,
trapping me in this gilded prison forever?

No. I pushed that fear aside. With what I had planned, he would
definitely not choose me.

Hegai's story about why Vashti had been banished still caused a
knot of fear to form in my stomach. To be married to a man who
would humiliate you in such a way was terrifying. Being as drunk as
they were, who knew what else they might have done to her had she
obeyed. The thought sent a chill down my spine.

These other women wanted to be queen, wanted to be chosen,
wanted to please him. I did not. I had no desire to sit on the throne.
Especially not with this King and his fiery temper and drunken
escapades. I yearned for my simple life back with my cousin.

I had resolved that death was better than life in the palace, subject
to the whims of this mad king. If defiance was what the King
despised, defiance is what he would get.

The guards escorted me through a series of opulent hallways until we reached the grand throne room. My knees threatened to buckle as I entered, and I only prayed that I had the courage to say what I intended to say. The space was vast, with towering columns and walls covered in gold. King Xerxes sat sprawled on an elaborate throne at the far end, a goblet of wine dangling from his hand; the weight of his piercing gaze fixed on me as I approached.

Those sharp, restless eyes suddenly darted between the eunuchs, the guards, and the women who had already been paraded before him. A man of extremes, they said—generous one moment, wrathful the next. Even his posture spoke of indulgence and power: his robes, heavy with gold and jewels, spilled over the arms of his throne like molten sunlight.

He was tall and broad-shouldered, his imposing stature designed to intimidate. His skin, bronzed by the Persian sun, seemed to glow under the golden light of the throne room. His hair, jet-black and thick, was meticulously groomed, cascading to his shoulders in smooth waves, with a single braid adorned with gold threading along the side—a symbol of his status and vanity. Wisps of silvery gray were fringed around his temples, reminding me how much older he was than I. His beard, neatly trimmed and oiled, was as black as his hair, accentuating the sharpness of his jawline, with only the faintest hint of gray around the edges.

Those eyes that were boring into me were perhaps his most striking feature—piercing and dark, like the depths of a stormy sea. They flicked quickly, taking in everything and everyone, betraying the restless mind of a man who was always calculating, even in his moments of leisure. His gaze had a dual nature; it could be both cold and fiery, depending on his mood, making it nearly impossible to predict his temper.

Xerxes dressed like a man who wanted the world to know he ruled it. His robes were made of the finest purple and gold silk, embroidered with intricate patterns of lions and lotus flowers—symbols of his divine kingship. Golden arm cuffs encircled his biceps, and jeweled rings adorned nearly every finger. Around his neck hung a heavy gold chain inlaid with emeralds and sapphires, glinting with every movement he made. A towering golden crown sat atop his head, its intricate spires mimicking the peaks of distant mountains.

Despite his regal appearance, there was an air of volatility about him, a barely restrained chaos beneath the polished surface.

He was surrounded by his advisors and friends, most of whom were already drunk. The smell of wine hung heavy in the air, mingling with the perfume that clung to my skin. I had watched girl after girl walk this path before me, some trembling, some smiling sweetly, but none had captured his favor for more than a fleeting moment.

My knees trembled, but I forced myself to take steady steps. Mordecai's words echoed in my mind: *"Do not fear men. Fear God, and God will guide your steps."*

I reached the center of the room and stopped, bowing low before him. I could hear his advisors chuckling and whispering to each other, their drunken voices barely muffled. I expected him to dismiss me immediately, as he had so many others. But when I straightened and met his gaze, he was staring at me with an unreadable expression.

"Another one?" he drawled, swirling his wine lazily. "What makes you any different from the others?"

His tone was sharp, laced with mockery. My heart pounded, but I refused to lower my gaze. "Perhaps nothing, Your Majesty," I replied evenly. "Or perhaps everything."

The room fell silent. His advisors exchanged glances, some smirking, others frowning. No one dared speak to Xerxes with anything less than utter submission. But something in me refused to cower, even before this unpredictable man. If he was going to dismiss me, so be it—but I would not grovel like the others.

He raised an eyebrow, clearly intrigued. "Everything, you say?" His voice was like silk, dangerous and soft. "Explain yourself."

I took a slow, deliberate breath, steadying my nerves. "I cannot tell you, my King, because words mean little. I do not know what you seek, but I do know that you are a man of great power, and power does not seek what it already has. If you find favor in me, it will not be because I am like the others. It will be because I am something new."

The room erupted in laughter. I could feel the flush rising to my cheeks, but I kept my head high. Let them laugh. I wasn't speaking to them—I was speaking to him.

Xerxes leaned forward, resting his elbows on his knees. The laughter died down as he studied me, his piercing eyes narrowing. "You have an interesting tongue," he said slowly, a faint smile playing on his lips. "But perhaps you mistake this for a debate. I am the King. I ask the questions, and you answer them. So, I ask you again: What makes you different?"

"What makes me different is I am not afraid to tell you that if you ever demand of me what you demanded of Vashti, you shall have to do to me as you did to her."

The throne room fell silent, the kind of silence that makes the air feel heavy. King Xerxes' eyes narrowed as if to make sure he had heard correctly. The murmur of his advisors in the adjoining corridor ceased, their curiosity surely piqued by my boldness. My hands trembled slightly at my sides, but I stood tall, refusing to show fear.

"What," he said slowly, his voice low and dangerously calm, "did you just say?"

I met his gaze head-on, the fear in my chest warring with the conviction in my heart. "I said, if you demand of me what you demanded of Vashti, I will not obey any more than she did."

For a moment, he said nothing, his expression unreadable. Everyone in the room held their breath, their eyes riveted on the King, wondering how he was going to respond to this challenge.

I caught sight of Hegai. His almond-shaped eyes were glued on me —dark and angry. He knew what I was doing and did not approve. I understood that Hegai's role and desire had been to prepare me to behave like a future queen; I was destroying his months of training.

The tension in the room was palpable, but I refused to back down. I could see the flicker of something in the king's eyes—anger, yes, but also something else. Curiosity? Admiration? It was hard to tell.

Then, slowly, a grin spread across his lips. He laughed—a deep, genuine laugh that startled even his advisors.

"Well," he said, setting his goblet down. "At least this one isn't boring." The room erupted again, only this time in nervous, halting laughter.

"Leave us," he suddenly commanded.

The room emptied quickly, the murmurs of his advisors fading into the distance. I was left standing before him, alone. My pulse thundered in my ears, but I remained still, waiting for him to speak.

Xerxes rose from his throne, his gaze never leaving mine. He walked down the steps slowly, his robes trailing behind him. When he stood before me, I realized how tall he was, how imposing. Yet I did not flinch. He walked with the confidence of a man who had never been challenged, yet his sharp movements and frequent scowl revealed the impatience of one who demanded constant control. His every step seemed to carry both the weight of an empire and the whims of a man who was used to having his desires met instantly.

"What is your name?" he asked, his voice softer now, circling around me like a predator stalks its prey.

"Esther," I said.

He nodded, as if committing it to memory. "You are bold, Esther. Foolishly so, perhaps. But, contrary to popular opinion, I prefer boldness to flattery."

I swallowed hard, unsure whether his words were a compliment or a warning.

"Do not mistake my interest for leniency," he continued, his tone sharpening. "I will not tolerate open defiance."

When he stopped in front of me, he was so close I could see the faint lines around his eyes, the subtle tension in his jaw. "Do you know what happened to Vashti when she defied me?" he asked, his voice as sharp as a blade.

"I do," I said evenly. "And yet I stand here before you, saying the same."

His lips twitched, and for a moment, I couldn't tell whether he was about to explode in anger or laugh in disbelief.

"You are either very brave," Xerxes said finally, "or very foolish."

"Perhaps both," I replied. "But if I may speak freely, my King, a ruler as great as yourself should not have to demand obedience in matters that strip a person of their dignity. If Vashti failed you, it was not because of her defiance. It was because you asked something unworthy of a queen—and of yourself."

"You presume to lecture me on what is worthy?" he said, his tone cold but measured.

"I presume to tell you the truth," I said. "Because a ruler who surrounds himself with only those who tell him what he wants to hear is a ruler who will find himself alone when the truth finally arrives."

For a long, excruciating moment, the King said nothing. He merely stared at me, contemplating how to respond. Then, to my shock, he once again laughed. It wasn't the kind of laugh one gives when genuinely amused, but rather the laugh of someone who has just been challenged in a way they didn't expect.

"It wasn't you who wanted to dismiss your Queen, was it?" I said, suddenly feeling emboldened. "You felt pressured by your men because she had dared to defy you publicly and you had to save face. But you know, deep down, you should have never asked that of her in the first place."

His smile faded, his eyes seeming to twitch. But as he looked at me, I knew I had spoken truth to him.

"You perhaps presume too much," he said in a low, warning tone. But then the smile returned as he shook his head in amazement. "You are a strange woman, Esther. Most would have begged for mercy by now, yet here you stand, lecturing me like some philosopher."

I didn't reply, sensing that anything more I said might push him over the edge. The danger was unmistakable.

Finally, he turned and strode back to his throne, calling for his advisors to return. "Perhaps there is something to be said for a woman who does not grovel," he mused aloud, though his tone carried a hint of warning. "But do not mistake my amusement for permission to defy me. You are bold, Esther, but even boldness has its limits."

I bowed my head, though my heart soared with relief. I had displeased him. Surely he would send me away.

For a moment, he said nothing as he continued to stare at me with an intense gaze. Then he chuckled, the sound low and rumbling. "Perhaps I have finally found something worth my time," he said, flopping with both grace and abandon back into his throne, picking the wine goblet back up as he regarded me with an amused smile and gestured to Hegai. "She pleases me," he said. "Take her to my chambers."

I blinked in surprise, then glanced in horror at Hegai as he came to escort me out of the throne room.

I had...pleased him? How? In front of everyone I had openly stated my intention to disobey him. Surely that should have removed me from contention!

I followed in a daze and barely heard the chattering of the attendants who were excitedly trying to explain to me how I should be with the King once he arrived. Were they really trying to tell me how to please the King in bed? And how did they know?

I decided I didn't want to know the answer to that particular question. He was the King. He took whomever he wanted into his bed. Most likely, including his attendants.

"My Queen." The sound of my maid's voice brought me back to the present. Somehow, I was the one he chose. "It is time," she said softly.

I blinked, realizing that the maids had finished dressing me. My reflection stared back at me, regal and composed, though inside I felt anything but. I reached for the crown and placed it on my head, its weight having become a familiar burden.

Today, I would risk everything. Today, I would step into the throne room once more—not as a girl seeking to be cast aside, but as a woman pleading for the lives of her people.

I would once again challenge him publicly, force him to either show me mercy, or kill me where I stood. Since my marriage, I had learned of a plot to commit genocide against my people by one of the King's most trusted advisers. My cousin, Mordecai, had overheard the plans of Haman, the king's vizier, and I still held Mordecai's note tightly in my hand, its words playing over and over in my head.

"Do not think that because you are in the king's house you alone of all the Jews will escape. For if you remain silent at this time, relief and deliverance for the Jews will arise from another place, but you and your father's family will perish. And who knows but that you have come to your royal position for such a time as this?"

I had not seen the King in person in over a month. I hadn't quite figured out if I had pleased or displeased him.

Though the reality was he had likely been spending it in the harem chambers. He knew I would not put up with some of his…proclivities…so he took them out on the other women in the harem.

I had not visited the harem since that night Hegai escorted me to meet the King for the first time, as the following morning Xerxes had declared that I was his favorite among all the women and would be named queen. I had instead been led directly to my own room and was kept apart from the others.

Even though I was now the King's wife—and the Queen—that did not mean the other women went away. Rather, they remained in the lower chambers of the palace, essentially his slaves. We had initially fought over this, but finally reached an agreement. I was his favorite, for reasons that still baffled me. I am the most stubborn and obstinate and…disobedient…of all the women. Yet, he even at times professed some form of what passed for love—at least his version of it.

I appreciated the irony that in my naive ploy to try and get him to send me away—which was never going to happen I later realized—I had inadvertently impressed him so much he respected me in a way he never had any other woman. I now thanked my God for that naivete, because my boldness had saved me from a much worse fate —the fate of the women down in the lower chambers.

My thoughts occasionally drifted to those other women. As Queen, I had some modicum of freedom, while they were forever trapped in their golden, gilded prison. They had no choice in their captivity, but there was nothing I could do. Whatever influence I had over the King ended at the stairwell that led down to the lower chambers. That was his domain now. Not mine.

I pushed thoughts of the other women out of my mind. They were minor and inconsequential as at the moment, I had much bigger problems. I must approach my husband unbidden.

The opposite offense as Vashti, who had refused to answer his summons. To approach the King without permission or invitation risked death unless he extended his scepter toward you in mercy. I did not believe that my husband was done with me yet. I think he took too much pleasure from our banter when we were together.

Still, I might catch him in a bad mood or at an inopportune moment and his whim might be to have me killed.

Well, so be it. I needed to at least try and save my people from being exterminated throughout the land of Persia.

I took a deep breath, straightened my shoulders, and walked toward the doors, praying that the God who had brought me this far would not abandon me now.

Discussion Questions

1. Esther and Vashti both challenge the King's authority in different ways. How do their approaches to defiance compare, and what does this say about the limited agency of women in the Persian Empire?

2. Do you think Esther made the right choices in order to survive? What would you have done in her place?

3. Hegai plays a key role in Esther's preparation and survival in the palace. What do you think his true motivations were in helping Esther?

4. God is never mentioned in the actual story of Esther (Mordecai tells Esther to trust in God in this story, but it is not in the original Biblical account), nor does God play any sort of role in terms of speaking through prophets or performing miracles. How might faith (or the struggle with faith) have shaped Esther's journey and decisions?

5. King Xerxes is portrayed as unpredictable, indulgent, and easily manipulated by his advisors. What does his character reveal about the nature of absolute power? Is he truly in control or is he controlled by those around him?

6. By risking her life to approach the King, Esther chooses to fight for her people rather than remain safe in her position in the palace. What does her decision reveal about her sense of duty and how does it contrast with her earlier reluctance?

7. Mordecai tells Esther that she may have been placed in her position "for such a time as this." Do you believe people have destinies or do they create their own fate through their choices?

Mary

(Matthew 1-2; Luke 1-2)

THE DONKEY RIDE WAS EXCRUCIATING. At almost nine months pregnant, making the trek from Nazareth to Bethlehem was hardly easy. Mary winced as they came to a stop at the city gates.

Finally. They'd arrived. The sun was setting, and Mary was relieved that they had made it to town before nightfall. The roads were not exactly the safest places to be at night, especially not for a pregnant woman.

Her back deeply ached, her ankles were swollen beyond the point of her sandals fitting, and her insides felt like the baby had displaced her internal organs. At the end of the journey, she'd felt a cramping that might have been contractions, but it was hard to tell as her body was in constant pain.

Joseph supposedly had family here they would be able to stay with. She silently cursed Caesar, demanding a census of the provinces. Joseph had suggested she stay back in Nazareth, but something inside her told her she needed to travel with him.

Mary had long since quit questioning her internal voice, and grudgingly informed Joseph that she had to accompany him.

Joseph had likewise long ago stopped asking questions of Mary. Neither one of them had any rational explanation for the situation they found themselves in. Angels. Dreams. Unexpected pregnancy of a virgin.

Mary was young and had no older siblings, so she didn't fully understand how men and women came together to make a child. She understood enough to know she and Joseph had never done what was necessary. Yet an angel had appeared and told her she would have a child. Born of the Holy Spirit, it had said.

Angels. Now there was a terrifying thing to behold. No wonder the stories about them were always accompanied by the words, "Fear not!"

Because that was one frightful sight. Bright, burning light like fire with a disembodied voice that reverberated through her skull. The sight was terrifying. And its words told her equally unbelievable things.

The next day she had figured it simply a strange dream. No one would believe what the angel had told her. Certainly not Joseph.

But when she missed her menstruation, and soon after felt cramping not accompanied by blood but rather swollen breasts swelling and nausea, she knew.

Panicked, she ran away to visit her cousin Elizabeth. Maybe Elizabeth could help. She didn't know what else to do. Staying in Nazareth would not be safe. Maybe…maybe she could just stay with Elizabeth long enough and they'd hide the fact that she was somehow with child. She didn't know what was running through her head. She just knew, there was no way Joseph wasn't going to have her stoned to death when he discovered she was pregnant.

Then there'd been Elizabeth's surprise. She, too, was pregnant against all odds in her old age, long past the time she should have been able to have children. Another Sarah.

Her faith strengthened, she returned to Nazareth and informed Joseph of what had happened.

He responded...better than she'd anticipated, but certainly not great. He was still going to terminate their engagement and set about starting the divorce proceedings, when he suddenly had a change of heart. Said an angel had come to him in a dream and told him to still marry her.

Why Joseph just got that terrifying image in a dream and not in person like she did, she didn't know, but she secretly believed it was because as a woman she was perhaps strong enough to face the angel awake, not through the protection of a dream. Still, despite the divine visit, Joseph looked at her differently. He was cautious, and a bit wary. She could tell he struggled to believe her unbelievable tale. Who wouldn't, though? If it hadn't happened to her, she wouldn't have believed it either. Likely story, right?

Mary remembered Abigail, a young woman who had been a few years older than she and found herself pregnant by someone other than her betrothed. Her fiancé had not responded as generously as Joseph. They'd dragged her out into the city square and stoned her to death for the infidelity. Mary had felt it quite unjust as nothing had happened to the man who had impregnated her. Of course, Abigail had refused to tell who it was, probably for that very reason —to protect him. Because she thought she loved him, no doubt. Mary never knew who the man was. That had been a secret Abigail had taken to her grave.

A strange thought occurred to Mary. Had she been the first to whom the angel had appeared? Or simply the one who survived to tell the tale? She shivered thinking about it.

While this trek to Bethlehem was painful, inconvenient, and honestly annoying, Mary did her best not to take her anger and frustration out on Joseph. He had been understanding beyond what any man should have.

Though her temper was tested when they arrived at the home of some of Joseph's cousins, only to discover they had no room for them. Unless they wanted to stay in the lower room of the house, the stable, with the animals. Mary kept her mouth shut, but couldn't help thinking what kind of family would put a pregnant woman in the stable?

Then she saw the looks they gave her, and one of Joseph's aunts sniffed in disgust. "You take that little whore of yours someplace else," she spat.

Joseph's cousin held up a hand, silencing the woman. "The stable is the best I can offer you." He gave Mary a reproachful, sidelong glance, though, as he said it.

Of course. They assumed, since he'd gone ahead and married her, that he'd slept with her prior to the wedding. He'd silently let people assume such things. He knew better than anyone what would and wouldn't be believed. By omission, they'd lived with the stigma.

"Capernaum." Joseph said as they made their way into the lower room of the stable and reached up to help her down off the donkey.

Mary frowned as she looked at him. "What?"

"Capernaum," he repeated. "That's where we should go live. People won't know us there."

Tears welled in her eyes. Of course. The reaction of Joseph's family here mirrored what many of the people of Nazareth who knew them—and even some who didn't—were saying and thinking. They'd long since stopped bothering Mary, but Joseph...

"It won't be good for the child to be raised in Nazareth," he said bluntly.

"Something to consider," she agreed wearily.

As her feet hit the straw on the ground, she suddenly felt a gush of warm water between her legs, and glanced down to see she was standing in a pool of fluid. She sighed heavily and looked back up at Joseph.

"Great," she said. "Just what we needed tonight."

For a moment, Joseph just stood there, stunned, staring at the mess beneath her feet. He turned his wide eyes finally on Mary and stammered, "N-n-now?"

Mary nodded her head. "I'm afraid so."

The first contraction that she recognized as labor hit her suddenly and doubled her over as she groaned in pain. Joseph looked around wildly. "Should, should I go get someone?"

"Someone like your aunt?" Mary said sarcastically. "No, we'll...we'll do this on our own. Just...get some clean hay and a blanket for me to lie down on.

Mary had seen the midwives birth babies before. She at least had some idea of what to expect. Still, it would have been nice to have had one here helping her instead of only Joseph, who was frantically trying to create a makeshift bed for her to lie on. If the contractions hadn't been wracking her body she'd have helped him, but instead she was doubled over, the wave of pain washing over her reminding her of her worst menstrual cramps, only a thousand times worse and shooting through her entire body, causing her to roar gutturally. After what felt like a millennia, the contraction ended, and she wobbled over to the improvised bed Joseph had prepared.

"What...can I get you?" he asked helplessly as she slowly laid down, her back perched up, her feet spread apart, breathing in and out slowly and deeply through the nausea and pain.

"A basin of water," she said. "You're going to need water when he's born to clean him."

Joseph nodded and disappeared. She let out a long sigh of relief. She loved him, if for no other reason than he tried so hard, but she was also glad to have a moment to herself.

"Well, I guess this is how you're going to arrive, little one," she said, placing her hand on her belly which had relaxed somewhat following the contraction. "In a stable. With…" she glanced over at where another donkey stood tethered and a couple of chickens were squawking at having been disturbed. A goat stared at her from behind the slats of his pen. The room smelled strongly of feces.

"…goats and donkey dung," she sighed in resignation.

Another contraction seized her and she hollered like a savage animal, noises that emanated from her very core. The flickering light of the small oil lamp Joseph had lit before he left cast shadows on the walls, offering little solace or comfort. The world outside seemed distant, oblivious to her not-so-silent battle.

Another contraction wracked her body, causing her to scream even louder, her determination faltering as she wished Joseph would return. He may not have been a midwife, but he was better than being alone, with no hand to grip as the pain roiled through her body. She cried out his name, but was met with silence, only the lowing of the animals that had begun to shift, agitated in their stalls with this loud intruder.

Panic seized her. Was she going to deliver this baby alone? The contractions had sped up and were coming more rapidly and more quickly now. Where was Joseph?

Beads of sweat dotted her brow, mingling with the dust of the straw-covered floor beneath her. Her breaths now came in ragged gasps, alternating with painful groans as cramps seized her, echoing off the stone walls as she rode the waves of pain that surged through her entire body. The air was heavy with the scent of hay and the distant musk of livestock.

As the moment of birth drew near, she stood, squatting, grabbing hold of the feeding trough that lay beside her. She reached down tentatively, pulling her hand away as she felt a soft head at the base of her pubic bone. The life within her was beginning to emerge.

A shaft of moonlight suddenly pierced through the stable as the door creaked open and broke the stillness as Joseph stepped inside holding the bucket of water. His eyes widened in shock as he took in the sight before him, lines of worry etched deep into his brow. Without a word, he hurried to her side, setting the bucket down with shaking hands.

"What…what can I do?" he asked, turning to her and reaching out to help, but stopping just short of actually touching her. She let out a scream as another contraction surged through her body and she felt herself unable to stop from pushing…pushing.

"Catch him," she gasped breathlessly as she could feel the child beginning to slide out. Joseph quickly shoved his hands between her legs just in time to feel the wet, slimy, bloody head of a squalling child.

He laughed and smiled despite himself as both hands grasped the newborn's body.

"Find a knife and cut his cord," she said tiredly as he gently wiped the newborn down and laid him on some hay to search in his satchel for a knife. Upon cutting the cord, he quickly began to use the water to wash the screaming baby's face, clearing away the afterbirth that clung to its red, tiny body.

Mary sank back down into the hay—exhausted. The labor had been blessedly short, she knew, compared to many women. Still, it had zapped all of her strength as she lay there, watching Joseph cradle the newborn child as he continued to wipe the blood away. She allowed herself a small, weary smile as the child was no longer screaming, but looking up at Joseph with his large, brown eyes and thin tufts of dark hair.

Suddenly, she became aware of another sound, and she turned her head to see the animals nearby had begun to…kneel? She frowned as she watched the goats and lambs and camels, even their donkey, all lower their heads, bending their legs to rest on their front knees.

Joseph paused as well, his eyes widening in surprise as he watched them one by one bow before them. He glanced at Mary nervously and she simply shrugged and shook her head as if to say, "I have no idea, either."

The moment of reverence only lasted a few heart beats before they stood and resumed eating. Mary continued to watch them in awe as Joseph finally sidled up next to her and lay her son in her arms.

A flood of emotions washed over her as she gazed into those dark eyes, that seemed like endless pools of wisdom and love. She felt a surge of overwhelming love, so powerful it took her breath away. Tears welled in her eyes, mingling with the sweat and dust on her cheeks. In that moment, everything else faded away. All the jeers. All the taunts. All the pointing fingers. All the accusations. All the pain of labor, the solitude of the stable, the uncertainties of the night and the future. All that mattered was this precious bundle in her arms, the culmination of months of anticipation, struggle—and a promise. She marveled at the miracle of his existence, at the perfect symmetry of his features, at the softness of his newborn skin that seemed to almost radiate with an inner light.

A sense of awe filled her heart as she realized the enormity of the responsibility that now rested in her hands—to nurture and protect this tiny miraculous life, to guide him through all the trials that would lie ahead.

As she pressed her cheek against his, she whispered words of love and devotion. In that quiet moment, amidst the hay and the scent of animals, she knew they were both headed down a path that was destined for heartache and pain. It was as though he was able to project that understanding into her mind. A somber knowledge that his life would alter the world as she—and everyone else—knew it.

Her tears of joy were suddenly also tears of sorrow.

He would be equally loved and despised by the world. She saw grief mingled with joy in their futures. What did it all mean? Who was this child exactly? What was he? Yes, he was her own flesh and blood. And he was something much more than that.

"An evolution," she heard whispered into her mind. A long distant voice of another primordial mother, a shadow of Mother Eve, lingering on the edges of her mind. *"Humanity, through him, must evolve and change."*

Those dark, wise beyond his newborn eyes gazed into hers for a few more languishing moments, before closing and falling asleep against her breast. She shuddered slightly from the chill in the night air as glimpses of the trials and tribulations that awaited him, the pain and suffering he would endure, permeated her mind.

She held him close. Even though her heart ached at the thought of what lay ahead, she also felt fierce pride swelling within her, born of the knowledge he was destined for a purpose greater than she could ever imagine.

Discussion Questions

1. Mary and Joseph likely faced judgment and rejection from their community. How do you think societal perceptions influenced their experience and how does this compare to social judgments people face today?

2. How do you interpret Joseph's reaction to Mary's pregnancy? How does his decision to stay with her demonstrate his character?

3. Why do you think Mary and Joseph had different angelic encounters? (Mary's was in person, Joseph's was in a dream.)

4. Why do you think it's significant that *both* Elizabeth and Mary experienced miraculous pregnancies?

5. What does the setting of Jesus' birth say about Jesus' arrival into the world and how does it contrast with expectations of a "kingly" birth?

6. What do you think the symbolism is of even the animals kneeling?

7. The story hints at Jesus bringing change and evolution to humanity. What do you think this means in the context of faith and human development?

8. What aspects of Mary's story do you think still resonate with people today?

The Adulterous Woman

———— ∞ ————

(John 8:1-11)

I AM AWAKENED SUDDENLY as rough hands tear the blanket from my body. I hear the sound of voices—angry, urgent, and far too many. The room is still dark, the faintest gray of morning creeping through the slats in the window, but the men in my doorway don't care about the hour.

They grab me.

I barely have time to cry out before fingers dig into my arms, yanking me from my mat. My head spins, my body tangled in sleep and confusion.

"What—?" My voice is hoarse. "What are you doing?"

No one answers.

I struggle, but the grip tightens. The first hand strikes my cheek, sending a hot sting across my skin.

"Silence, whore," one of them spits. "You've been caught."

The words don't make sense.

Caught? What I do isn't a secret.

I blink hard, trying to push through the fog in my mind. My bed is empty. The man who paid for my time is gone—he always leaves before dawn. He knows better. They all do.

So what are they talking about?

Another hand—this one tangled in my hair—drags me forward. My feet scrape against the floor as I stumble, my heart pounding. My thin tunic offers no protection from the cold or their eyes, and shame burns through me as I realize I know these men.

Not by name, not in daylight, but I know them. Some of them have stood at my doorway before, glancing left and right to make sure no one sees. Some of them have pressed silver into my palm, their eyes dark with something they refuse to name.

And now they have come for me in the open.

They shove me into the street, dragging me through the waking city. The sun is rising, and people are beginning to stare. Whispers ripple through the air, sharp as knives.

I begin to see it as they drag me toward the temple where another Rabbi is standing teaching, my bare feet scraping against the stones. The temple courtyard is already full. They shove me forward, and I stumble, falling hard onto the ground. Dust fills my mouth, my hands scraping against the stone. My hair falls over my face, and I do not lift my head.

I feel them around me, looming. I hear their voices, sharp and eager.

"Teacher," one of them says, his voice slick with something I cannot name. "This woman was caught in the very act of adultery."

A cold wave crashes over me.

That is not who I am. That is not my crime. The Law of Moses is clear—adultery requires a married woman and a man who is not her husband. But I am no man's wife. I belong to no one.

They know this. And yet they say the words anyway. Because the truth doesn't matter.

Only the spectacle.

Only the trap.

A pause. A carefully timed silence.

"In the Law, Moses commands us to stone such women," they continue. "What do you say?"

The trap is laid. I suddenly realize this isn't about justice, it's about power. This isn't about me. I am nothing to them. I am only the bait. If this rabbi knows that there has been no actual crime, that means he knows who I am. And if he knows who I am, then that is a confession that he sleeps with prostitutes.

I force myself to breathe, my fingers curling into the dirt. My body is trembling, but not from cold.

They do not care about my punishment. If they did, they would have brought the man as well. If it were truly adultery, we would both be guilty. He would be committing a crime against my husband and would be just as culpable.

But there is no man.

Only me.

Because I am not the real target.

I do not look at him—this man they have taken me to for judgment. I cannot.

But then—silence.

Not the kind that waits, but the kind that confounds.

I risk a glance.

He is kneeling. Not speaking. Not judging. Not even looking at them.

He kneels in front of me in the dust, pressing his fingers into the earth. Writing something I cannot see.

The group of men shift impatiently. "Well?" one of them demands. "What do you say?"

The man lifts his head. His gaze sweeps over them, steady, knowing.

"If any one of you is without sin," he says softly, "let him be the first to throw a stone at her." A blade of silence cuts through the courtyard.

I hold my breath. No one moves.

And then—one by one—I hear the stones drop.

The oldest leaves first, then another, then another.

I glance back, watching them go, my heart pounding in my throat. These men who tore me from my bed, who dragged me here in the name of righteousness, who condemned me with their mouths but not their hands...

They walk away.

Because they know.

Some of them have touched me. Some of them have whispered my name in the dark. Some of them have left my bed only to stand in judgment.

They cannot throw the first stone because they are just as guilty.

Until, at last, no one remains but him.

And me.

I remain kneeling in the dust, my whole body shaking. I do not know what to say. What to do. And then—his voice.

"Woman."

Not whore. Not adulteress.

"Woman, where are they? Has no one condemned you?"

I lift my eyes. "No one, Lord," I whisper.

And then he says the words I never expected.

"Neither do I condemn you."

I nearly collapse with relief. My vision blurs, my breath comes fast, and I am not sure if I want to weep or laugh.

But then his voice changes. Not unkind, not harsh—but firm.

"Go now," he says. "And sin no more."

The words strike deep. Not because I do not know my sins, but because I do. Yet I am at a loss—what does he expect me to do? Women like me...we have few options. We don't simply stop what we do. Society does not accept us. We cannot just live normal lives, have families, and be respectable.

Then I realize there is something deeper in his voice.

A warning. I do not miss it.

"Or something worse may happen to you."

He is not speaking of God or the law. He is speaking of men. Of the ones who dragged me here.

They did not get what they wanted today. They could not trap him, could not use me to destroy him. But men like that do not like being humiliated. They will have to find other ways to deal with him.

But me? I am nothing to them. And men like that do not forget.

I swallow hard. He is right.

If I keep living this life, if I keep putting myself at the mercy of men who have none, one day I may not leave the courtyard alive. One day, there may be no one to kneel beside me in the dust. Still...what are my options?

As he turns to leave, I call out.

"Where do I go? What do I do?"

He pauses, turns around and looks at me, then, after a long moment, extends a hand.

"Come and follow me."

It is not the same kind of invitation that men normally mean when they extend a hand and want me to follow them. There is gentleness in those eyes. I have no idea what it means exactly to follow him, but I extend my hand out as well.

I don't know where following this Rabbi will lead, I only know that I must follow where he guides me.

And so I rise. Not just from the dirt. Not just from the temple courtyard.

But from the life that nearly became my death.

Discussion Questions

1. According to Jewish law, it was not adultery for an unmarried woman to sleep with a man, though if the man was married, it was definitely viewed as morally wrong and was still prohibited. However, the one in the wrong would be the man, not the woman necessarily. If the woman was married, both would be considered guilty of adultery as it would not matter if the man was married or not, he was committing adultery with the woman regardless because she belonged to another man (it's a property issue). Which scenario do you think is most likely?

2. We hear Jesus say, "go and sin no more" all the time when we want to try and correct someone else's behavior, or in particular, their "lifestyle choices." Regardless of whether she was married to another man or if she was a prostitute, this woman's life was likely still in danger. So what might Jesus really be getting at?

3. The only other place Jesus tells someone to "sin no more" is with the man he heals, and he adds "so that something worse will not happen to you." We don't know what the man had been doing for Jesus to state that, but it might be safe to assume that Jesus' point was there were worse things than being crippled. That phrase is added here to this story as well (though it is not in the original Biblical text) as a caution to the woman that she is leading a dangerous life that could result in "something worse." What dangers do you think she might have faced?

4. The woman is used as bait to trap Jesus rather than being the true focus of justice. How does this reflect the way marginalized individuals are often exploited in larger power struggles?

5. Given the man is not present, what does this suggest about gender dynamics and accountability in the enforcement of laws and morality? What double-standards today continue to exist between men and women when it comes to sexual behavior?

6. If the woman was truly an adulteress and was a married woman, the law does indeed call for punishment. But Jesus still showed mercy rather than enforcing the law. How do justice and mercy interact and what lessons can be applied to modern life?

7. In this story, the woman winds up following Jesus (many since the sixth century conflate this story with Mary Magdalene when Pope Gregory the Great identified her as a prostitute, giving more credence to the idea that the woman in this story actually was a prostitute, but there's no evidence they are the same woman). What do you think might have really happened to her following this incident?

8. The woman's situation is used to try and discredit and trap Jesus. Can you think of modern examples where religious or political figures manipulate situations to undermine others? What parallels do you see?

Mary—The Magdalene

(*Matthew 27:56-28:11; Mark 15:40-16:9; Luke 8:2; 24:10; John 20:11-18*)

PRE-DAWN LIGHT IS JUST BEGINNING to illuminate the eastern skies as Mary shuffles her way out of the city gates of Jerusalem toward the tomb.

The tomb. The hole dug out of the rock face that lines the road leading into the city. She watched two nights earlier as the rock was rolled across the entrance with his beaten, bloodied, crucified body. There had been no time to properly prepare it before the sun went down for Sabbath. The body would surely stink by now, having spent an entire Sabbath day inside the tomb. The days had been warm, no doubt turning the rock into a near oven-like structure.

Still. He deserved a proper burial. He deserved something so much better than what he had received. Images of him hanging on that cross, crying out, will haunt her forever. Haunt her the same way the images of her own family hanging on similar crosses years earlier haunted her.

She'd watched them get crucified as well. Watched as the soldiers strung her father and brother and husband up on crosses and called them insurrectionists.

Watched and then suffered her own hell on earth. Until this man had saved her life.

Saved her from the voices that had screamed at her constantly, accused her, fought with her.

Now that he is gone…would the demons return? Would she go back to her life of squalor and anguish? Were the mental chains he had released fully released now that he is dead? Or would the torment begin anew? Does her grief and anguish open yet another window into her soul that will allow the dark thoughts and voices to enter once again?

Her breath catches slightly, stifling a sob as she trudges up the hill.

Is she prepared for this? Is she ready to see him again? She grips the jar of myrrh and spices in her hands tightly, holding them against her chest as she draws in a deep breath and lets it out slowly.

I can do this, she tells herself. She has to do this. She owes him this at least. Still, she'd been so certain that this was not how all of this was going to end. She'd stood and watched at the foot of the cross with his mother, confident even in her grief that somehow, he was going to survive this. That his angels would descend and lift him off that cross so that every eye could see what she saw, know what she knew.

But that hadn't happened. He'd died, just like every other human she cared about in her life had died.

They'd wrapped his body and placed it in the tomb and slid the large stone into place at the entrance.

As she crests the hill and can see in the dim morning light the outlines of the tomb, she stops dead in her tracks and blinks.

The stone they had rolled in front of it is…gone. The tomb lies vacant and empty.

Horror slowly dawns on her and threatens to overwhelm her as she stares in numb disbelief.

They've stolen his body. They've taken him and buried him…where?

She stands there a few moments and simply blinks before she drops the jar of burial spices and runs back the way she came.

Wild thoughts race through her mind as she runs back toward the city gates. They've taken even this from her. Taken her ability to give him a proper burial. Taken away her ability to have somewhere to come to mourn him in the months and years to come.

Rome did this. Rome…who has taken everything she's ever loved from her.

Rome. Will her mind be able to handle this latest violation? This latest blow to her already fragile psyche?

This isn't how this is supposed to end. She's not had enough time. She's only been free from her demons for a short time.

Not. Enough. Time.

As she runs back to find the other disciples, her memory of the first time she met him floods through her mind…

Her head was hurting again. It had been a particularly bad day as she sat inside the city gate, a filthy blanket, her only garment aside from the tattered shift beneath, wrapped around her shoulders. People walked by and would step wide to avoid getting too close as she muttered to herself, then suddenly would begin to slam her head against the wall. Sometimes, smashing her head against the stones made the voices stop for a while.

Sometimes.

She had wished for death. Death had to be better. The voices kept telling her that.

Surely in death she would no longer see the images of her husband and father, puffy and putrefying in the sun. Their cold, dead eyes sunken in their sockets but still somehow staring almost accusingly down at her; their tongues lolling swollen and purple out of their mouths; their arms strung out to either side and nailed to the crosses they hung from.

In death she would no longer feel her mother's blood slick and coppery against her hands as she lay dying in Mary's arms, a Roman spear through her midsection.

In death she would no longer feel the violation of her body as the soldiers had taken her, repeatedly. At times she could still smell their sour, hot breath against her face, feel the knee against the back of her neck, pinning her down to the ground and smashing her face into the floorboards. She could hear their laughs and jeers as they echoed through her memories.

In death she would not still smell the tiny cell she had been held captive in for weeks or possibly months—time had lost meaning inside those small, stone walls—that reeked heavily from her own urine and feces. Despite her attempts to keep her waste confined to a corner, the stench had continued to build, mingled with the subtle stink of decay from the molding straw that had covered the ground to serve as her bed, and the pungent odor of the bucket of vile putrid glop that was tossed into her cell for food.

In death she would no longer smell her daughter's stillborn corpse as it rotted in the cell with her before she was tossed back into the streets.

In death, everything that she had become would be wiped away, the accusatory voices would stop haunting and hounding her both waking and sleeping.

In death, she would not be scrambling across the ground trying to gobble up the small morsels of bread passersby would throw at her before some other homeless indigent. At least she still had the use of her legs, which was more than she could say for some of her gate-sitting companions.

Occasionally, someone would throw her a few coins that she would hoard so that on good days, when the voices didn't torment her as much, she could go inside the town and actually purchase fruit.

Such treks were always equally painful experiences. While the voices in her head may have momentarily paused their taunts, the disdainful looks of the people she had once called her neighbors and friends followed her wherever she went. Magdala was not a large city, so everyone knew everyone else. There was no anonymity in such a place.

Yet she would never forget that they had left her alone, outside the city gates, clawing her way through the mud, nearly starving and beaten to death, at the foot of her father and brother's and husband's crosses. Most had left her there to die. After all, her family had been convicted and sentenced to death as traitors against the Roman Empire. Traitors because a wall her husband had been working on fortifying at the fortress outside of Magdala had collapsed and killed several Roman soldiers. It had been an accident, but that didn't matter.

No one wanted to be seen with a traitor.

In the evenings, when the city gates were closed, she made her way to the home she had once shared with her husband, shared not only their lives but their dreams of a family. Dreams for the unborn child that she had still been carrying inside her when the Romans had come.

All that remained was a black, charred skeleton of a dwelling that had been torched and burned to the ground. She wasn't sure why she returned here night after night. The voices were worse here more than anywhere else.

This is all that's left of your life. Charred remains. Gone. All of it. Gone. No family. No husband. No baby. No friends. No life. You're a walking corpse, nothing more.

Yet every night she would sit down in the middle of the rubble, hoping that maybe she could just lie down here and die.

That afternoon, she wandered home early. Not for any particular reason, she just hadn't felt the need to stay until the gates closed. She saw a glint nearby, the late afternoon sun just catching the edge of something metallic. She crawled across the jagged debris and scraped away blackened dust to reveal what had once been her husband's dagger, the one he had used to skin animals. She held the gleaming blade in her hands almost reverently.

You cannot escape. Your death is near.

The voices hummed inside her brain, rising in a steady crescendo.

People walked by and stared as she sat in the middle of the burned down house holding the dagger. When they realized what she was holding, they hurried along quickly.

They all hate you. They all blame you. It's your fault.

What's my fault?

That they're all dead.

How is that my fault?

You didn't do enough to protect them. You couldn't even keep your own child inside of you safe. You didn't warn your parents fast enough. You hesitated. You didn't demand your husband flee with you. You're a failure. You're filthy. You're an outcast. You're better off dead. Just take that dagger and stab yourself.

"NO!" she screamed aloud and threw the dagger, garnering stares from passersby who hastened their steps.

No? NO? You can't even do that right can you!

The voices started laughing at her. She covered her ears with her hands and squeezed her eyes shut as she shook her head, trying to make the laughter go away. But they only got louder and louder. First cackling, then roaring.

"Fine!" she yelled at last and scrambled over to where she had tossed the dagger. Picking it up the voices again shifted. The laughter died down, replaced again by the taunting.

Do it. Slice your wrists. Plunge the blade into your bowels. Your neck, your heart. Join your husband. Join your daughter. Join us all in death's eternal dance.

The cackling, taunting laughter began again. She raised the blade before her, taking deep breaths, her hands shaking, tears flowing from her eyes.

"Mary. Stop."

She had paused, blinking. *Don't listen. He only wants to prolong your agony.*

"Mary. Come to me."

Blinking through the haze of pain and tears, she saw someone standing before her, his hand outstretched. She no more believed he was anything more than a figment of her imagination than anyone else she imagined talking to her. That didn't matter though. She spoke to them, she'd speak to him.

"Why?" she whispered. "I want to end the torment."

The man took a step toward her, grasping her hand. It was as though a bolt of lightning shot through her, and the voices in her head howled with anger.

The man said something more, though she couldn't make it out through the cacophony of shrieks and howls that now assailed her senses. She crumpled to the ground, writhing in pain and agony.

Nooooooo! she could hear them howling. *NOOOOOO! SHE'S OURS! WE WON'T LET GO! NOOOOOOO!*...and then suddenly...silence.

Her body heaved as she gulped in air and curled up into the fetal position, just waiting for the voices to attack her again.

Suddenly, after several moments, the silence remained. There was nothing.

Cautiously, she opened her eyes, confused as to where she was and what she was doing.

The man she had seen remained, however, and knelt down next to her and helped her sit up.

"You're...you're real?" she croaked through her dry throat, as she hadn't truly spoken except in grunts and screams for some time. Her voice sounded strange in her own ears.

"What...what happened?" she asked, looking around, bewildered.

"Do you feel better?" the man asked.

Mary nodded, frowning. They were gone. The voices were completely silent now, not even sitting in the back of her mind threatening to overwhelm her anymore.

She looked up in awe at the man before her. "Yes," she said softly. "How did you...?" She stared into his dark eyes, which were filled with kindness and compassion. He smiled gently and helped her to her feet, which is when she realized all she was wearing was a filthy blanket. She held the edges tight around her shoulders.

As she gazed around the burned out house she realized not only were the voices gone, the pain was gone as well. The sharp stabbing pain that cut its way through her brain on a regular basis was just suddenly...gone.

Then she felt it. A sudden wave of grief that threatened to over-power her. She bent over and vomited. The man did not shy away. Instead he reached out and gently held her arm, and the wave of nausea seemed to abate. Even the intense grief and pain that she had been forced to bury for the past weeks and months seemed to dissipate as quickly as it had risen.

"I...I was ready to die. You...you saved me," she finally said, looking up at him.

He nodded and Mary resisted the urge to throw her arms around him.

"What happened was not your fault, you know," he said after a moment. "None of this—your father, husband, mother, child—none of it was your fault."

"Then whose fault was it?" Mary demanded, tears welling in her eyes.

The man shrugged and let out a sad sigh. "It is the fault of many. But not yours. I have relieved you of your demons."

She stared at him in wonder and awe. He wasn't one of the towns-people. She'd have remembered him. Yet, he seemed familiar. Like she knew him even though she also knew she had never met him before.

"But...how...?" she began, still bewildered. "I mean...who are you?"

The smile returned as he held out his hand. "I am the way. Come, follow me now."

She tentatively accepted his outstretched hand and followed him through the streets of Magdala, despite his strange and enigmatic response. Twilight had fallen and they hurried toward the gates of the city before they closed. He led her to a small encampment outside the town where a group of men and women sat around a small campfire.

One of them, a gruff looking fisherman—he had to be a fisherman, she had grown up in a fishing village and spent all of her time around them—stood and appeared both relieved and annoyed. "I really wish you would tell us when you're just going to disappear like that," he grumbled.

The man beside her smiled and chuckled. "Then how would you learn faith and trust?" he answered enigmatically. Then he turned to Mary and pulled her forward.

"This is Mary. She's going to be one of us from now on. Though, if your wife could see to maybe helping clean her up a bit. She's had a rough go of it for some time, I'm afraid."

A woman who had also been sitting near the fire stood and wrapped an arm around her. Like the man, she didn't shy away from the stench and filth that coated Mary. "You dear thing. Come, let's clean you up. It's all right. I promise, you're safe now. Everything will be fine."

Mary reluctantly released the man's hand and allowed the woman to guide her away.

"Who…who is he?" Mary asked once they were out of earshot from the men.

The woman's eyes twinkled with excitement. "That? That is Jesus of Nazareth."

"Who?" Mary looked confused. This woman seemed to think she should know who he was or that she should have heard of him. Nazareth was a nearby town so perhaps the name should be familiar.

"Jesus of Nazareth," she repeated. "My husband, Peter, thinks he's the messiah." The other woman lowered her voice as she continued: "And from everything I've seen thus far, I think he's right."

"The messiah?" Mary's eyes widened in surprise. And yet…the moment the other woman said it, she knew it to be true. No one could have done what he had done. No one but God.

Mary shook her head. "No…he's more than the messiah. So much more."

So much more.

Those words echo in her mind as she now stands before the empty tomb. She slides down outside of it and begins to finally sob. The tears that she has not allowed herself to shed finally come. Peter and the others—they rushed to the tomb when she ran and told them that their Lord was gone. Came, saw, and left.

But she remains. She still sits here, outside the tomb. Sobbing. Grief wracks her body as she tries to comprehend this new horror being inflicted upon her. She glances into the empty tomb once again and…her breath catches.

The tomb is not empty. Two men are standing there in white robes that seem to gleam and shimmer in the morning light. Angry, she stands. How dare these men desecrate this tomb like this!

As she stands, ready to speak, one of them turns and gazes at her with golden eyes. Golden eyes.

She pauses. Who are these men?

"Mary, why are you crying?" the first one asks. She blinks in disbelief for a moment before responding.

"They…they have taken my Lord away and I don't know where they have laid him!" she wails louder than she intended, hysteria threatening to overwhelm her as she turns, ready to run again when she sees another man who was more plainly dressed, like a gardener. She stops short and gasps. There is something…familiar about him. But terror seizes her.

Like the men in the tomb, he gazes calmly at her and asks, "Why are you weeping? Whom are you looking for?"

Anger now bubbles up inside of her. Why do people keep asking her that stupid question? She is standing outside a tomb. Why do they think she is weeping? They surely know whose tomb this is… was.

Taking a deep breath, she tries to stamp her anger down. She still feels they were solely being rude and toying with her, so her voice shakes as she demands, "You're the gardener here. You tend to these tombs. Tell me what you have done with him! Where have you laid him? I must go retrieve him!" Hysteria nearly overtakes her trembling voice.

For a long moment, the man says nothing, just stares at her curiously. Angrily she turns aside and tries to move past him. If he won't answer that simple question…

"Mary…" She stops. That voice. She knows that voice! Could it be…? No, that's impossible.

She whirls around, her eyes wide in disbelief. But…it is him! How… how had she not recognized him! *Because you thought he was dead,* she reasons with herself. *Why would you think he was wandering around tending to the garden when he's dead?*

And he is dead. She'd watched him die. Yet here he is! Standing in front of her. She could not deny what her eyes were showing her. Tears spring to her eyes. Tears of joy this time as she moves to fling her arms around him as she cries, "Rabbi!"

But he holds a hand up, stopping her from embracing him. "Do not touch me, Mary. For I have not yet ascended. Go to my brothers and say to them, 'I am ascending to my God and your God.'"

She pauses, trying to absorb it all. But then, as suddenly as he had just appeared before her, he vanishes. She blinks. Did she really see him? Really talk to him? Was he just an apparition?

She shakes her head and turns back toward the tomb where the two men...angels?...had been standing. They, too, have vanished. She frowns.

Is it the demons? Have they come back and are making me see things? she wonders. Peter and the rest...will they believe her or think that her psyche has broken again?

Well, she'd been right about the empty tomb, and they'd verified that. Maybe they would believe her this time?

She shakes her head. Would she believe her? Not likely.

"Go, Mary."

Startled, she whirls around, hearing the Rabbi's voice again, but this time, sees nothing. Frightened, but somehow also joyful and hopeful, she takes off running once again toward the city gate. Back to once again tell Peter and the others the good news.

Discussion Questions

1. How does Mary's past suffering—including her demonic possession—influence her faith?

2. Mary expected Jesus to miraculously save himself from death. How does her initial reaction to the empty tomb reflect the struggle between human expectation and divine reality?

3. Why do you think Mary is the first person Jesus appeared to after his resurrection? What does this say about her significance and role in Jesus' ministry?

4. Unlike Peter and the others who left the tomb, Mary stayed and wept. What does her persistence teach us about faith and devotion?

5. Mary did not immediately recognize Jesus (nor do the disciples on the road to Emmaus in Luke's gospel). Why do you think that is? What does this tell us about how we sometimes struggle to recognize God's presence in our own lives?

6. Why do you think Jesus told Mary not to touch him because he had not yet ascended? How does this moment shape our understanding of Jesus' resurrection and ascension compared to how he later invites Thomas to touch him? (Both accounts are part of John's Gospel.)

7. How do you think Mary's encounter with the risen Christ transformed her mission and identity? How might it have redefined her role among the disciples?

Lydia

(Acts 16:11-40)

A LOUD POUNDING noise jolted me awake. I sat up in my bed, disoriented, the light of the moon spilling through the window. My mind raced. Was something wrong? Another riot in the city? I grabbed a shawl, wrapping it tightly around me as the knocking came again, more urgent this time.

I hurried to the door, my bare feet cold against the tiled floor. Other than the intermittent pounding, the house was quiet, the servants still asleep in their quarters. As I reached the heavy wooden door, I heard a familiar voice call out softly, "Lydia, it's us."

I unbolted the door and pulled it open. There stood Paul and Silas, both looking like they'd wrestled with a pack of wild dogs—and lost. Their clothes were torn, their faces bruised, and Silas was limping slightly. Paul's tunic was streaked with blood and dirt, and his usually confident stance sagged with exhaustion.

"God Almighty," I breathed. "What happened to you two?"

"Good evening to you, too," Paul said, his voice dry. "Would you believe we had a little misunderstanding with the local authorities?"

"A misunderstanding?" I said, arching an eyebrow. "You look like you've been flogged."

"Ah," Silas said with a wince as he stepped past me into the house. "You're quick. That's exactly what happened."

I rolled my eyes, motioning them inside. "Come in before someone sees you. I'm already housing a church the authorities are suspicious of; I don't need to be accused of harboring fugitives," I said, glancing furtively into the street in front of my home, looking for signs that someone might be spying from the shadows.

Paul gave me a wry smile as he crossed the threshold. "We were released, actually. Not fugitives. Just…battered."

"Semantics," I muttered, closing the door behind them. "Sit down before you fall down. I'll fetch some water."

My home wasn't modest by any means. As a successful merchant in purple cloth, I'd built a house that could accommodate both my business and my newfound role in the church. The main hall was spacious, with polished wooden beams and a long table that could seat a dozen people. On most days, it was filled with laughter, prayers, and the clatter of shared meals. Tonight, it felt far too quiet as Paul and Silas collapsed onto the cushioned benches by the hearth.

I returned with a basin of water and clean cloths, setting them down on the table. "All right," I said, hands on my hips. "Explain. And don't leave out the part where you managed to get yourselves arrested and beaten half to death."

Paul leaned his head back against the wall, sighing. "We were preaching—peacefully, I might add—when a group stirred up trouble. They dragged us before the magistrates, accused us of all sorts of nonsense. Next thing we knew, we were stripped, beaten with rods, and thrown into the inner cell of the prison."

"And you just sat there?" I asked, dipping a cloth into the water and handing it to Silas, who grimaced as he began cleaning the cut on his cheek.

"We prayed," Silas said simply, his voice calm despite the bruises. "And sang hymns."

I stared at him. "You sang? While locked in stocks?"

Paul's lips quirked into a faint smile. "It seemed appropriate at the time."

"Appropriate," I repeated, shaking my head and rolling my eyes in exasperation. "I'll never understand you."

"The other prisoners appreciated it," Silas added with a weak grin. "And then there was the earthquake."

I paused mid-step. "The what?"

Paul straightened slightly, the firelight flickering across his battered face. "An earthquake shook the prison. The doors flew open, and our chains fell off. The jailer thought we'd escaped and was ready to kill himself."

"But of course you didn't escape," I said, giving him a pointed look. "Because that would've been too simple."

He smiled faintly. "No. We stayed. The jailer ended up asking how he could be saved, and his whole household was baptized that night."

I sank into the chair across from them, staring at the two of them in disbelief. "You two are either the most stubborn men I've met, or the most faithful. I'm leaning toward stubborn."

"Why not both?" Silas said, wincing as he shifted his weight.

I sighed, standing again to fetch more bandages. "You're lucky the Lord clearly loves you. Otherwise, you'd be dead by now."

Paul chuckled, though it sounded more like a groan. "We don't deserve any of it, Lydia. But here we are."

"Here you are indeed," I said, glancing back at them. "And now, you're under my roof again. Which means I'm responsible for keeping you alive. Try not to make it harder than it already is."

Paul nodded, his smile softening. "We'll try, Lydia. Thank you—for everything."

I shook my head as I wrung out a cloth. "Don't thank me yet. Wait until you see what I make you eat in the morning."

For a moment, the three of us laughed, a brief reprieve from the weight of their suffering. Even in their pain, they carried themselves with a faith that steadied me, and as I tended to their wounds, I felt a deep sense of gratitude that they had been brought to my doorstep once again.

I honestly hadn't believed I would ever see either of them again after our first meeting a few months earlier on the banks of the river just outside of the city of Philippi.

The sun had been warm that Sabbath morning as it filtered through the trees lining the riverbank. The air carried the scent of wild-flowers and fresh water, mingling with the hum of insects and the murmur of the stream. It was a quiet place, away from the bustling Roman colony, where my little group of women gathered each week to pray and reflect on the Scriptures.

We had been seated in a circle on smooth stones, our heads bent in prayer, when I heard the rustling of footsteps approaching. Opening my eyes, I looked up to see four men coming toward us. They weren't locals—that much was clear from their worn traveling cloaks and the way their eyes scanned the area as though looking for someone specific. The leader, a man with a commanding presence, a balding head with a small circlet of graying, short-cropped curly hair forming soft tufts around the crown of his head, but kind eyes, stopped a few paces away, clearly surprised to find us.

"Good morning," I called out, breaking the silence. "Are you lost?"

The man hesitated, then stepped forward. "Not lost, no," he said. "We were told there's a place of prayer outside the city. I didn't expect..."

"A group of women?" I finished for him, arching an eyebrow.

He eyed me curiously, but with a hint of amusement. I found myself blushing slightly at my directness. I was used to working with men as a merchant, and I forgot that my forthrightness sometimes caught other men by surprise.

His companion, a younger man, with a taller, broader, sturdier build, but with a friendly face, stifled a laugh. "Paul thought he'd find a synagogue full of men debating theology."

Paul shot him a look but didn't deny it. "We've traveled a long way," he said, his voice calm but firm. "I had a vision—of a man from Macedonia, calling for help."

"Well, I hate to disappoint you," I said, motioning to the women around me, "but we're the only ones praying out here. Unless your Macedonian man is hiding in the bushes, I think you've found us instead. And...we are most definitely not in need of any help."

That earned me a small smile, though he quickly composed himself. "Then perhaps God has a different purpose for us being here."

I gestured for them to sit. "Come, tell us about this vision. You've piqued my curiosity."

The men settled on the stones across from us, and Paul introduced himself and his companions—Silas, Timothy, and Luke. He began to speak, explaining how they had been traveling through the region, preaching about Jesus of Nazareth, the Messiah who fulfilled the Hebrew Scriptures.

As he spoke, I studied him. He wasn't what I expected in a preacher —his manner was straightforward, almost blunt, but his words carried a conviction that was hard to ignore. He spoke of Jesus with such clarity and passion that I found myself leaning closer, hanging on his every word. His most striking feature, I noticed, were his eyes.

They were intense and piercing, dark with an almost burning focus, as though he was always pondering the next argument or sermon. His complexion was a dark olive tone, tanned and weathered from his journeys under the Mediterranean sun.

As he continued to speak, I turned my attention momentarily to his companions. The other one who had spoken—Silas—whose complexion was considerably lighter than that of Paul's, was clearly much younger. His hair was thick, dark and wavy, often falling into his eyes, which he pushed back with a hand regularly out of seeming habit. His beard was fuller than Paul's slightly untamed and he carried himself with a laid-back confidence that contrasted Paul's intensity. His soft brown eyes glimmered with humor, and when he moved, he moved with the ease of someone who was used to carrying heavy loads—both physically and emotionally.

"You're saying this Jesus is the fulfillment of everything the prophets spoke about?" I asked, turning my attention back to Paul and interrupting him mid-sentence.

Paul paused, his expression unreadable. "Yes," he said simply. "He is the Messiah, sent to reconcile us to God. Through Him, all—Jew and Gentile alike—are welcomed into the family of God."

"Even us?" I asked, gesturing to myself and the other women. "Even Gentile women who've spent their lives on the fringes of the faith?"

He met my gaze, his voice steady. "Especially you. In Christ, there is no Jew or Gentile, no male or female. You are all one in Him."

The words struck me like a bolt of lightning. I had always believed in the God of Israel, even as a Gentile woman from Thyatira, but there had always been a distance—a sense that I could only come so close. Now, here was a man telling me that the Messiah himself had made a way for me to be fully accepted, fully known.

I stared at him in suspicion. "You'd better explain that in more detail," I said, narrowing my eyes.

Paul smiled then—a real smile, warm and genuine. "I think you're ready to hear more."

Later, as we walked together along the riverbank, I shared my story with him. I told him how I had come to Philippi from Thyatira, a city known for its trade in purple dye. My family had been in the dye business for generations, and I had taken over after my father's death. But Thyatira was a city of idols, steeped in pagan practices, and I had always felt out of place there. Plus, to be a merchant in Thyatira, you had to join one of the trade guilds—which required making sacrifices and paying tribute to the Nona, the patron goddess of textiles.

When I heard there was a market for purple cloth in Philippi, I saw an opportunity to start fresh.

"Business brought me here," I admitted, "but faith is what keeps me here. I longed for a place where I could worship the one true God without compromise. This little group of women—you wouldn't think much of us, but it's been my refuge."

Paul nodded thoughtfully. "It seems God brought you here for more than business. He brought you here to prepare for today."

I glanced at him, skeptical. "You're sure of that?"

"Absolutely," he said without hesitation. "And judging by the way you've been asking questions, I'd say He's been preparing your heart for a long time."

I laughed, shaking my head. "You're an odd man, Paul."

He grinned. "I've been called worse."

Paul baptized me and my household soon after, and I insisted they stay at my home. My life, once centered on the trade of purple cloth, soon would revolve around something far greater: the growing church in Philippi, born that day by the riverside.

Now, as I tended to their wounds, I felt a sense of melancholy. I realized with some alarm that I deeply enjoyed Paul's company, but I knew he was married to his mission. He wasn't a man who lingered —his heart was always on the road, drawn to the next city, the next soul, the next church.

Silas winced as I wrapped a clean bandage around his arm. "You're too good to us, Lydia," he said, offering me a tired but genuine smile. "You should've thrown us back out and told us to fend for ourselves."

I smirked as I tied off the bandage. "Oh, don't tempt me, Silas. If I weren't so worried you'd bleed all over my doorstep, I might've considered it."

Paul chuckled, the sound low and rough from exhaustion. "You're too practical for that, Lydia. Besides, you'd miss us."

"Miss you?" I said, raising an eyebrow. "I'd finally have some peace and quiet."

Silas laughed, though he winced again, clutching his ribs. "Peace and quiet? You're running a church out of this house. Don't tell me you've forgotten what that means."

I sighed, shaking my head. "Fair point. Between the endless questions, the arguments over Scripture, and the children running underfoot, quiet is a luxury I haven't had in months. And now here you are, adding your bruises and battered pride to the chaos."

Paul smiled faintly, leaning forward on the bench. "Chaos is the price of the gospel, Lydia. You've been paying it since the day we met."

I looked at him then, my hands stilling as I met his gaze. His eyes, despite their weariness, held that same intensity I'd seen the first day by the river—the conviction that had turned my life upside down.

"I don't mind the cost," I said softly. "I just…" I hesitated, unsure how to put my thoughts into words.

Paul tilted his head, watching me carefully. "You just what?"

I shrugged, forcing a smile. "I just wish the price didn't include seeing you and Silas half-dead on my doorstep."

He smiled faintly. "We're still here, Lydia. And we'll keep coming back as long as the Lord allows."

I nodded, though the knot in my chest didn't loosen. I knew what he meant, but I also knew it wouldn't be forever. Men like Paul weren't meant to stay in one place. His calling was greater than Philippi—greater than anything I could offer.

I busied myself with cleaning up the bloodied rags and empty basin, needing a distraction. "Well," I said briskly, "if you're going to keep coming back, you'll need to stop making such dramatic entrances. Next time, try walking in during daylight hours, preferably without the bruises."

Paul chuckled again, leaning back against the wall. "I'll see what I can do."

Silas stretched, wincing as he moved. "Speaking of daylight, we should probably try to sleep before it gets here."

"You should've done that in the prison instead of singing," I said, smirking as I carried the basin to the kitchen.

Paul gave me a look that was almost grateful when I returned. "Thank you, Lydia," he said softly. "For everything."

I nodded, my voice catching slightly as I replied. "You're welcome. Now, get some rest."

As I walked away to prepare their sleeping arrangements, I couldn't help but glance back at them. Despite their pain and weariness, they radiated a quiet strength, a deep sense of purpose that inspired everyone around them—including me.

And though I knew they wouldn't stay, that Paul's path would eventually lead him far from here, I decided not to dwell on it. For tonight, they were here. They were safe. And that was enough.

Discussion Questions

1. Lydia welcomes Paul and Silas into her home despite the danger. What does this say about her faith and courage? How can we apply this kind of bold hospitality in our own lives?

2. Lydia was a significant female leader in the early church. What does her story reveal about the role of women in spreading the gospel? How does her leadership compare to the expectations of women both in that time and in our own?

3. Paul originally had a vision of a Macedonian man, but instead he meets Lydia and her group of women. What does this tell us about human expectations? Would Paul have been moved to find a group of women?

4. Lydia comes to faith through asking questions and being curious. What role does curiosity play in spiritual growth?

5. Lydia's home becomes a center for the new church and she risks her reputation and safety. What sacrifices might we be called to make for the sake of our faith?

6. Paul tells Lydia in this story (which he writes down in reality in his letter to the Galatians) that there is no distinction between Jew and Gentile, male and female. How does this truth challenge cultural and societal divisions today?

7. How do Lydia, Paul and Silas support each other in this story? What can we learn about the importance of community in our own spiritual lives?

Priscilla

(Acts 18; Romans 16:3; 1 Corinthians 16:19; 2 Timothy 4:19)

IT WAS hard to know what time it was exactly, but the damp caverns of the catacombs had fallen silent except for the sound of breathing and snoring from the other followers who were in hiding. Carefully, Priscilla slipped out from under the blanket she had been sharing with her husband, Aquila, wrapping her cloak tightly around her shoulders, the fabric absorbing the chill of the subterranean air. A single oil lamp flickered nearby, casting gentle shadows on the earthen walls, creating a fragile sense of peace in their hidden refuge.

Aquila grunted and rolled over in his sleep, immediately falling back into his gentle, soft, rhythmic snoring. She whispered a silent prayer before gingerly tip-toeing her way through the narrow labyrinth of passages. Moving swiftly, but silently, mindful of every step, her sandals made almost no sound on the cold stone floor. As she expertly wove her way through the intricate network of tunnels, she tried to ignore the strong scent of earth and decay—a constant reminder of the catacombs' primary purpose as a burial site.

Reaching a concealed exit known only to the leaders of their community, she pushed aside a cleverly disguised stone and slipped through the narrow opening.

Emerging into the cool night air, the city of Rome lay relatively silent, the rain from earlier in the day driving everyone indoors. The rain had stopped for the moment, however, and a pale full moon was peeking out from behind the cloud cover, the streets glistening with moisture. As she walked, her sandals splashed lightly in the puddles that dotted the cobblestone streets.

She glanced up toward the majestic Palatine Hill, shivering slightly as its silhouette loomed darkly against the moonlit sky. It contained the homes of Rome's elite. Emperor Nero himself resided some-where on that hill in all his pomposity and cruelty. The remnants of rain clung to the lush greenery, glistening in the torch light from the lamps that lined the winding streets. The hill seemed almost other-worldly in the quiet of the late night.

While she knew it was simply her imagination, she could almost feel tendrils of oppressive evil reaching out of the darkness from those homes toward her. She quickened her step and hurried down the hill toward the Roman Forum. The Forum, usually teeming with life and activity, was eerily serene. The grand temples stood silent, their columns and arches slick with rainwater, reflecting the burgeoning light of dawn. As she passed the imposing Temple of Saturn, she marveled at the juxtaposition of the imposing structures and her own, humble mission.

Priscilla paused briefly at the edge of the Forum, gazing in both awe and horror at the massive Colosseum with its towering arches and intricate stonework. She contemplated the countless spectacles of violence and triumph that had played out within its walls—spectacles she herself had sat in the stands and cheered on prior to their expul-sion by emperor Claudius nearly twenty years earlier. Bloody gladia-tors, deadly chariot races, wild animals ripping slaves apart all for the entertainment of Rome's citizens. The structure stood as a stark reminder of Rome's power and the often harsh reality of its rule.

Leaving the Colosseum behind, she made her way towards the Mamertine Prison, nestled in the heart of the city. As she drew closer, the streets narrowed and the buildings became more imposing, their shadows long and foreboding in the dim light. The prison itself was a grim structure, its walls thick and unyielding, designed to contain those deemed a threat to the empire.

A threat to the empire.

She almost wanted to laugh at the absurdity of the Imperial forces counting the man she was on her way to see being considered a threat to Rome's power and might.

Priscilla's heart quickened as she approached the entrance. As she drew near, two other forms stepped out of the shadows and startled her, grabbing her and dragging her off the street. She stifled a scream as the two cloaked figures removed their hoods. She breathed a sigh of relief as she recognized the stern, angry faces of Phoebe and Junia, two women she had met while living in Corinth and had returned to Rome with almost a year earlier.

"You nearly scared me to death!" she hissed at them, trying to calm her now racing heart.

Phoebe's glower only deepened, unimpressed and unsympathetic. "What do you think you're doing?" she hissed back. "Wandering the streets of Rome this early in the morning?"

She folded her arms across her bosom, cocking her head to one side as she regarded the other two women. "I might ask you the same thing."

"We saw you slip out and followed you until we realized where you were headed." Phoebe gestured toward the prison at the foot of Capitoline Hill.

"Are you mad?" Junia demanded.

Priscilla set her jaw and straightened her back in defiance, though even she had to agree that perhaps her mission was folly. She relaxed slightly after her moment of bristling, lowering her arms as she sighed.

"I know one of the guards," she said at last. "He said he'd let me in to see him."

Junia and Phoebe's eyes widened in surprise.

"I...I wanted to see him one last time before...before they took him to the Circus for execution." She choked on that last word, still hardly believing it. Though, she did believe it. She had seen so many of her brothers and sisters in the faith brought into the Circus to either be beheaded or torn apart by wild animals. Or hung on crosses and set on fire throughout the city. Of course, the last time that happened it had resulted in a large part of the city actually catching on fire, thus only adding to their persecution as Nero had then blamed the fire on them. Technically, he was correct. Their burning bodies had started the fire. Rome had become a very dangerous place for Followers of the Way to live in recent months. Hence why they had been hiding out in the catacombs, thus far undetected by the Roman guards. Why on earth Paul had demanded an audience before the emperor was still a mystery to the community in Rome.

The other two women's eyes softened, and even glistened slightly with tears of their own. They had all seen too many horrors of late.

"How do you know this guard?" Junia demanded, though the anger had diminished from her voice.

"He's...an old friend," she said cautiously.

Phoebe raised a curious eyebrow while Junia scowled.

"Not like that," she said, exasperated. "I'm a married woman. He's a childhood friend who has been...curious...about The Way."

Phoebe and Junia exchanged a skeptical glance and Priscilla resisted the urge to roll her eyes in annoyance. She absolutely understood their concern. A Roman guard who was cozying up to one of the primary leaders of their movement might not have the best of intentions. A spy for Nero, possibly trying to find out the location of their hideout. Priscilla might unknowingly lead them right back to the catacombs.

"One of us should go with you," Junia said at last. Priscilla frowned. "Guards are rarely on duty alone," she continued. "Your friend's... friend...might need some distracting."

Priscilla hadn't thought about that. She had simply assumed that Gaius would figure a way around the other guard on duty. Reluctantly, she nodded, biting her lower lip and hoping this wouldn't mess up whatever story or plan Gaius had concocted to get her inside the prison. But she knew that look on Junia's face. She either let her come with her, or she wouldn't allow her to go at all.

"I'll stay back here in the shadows and watch to make sure you come back," Phoebe stated.

The two women quietly made their way toward the prison entrance where one of the guards, clad in his armor and helmet, watched her with a mixture of curiosity and suspicion.

Priscilla smiled as she stepped toward him, batting her eyelashes under her cloak.

"I'm here to see Gaius," she said, flashing her sweetest smile. His eyes narrowed with skepticism, then glanced at Junia.

"You both here to see Gaius?" he asked after a moment. Priscilla started to open her mouth, but Junia stepped forward, lowering the hood of her cloak and shaking out her long mane of thick, curly black hair, traced a finger along his armor.

"Oh no, Prissy here is for Gaius. I'm here for you." She smiled coyly.

Priscilla blinked in astonishment, her jaw dropping open momentarily before she snapped it shut again. Junia was a strikingly beautiful woman, compared to Priscilla's understated plainness. She wasn't ugly, but next to Junia's dark Greek features, her own wavy chestnut hair and relatively flat chest seemed underwhelming.

The other woman's voice dropped as she continued. "It's rather chilly out here tonight. Wouldn't you like to tell me more about some of your duties? I've always found the lives of soldiers fascinating!"

The guard's suspicion faltered as he gazed at Junia.

At that moment, Gaius appeared and the other guard stepped back and to attention. Gaius frowned slightly at the guard and then over at the two women. His eyes flickered with recognition as he saw Priscilla, but looked questioningly at Junia.

"Go on my sister," Junia said in a throaty voice. "You take care of him and I'll...entertain this big guy."

The guard glanced fearfully at Gaius, who relaxed visibly as he realized the ploy. Priscilla let out a slight sigh as she knew the look on his face. He was going to play along.

The corners of his lips quirked up in a crooked smile and he nodded toward the other man. "Consider this on me," Gaius stated, nodding toward Junia. He grabbed Priscilla's hand and led her past the heavy iron gate that led into the entrance of the prison.

The stench of the prison hit her immediately, a rancid mixture of sweat, filth, and despair. She steeled herself as the gate shut behind them. She could still hear Junia cooing with the guard.

"We don't have long," Gaius whispered, glancing back at the two. "Though, that was brilliant bringing your friend along. Much better than the story I was concocting. But I assume she doesn't want to have to actually...you know..." He let the thought trail off.

Priscilla's eyes widened. "Oh, definitely not!" she agreed. He opened a heavy wooden door and led her through it into the upper level of the prison that was clearly some sort of holding area. The heavy door groaned as it closed behind them, sealing off the outside world. The transition from the cool night air to the oppressive atmosphere of the prison was immediate and jarring.

The holding area was a stark contrast to the streets outside. Rough-hewn stone walls surrounded them, and narrow slit-like windows allowed only sparse shafts of moonlight. The stench she'd caught only a whiff of a few moments earlier now assaulted her nostrils. The air was thick with the smell of mildew, sweat, unwashed bodies, and, of course, excrement. The flickering light of torches mounted on the walls cast eerie shadows, making the space feel both confined and foreboding.

She followed Gaius down a long, narrow corridor; the uneven smooth stones beneath her feet nearly causing her to trip. The murmur of voices and the clanking of chains echoed through the hall, creating a haunting symphony that reverberated through the air.

At the end of the corridor was another large, heavy iron door. Inserting a large key in the lock, the door swung open with a loud creak, revealing a steep, winding staircase descending into the darkness.

"This way," Gaius murmured, his voice low and somber.

Taking a deep breath and nearly gagging from the odor of human filth, she began her descent down the narrow steps that were slick with moisture. The deeper they went, the colder, darker, and damper it became.

The stairwell finally ended with a small landing where yet another iron door stood open and the stepped into the dungeon-like lower level of the prison. Like the catacombs she had been living in the past few months, the prison was a labyrinth of narrow passageways and cramped cells, each one a stark reminder of the harsh conditions faced by its inhabitants. The walls, rough and unyielding, were covered in grime and mold. The floor was damp and uneven, with puddles of stagnant water reflecting in the flickering torchlight.

Low moans echoed throughout the subterranean chamber, along with the faint sounds of chains clinking as people shifted restlessly. She shivered at the sound of the occasional wail of suffering and desperation. She tried hard not to glare at Gaius, silently wondering how he could stomach holding his fellow human beings in conditions such as these.

Now was not the time to judge him, she recognized, and yet…how did one just ignore the palpable sights, sounds and smells of such desperate human suffering? How did you witness this inhumane treatment of your fellow human beings and continue to live with yourself? What sort of depraved indifference did one have to adopt in order to not go mad?

He led her through a series of winding passages. Each turn took them deeper into the bowels of the prison, the sense of isolation and despair growing with every step.

She wanted to weep as she thought of Paul locked away down here in the midst of all of this filth and decay. Finally, they reached a small cell at the end of a particularly dark corridor. Gauis paused, his hand resting on the door's heavy lock as he turned toward her.

"Why would you risk this?" he asked suddenly.

She blinked at him in confusion. "Risk what?" she asked.

"Risk getting caught and sent down here yourself?" he asked. "Just to see a condemned man before he dies?"

Priscilla's face relaxed into a gentle smile. "Would you want to see a kind face before you were executed?" she asked simply.

He stared at her for a long moment, before inserting his key into the locked cell door and swinging it open. She looked past him and stifled a gasp as the man in the room turned his grizzled features upon her.

She barely recognized the once confident, brash preacher who had so boldly taught them and led them at Corinth. The bald man before her was stooped, his long beard now a tangled mess of knots, his frame so thin that the filthy, tattered, feces-covered tunic hung loose on his nearly skeletal frame.

But those eyes. Those dark piercing eyes hadn't lost any of their sharpness. His body may have been beaten and seen better days, but those eyes were still alert as she remembered. Seeing her, a smile broke out across his sunken, dirt-covered features, and he tried to stand, though the shackles prevented his ability to even stand fully next to the bench he'd been sitting on.

"Make it fast," Gaius said in a low voice, and stepped away from the door to give them a moment of privacy.

"I had hoped that when I saw you again, it would be so that I could work alongside you and Aquila again here in Rome," he chuckled sitting back down on the bench rather than fighting against the chains that bound him.

"Things have changed since you sent us here," she said, glancing warily around the cell, fighting off a shiver. "We have been forced into the catacombs, living off the kindness of those who are able to move about Rome more freely than many of us."

Paul's eyes narrowed slightly as he regarded her. "Where…where is Aquila?"

"He's back in our hideout. Sleeping. He'd have…never let me come if he knew I was doing this."

Paul raised a curious eyebrow, the familiar glint of mischief twinkled briefly.

"Junia and Phoebe came with me," she continued.

The glint died and his shoulders sagged as he shook his head. "I don't wish any of you to watch my demise."

Priscilla shook her head sadly. "Why, Paul? Why on earth did you demand an audience with the emperor?"

A wry smile returned to his lips as he shook his head and rolled his eyes slightly. "Pride goeth before a fall," he muttered. "You know how I can get sometimes when I'm arguing, and I let my mouth get ahead of my brain. I threw my Roman citizenry around a little too boldly, I'm afraid. Governor Felix would have let me go but I went and opened my big mouth...which of course is now leading to my death. The emperor is far less concerned about whether or not I pose any sort of actual danger and whether or not he can make an example out of me as one of the primary leaders of The Way."

"Aren't you afraid that your execution will lead to the end of all of us? The end of the movement?" she asked.

Paul scoffed. "Hardly. I have done the work I was tasked with. What has begun cannot be stopped. Rome will see that one day. That fire will not be quenched, no matter how many of us he kills...or burns."

Priscilla stepped forward, producing a scroll of papyrus from the folds of her cloak. "I...I've written something, and I wanted to know your thoughts on it."

Paul raised a curious eyebrow, and extended his hand as far as he could as Priscilla slipped the scroll into them.

"You taught me so much about how Jesus is truly the embodiment of the Holy Temple that I thought it might be helpful to draw some of those correlations, how he's our High Priest, the Curtain, and the sacrifice all rolled into one. How we all, even us women, can now enter into the Holy Presence."

Now it was Paul's turn to have his eyes glisten with tears as he read over her writing.

"This is beautiful, Priscilla," he said at last. "Every Hebrew should read this to help them understand the presence of God in our lives. If they have trouble leaving the sacrificial system behind, this...this could help them."

Reluctantly, he handed it back to her, though he clearly wished to linger on the written work longer. She rolled it up and tucked it beneath the folds of her cloak once again.

"If you are agreeable, I'll simply tell them it's from you. It will be better accepted that way."

Paul let out a laugh. "No one is going to believe that came from me," he chuckled. "It doesn't have enough run-on sentences."

They both smiled for a moment. Priscilla's eyes suddenly welled with tears.

"When does this all end, Paul? When does the death, the persecution, the fighting just to exist…end?"

His smile faded as he slowly shook his head and looked upward toward the ceiling of his cell. "I suppose that is a question that might only be answered in the next life," he finally stated with a heavy sigh.

Priscilla opened her mouth to ask another question when Gaius suddenly reappeared, glancing nervously behind him.

"Priscilla!" he hissed. "You need to go. Now."

Paul glanced at the guard and shifted uncomfortably. "Is…it almost time?"

Gaius met the other man's gaze for a moment before nodding solemnly. Paul smiled sadly and patted Priscilla's hand. She glanced from one man to the other, sudden realization dawning on her.

"Wait, what? No!"

Gaius shook his head impatiently. "You knew this was coming, Priscilla. Now let's go before you join him in the arena."

"It's senseless for you to die alongside me," Paul stated simply, removing her hand from where it was tightly gripping his arm. "You need to witness this and tell others. I'm ready to meet my Lord. I've been ready ever since that day on the road to Damascus. I know what awaits me."

Priscilla bit her lower lip as she slowly stood, tears still threatening to spill from her eyes. Her voice trembled as she turned to face him.

"I've fought the good fight," he whispered.

She closed her eyes as she lost the battle with the tears, and they began to flow down her cheeks. "We will carry on your work," she said, barely audible.

Paul reached out and squeezed her hands, his grip firm despite the chains.

"Until we meet again, brother," she murmured.

Paul raised his bound hands and traced a sign of blessing in the air. "Go in peace, my sister."

She turned and followed Gaius out of the room, though paused at the threshold, looking back one last time. Paul met her gaze and nodded, his calm presence steadying her, before the heavy door swung shut, sealing him away.

Outside, the air was cold and sharp against her damp cheeks, though the early morning light had begun to peek over the horizon, bathing the cobblestone streets with a golden glow. Her chest tightened as she saw Junia and Phoebe waiting for her in the shadows of a nearby archway. The two women hurried to her side, their faces etched with the same grief that weighed on her heart.

"He's ready," she said, her voice breaking. "More ready than any of us could ever be."

They wrapped their arms around each other and waited as the streets slowly began to fill with Roman citizens preparing for their day. They made their way toward the Roman Circus, its arches and columns towering over the city like a monument to cruelty. As people gathered outside, the three women kept to the edges, the peoples' voices rising in a mix of anticipation and indifference.

Priscilla's heart ached as she saw Paul being led from the prison gates. His chains clinked with ever step, but his gait was steady. His shoulders, though stooped with suffering, bore no sign of fear. Around him the crowd jeered and shouted, but he seemed not to hear them. His focus was fixed ahead, as if he already saw the glory that awaited him.

The three women followed at a distance, staying in the shadows. They dared not draw attention to themselves, but neither could they turn away. Priscilla clenched her hands together, praying silently, her lips moving without sound.

Priscilla forced herself to keep moving, slipping through the chaos with her head bowed, her heart pounding like a drumbeat.

When she dared look over at her companions, their faces were both as pale and grim as her own. As they neared the outer wall, she leaned against the cool stone momentarily. But this was no time for weakness. They would bear witness. Together they would carry the story of Paul's final moments to the scattered believers who waited in fear and faith.

Above them, Nero's banners flapped in the wind, their bright crimson stark against the pale sky. The circus was a monument to death, but as Priscilla stood with her sisters, she held onto the truth that had sustained her through every trial. This was not the end. Not for Paul. Not for the movement. And not for the Kingdom they served.

When they reached the circus, the enormity of the arena pressed down upon them. Rows upon rows of spectators filled the seats, their faces blurred by distance but their collective fervor palpable. Men jostled for better views, women leaned forward eagerly, and children darted between legs, drawn by the morbid excitement. The sand in the center of the circus was stained with dark patches, remnants of earlier executions and battles. A shallow trench ringed the arena floor, its purpose both functional and sinister—designed to drain away what spilled here.

Everywhere they looked, there was motion: the sweeping robes of the senators in the upper tiers, the restless pacing of guards near the arena's edge, the nervous fidgeting of prisoners awaiting their fate. A loud trumpet blast silenced the crowd momentarily, a signal that the next spectacle was about to begin. Then the noise returned, louder and more frenzied, like the roar of an unholy beast.

Priscilla's breath quickened as she spotted Paul being led through a side gate, his chains glinting in the pale sunlight. The guards flanked him, their faces expressionless as they shoved him forward. She gripped the folds of her cloak tightly, willing herself to stay hidden in the shadows of the towering stone columns. The urge to cry out, to run to him, clawed at her chest, but she held back. To reveal themselves now would only ensure their own arrests—and Paul would not have wanted that.

The sharp smell of iron filled the air as a soldier tested the blade meant for Paul. The metallic scrape echoed in her ears, cutting through the crowd's anticipation.

The scene unfolded with brutal efficiency. Paul was forced to kneel, his head bowed, as Nero's soldiers prepared the execution. The crowd roared, but Priscilla could hear only her own heartbeat, pounding in her ears. Beside her, Junia and Phoebe stood rigid.

As the sword fell, Priscilla closed her eyes. Her hands trembled, but her lips continued to move in prayer. She didn't need to see what happened next. She already knew.

Paul was free.

When she finally opened her eyes, she was staring skyward into the bright, cloudless sky. The crowd was dispersing, their bloodlust sated. The three women remained where they were for a moment, silent and still. Then, turning to Junia and Phoebe, her voice barely audible, she spoke.

"Now it's our turn. We must carry the light."

They nodded and turned and made their way through the crowd toward the exit, slipping away into the shadows and carrying with them the weight of loss—and the unshakable hope of what was to come.

Discussion Questions

1. Priscilla, Junia, and Phoebe played a crucial role in supporting the movement. How does this challenge common perceptions of women's roles in the early church?

2. Paul accepted his impending execution with peace and conviction. How do you think Priscilla and the others processed witnessing such a loss?

3. Early Christians in Rome hid in the catacombs due to persecution. How does this compare to the struggles of persecuted believers in different parts of the world today?

4. Paul assured Priscilla that the movement would not die even if he did. What factors contributed to the spread of Christianity despite the persecution?

5. How do faith and fear interact in our own spiritual journeys?

6. Paul's execution was brutal, yet in this story, Priscilla and the others chose to watch and later share his story. Why is witnessing and retelling history so important in matters of faith?

7. Some scholars believe Priscilla may have been the author of Hebrews. How do the teachings of leaders continue to shape and inspire believers long after they're gone?

8. This story ends with Priscilla and her companions committing to carrying on Paul's mission. What does "carrying the light" look like in our lives today?

9. In the early centuries of the Roman Empire, Christians were often scapegoated during times of crisis—blamed for natural disasters, political unrest, and societal decay. They were portrayed as disloyal, immoral, or even dangerous, which justified their persecu-

tion in the eyes of many Roman citizens. Today, we continue to see certain groups within our own society blamed for complex social and economic problems, often through dehumanizing language or misleading narratives that turn public opinion against them. What can we learn from the scapegoating of early Christians in Imperial Rome about the dangers of using fear and blame to marginalize vulnerable groups? In what ways does the language we use about others shape our willingness to see them as neighbors—or as threats?

10. In Matthew 25, Jesus says, *"I was in prison and you visited me... Truly I tell you, whatever you did for one of the least of these brothers and sisters of mine, you did for me."* Yet throughout history—and even today—Christians have many times been complicit in or silent about systems that dehumanize prisoners or treat them with cruelty. How is it possible that people who follow Jesus, who so clearly identified himself with "the least of these," can justify or ignore the inhumane treatment of others, even those deemed criminals? What does Priscilla's question—*"What sort of depraved indifference did one have to adopt in order to not go mad?"*—reveal about the spiritual cost of turning away from suffering?

Acknowledgments

I want to thank some of the people who were instrumental in inspiring and helping me write this book. Professor Diane Jacobson at Luther Seminary whose *"Harlots and Heroines of the Old Testament"* course I took during my time there helped spark my imagination regarding these Biblical characters. My editor and friend, Laura Hennen, who I know had to balance her editing efforts between her day job, classes, family, and a bout with the flu. B.R. Dohle and Michelle Wahila who were both very helpful in the early stages when I was thinking through the theology of some of these stories. Maryanne Kehlenbach who has always been a staunch supporter of my writing. My parents whose unconditional love has always been instrumental in all my endeavors. My congregation that supports and inspires me on a daily basis. And, of course, God who supplies me with my imagination.

To contact Rebecca J. Craig for speaking engagements, or to view or purchase her artwork, please visit rebeccajcraig.com.

TEHOM CENTER

WWW.TEHOMCENTER.ORG